D1155770

HTML

PROGRAMMER'S REFERENCE
SECOND EDITION

Thomas A. Powell
and
Dan Whitworth

Osborne/**McGraw-Hill**

New York   Chicago   San Francisco
Lisbon   London   Madrid   Mexico City   Milan
New Delhi   San Juan   Seoul   Singapore   Sydney   Toronto

Osborne/**McGraw-Hill**
2600 Tenth Street
Berkeley, California 94710
U.S.A.

For information on translations or book distributors outside the U.S.A.,
or to arrange bulk purchase discounts for sales promotions, premiums, or
fund-raisers, please contact Osborne/**McGraw-Hill** at the above address.

HTML Programmer's Reference, Second Edition

Publisher   Brandon A. Nordin
Vice President & Associate Publisher   Scott Rogers
Acquisitions Editor   Ann Sellers
Project Editor   Mark Karmendy
Acquisitions Coordinator   Tim Madrid
Proofreader   Stefany Otis
Indexer   Rebecca Plunkett
Computer Designer   Melinda Moore Lytle
Illustrator   Robert Hansen
Series Design   Peter F. Hancik

1234567890 DOC DOC 01987654321

ISBN 0-07-213232-9

This book was composed with Corel VENTURA™ Publisher.

About the Authors

Thomas A. Powell is the author of Osborne's *HTML: The Complete Reference* and *Web Design: The Complete Reference*. His firm, PINT, Inc. (www.pint.com), designs Web sites for large corporate clients. He is the developer and lead instructor of the Web Publishing Program at the University of California, San Diego, Extension, and a lecturer for the UCSD Computer Science Department.

Dan Whitworth provides editorial, writing, and HTML services for PINT, Inc.

CONTENTS

vi　Contents

3   Special Characters 371

HTML is the core technology of the Web. Web pages rely on this markup language for structure and, unfortunately, often for presentation as well. There is a constant struggle between what HTML was designed to do and what the needs of the people are who use the technology. HTML has changed dramatically since its inception, and other technologies have been developed to complement its core facilities. Today HTML has many nuances and complexities that are unknown to all but those who study the specifications very carefully. This book describes the core elements of the HTML 4.01 specification and the many common elements introduced by Netscape, Microsoft, and WebTV. The book also provides notes on XHTML compliance, which today's Web designers should find useful.

Chapter 1
General HTML

Hypertext Markup Language (HTML) is a structured markup language used to create Web pages. A markup language like HTML is a collection of text codes, called *elements,* that indicate the structure and format of a document. A user agent, usually a Web browser, interprets the meaning of these codes and renders a Web page appropriately.

HTML Elements

Elements in HTML consist of alphanumeric tokens within angle brackets, such as **<b>**, **<html>**, **<img>**, and **<h1>**. A complete HTML element is defined by a start tag, an end tag (where applicable), possible attributes, and a content model. Figure 1-1 diagrams the syntax of a typical HTML element.

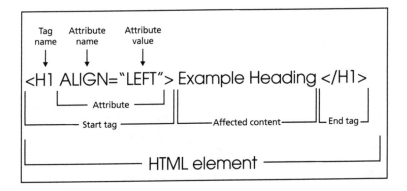

Figure 1-1. HTML element example

Content Model

HTML specifications define the type of content an element can enclose, or its *content model*. This can include other elements, text, elements and text combined, or nothing. The **<head>** element provides general information about an HTML document. Its content model only allows it to contain a small number of related elements, such as **<title>** and **<meta>**. The content model for the bold element **<b>** allows it to enclose text and some elements, such as the one for italic text (**<i>**), but not others like **<head>**.

Tag Pairs

As shown in Figure 1-1, most elements consist of a start tag and an end tag. The symbol for bold text is **b.** Its start tag is **<b>**. An end tag is identical to a basic start tag except that the symbol is preceded by a forward slash: **</b>**. An element's instruction applies to the content contained between its start and end tags:

```
<b>This text is bold</b> but this text is not.
```

For some elements, such as the paragraph element **<p>**, an end tag is optional. However, to be compliant with a more rule-enforcing form of HTML called XHTML, all end tags should be used. Various points about XHTML compliance will be made in this chapter. For a more complete discussion see Chapter 2.

Empty Elements

Some elements, called *empty* elements, require no end tag because they do not enclose content. One example is the break element **
, which indicates a line break. Other elements do not require an end tag because the end of the content they affect can be inferred from surrounding elements. An example is the element **<hr>, which indicates a horizontal rule that occupies a line all its own. XHTML conformance requires that you self-identify empty elements with an included slash, for example **<hr>** becomes **<hr />**.

Attributes

An HTML start tag may contain attributes that modify the element's meaning. Attributes within a tag's brackets must be separated from the element's name by at least one space. This makes it important to avoid accidental spaces in element names. A browser would not interpret **<i m g>** as the image element, but rather as the italic element **<i>** with two unknown attributes, **m** and **g**.

Some attributes are self-explanatory, like the **compact** attribute for the ordered list element: **<ol compact>**. Other attributes indicate an effect by assigning a value to their name. **<ol type="I">** assigns the bullet type of an ordered list to uppercase roman numerals. An element may contain multiple attributes if those attributes are separated by at least one space, as in **<ol compact type="I">**.

There are four core attributes common to most HTML elements: **id, class, style**, and **title**. These are discussed in Chapter 2 under "Core Attributes Reference."

Two more common attributes, **lang** and **dir**, are discussed in Chapter 2 under "Language Reference."

Another kind of attribute, called an *event handler,* is used to associate scripting events with HTML elements. There are many event handlers; a common one is the **onmouseover** attribute, which associates an event when a user's mouse passes over the affected element. Event handlers are listed and discussed in Chapter 2 under "Events Reference."

There are many more attributes available; some are used only with specific elements, such as the **<body>** element's **alink** attribute, while others, like the **align** attribute, may be used with numerous different elements (**<p>**, **<img>**, and **<table>**, among others).

Comments

One important aspect of coding HTML pages is often overlooked: comments. The contents of HTML comments are not displayed within a browser window. Comments are denoted by a start value of **<!--** and an end value of **-->**. Comments can be many lines long. For example,

```
<!--
         Document Name: Sample HTML Document
         Author: Thomas A. Powell
         Creation Date: 2/5/01

         (c) 2001 Demo Company, Inc.
    -->
```

is a valid comment. Be careful to avoid putting spaces between the dashes or any additional exclamation points in the comment. Comments are useful in the **<head>** of a document to describe information about a document as just shown. Comments might also be useful when trying to explain complex HTML markup.

Comments also can include HTML elements. This is very useful in hiding new HTML elements from older browsers, and is commonly used with the **<style>** element, discussed in the "Style Sheets" section later in this chapter.

HTML Syntax

All well-written HTML documents share a common structure (see Figure 1-2). An HTML document begins with a **<!DOCTYPE>** declaration indicating the version of HTML used by the document. Following this, the **<html>** element encloses the actual document. It contains two primary sections, enclosed respectively by the **<head>** and **<body>** elements. The *head* contains identifying and other meta-information about the document. It always contains the document's title, enclosed by the **<title>** element. The *body* contains the actual document content.

```
<!DOCTYPE HTML PUBLIC "html version">
<HTML>
<HEAD>
<TITLE>Document Title</TITLE>
     ...Other supplementary information goes here...
</HEAD>
<BODY>
     ...Marked-up text goes here...
</BODY>
</HTML>
```

Figure 1-2.   HTML document template

Document Types

HTML follows the SGML notation for defining structured documents. From SGML, HTML inherits the requirement that all documents begin with a **<!DOCTYPE>** declaration. This identifies the HTML "dialect" used in a document by referring to an external *document type declaration,* or *DTD.* A DTD defines the actual elements, attributes, and element relationships that are valid in the document. The **<!DOCTYPE>** declaration allows validation software to identify the HTML DTD being followed in a document and verify that the document is syntactically correct. Any HTML construct not defined in the document's DTD should not occur. The **<!DOCTYPE>** declaration for the strict version of HTML 4.01 is shown here:

```
<!DOCTYPE HTML PUBLIC "-//W3C//DTD HTML 4.01//EN">
```

The HTML document template suggests always using a **<!DOCTYPE>** declaration. In some cases this may not be practical. Including a DTD declaration conveys the intention to follow it. It is better to omit a **<!DOCTYPE>** declaration than to include one that will not be followed.

XHTML

A new variation of HTML, called XHTML, has been developed by the World Wide Web Consortium. The purpose of XHTML is to bring HTML into compliance with the rules associated with XML (Extensible Markup Language), another SGML-based markup language. XHTML is geared to smooth the transition to XML-compliant browsers, as well as to facilitate the reduction of display formatting done with HTML; XHTML is meant to use CSS for all display considerations. XHTML documents should start with the appropriate DTD:

```
<!DOCTYPE HTML PUBLIC "-//W3C//DTD XHTML 1.0 Transitional//EN">
```

XHTML is more rigorous in its enforcement of effective coding practices, and introduces a number of new rules as well; the basic rules are discussed in Chapter 2 under "XHTML Compatibility." XHTML's impact on specific elements is discussed throughout the listings in Chapter 2. Authors are encouraged to consider getting XHTML-ready now. For a more complete discussion of XML and XHTML, see Chapter 17 of *HTML: The Complete Reference* (http://www.htmlref.com/samples/chapt17/). The XHTML 1.0 specification can be found online at http://www.w3.org/TR/xhtml1/.

The <html> Element

The **<html>** element delimits the start and end of an HTML document. It contains only the **<head>** element and the **<body>** element. It can also contain the **<frameset>** element *instead* of **<body>**. The HTML document template shown in Figure 1-2 displays the typical use of the **<html>** element as a container for all other elements in a document.

The <head> Element

The **<head>** element contains identification and supplementary information about the document, as well as scripts and style sheets. The **<head>** element should always be included for document style and legibility. The following table lists the elements allowed within the **<head>** element according to the HTML 4.01 DTD.

Element	Description
<base>	Defines base URL for all relative URLs in a document
<isindex>	Indicates that a document has a searchable keyword index
<link>	Defines relationships between a document and other documents (table of contents, style sheets, etc.)

Element	Description
<meta>	Defines information about a document, usually for indexing
<object>	Defines an object to be included in an HTML document
<script>	Encloses scripting language statements for client-side processing
<style>	Encloses style sheet rules for a document
<title>	Defines the document title (See the following section.)

The <title> Element

The **<title>** element gives an HTML document a title by which it is known to browsers and indexing robots. Browsers display the document title while it is being viewed, generally at the top of the browser window. They also use the title in bookmark lists. A document title may contain standard text and character entities (for example, **©**), which are discussed later in this chapter. HTML markup is not permitted in a **<title>** element. There should be only one **<title>** element in a document, and it should always be placed as the first tag in the **<head>** element of the document.

The <frameset> Element

Instead of **<body>**, an HTML document can contain the **<frameset>** element, which in turn contains a number of **<frame>** elements. Here is a very simple frameset with two frames:

```
<frameset cols="150,*">
    <frame src="sidenav.htm" name="side">
    <frame src="index.htm" name="main">
</frameset>
```

Here's what this would look like in a browser, assuming that there are additional HTML documents to populate the frames.

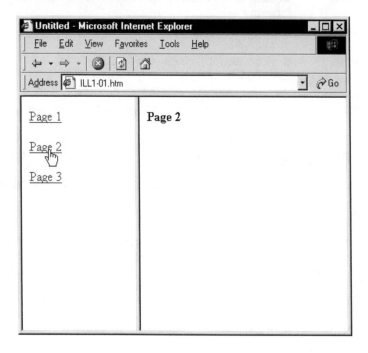

The **cols** attribute in the opening **<frameset>** tag defines how many frames there are in the frameset, and their width, using a comma-separated list. Values can be numerical (pixels), percentages (defined in relation to the size of the browser), or wildcards, defined with an asterisk. In this case, the frameset consists of one column that is 150 pixels wide, and another column that will automatically fill the rest of the browser window. (The **cols** attribute defines vertical columns; there is also a **rows** attribute that defines horizontal rows but otherwise works the same way.)

In their simplest form, the **<frame>** elements use the **src** attribute to "pull in" another HTML document; this can be a document with a standard body, or another frameset to create nested frames. Each frame should also be named for linking purposes. A link in the frame named "sidenav" should use the **<a>** element's target attribute to define which window the linked page will appear in:

```
<a href="page02.htm" target="main">Page 2</a>
```

When clicked, the link in the left-hand frame will open the document page02.htm in the frame named "main".

The <body> Element

The body of an HTML document is delimited by **<body>** and **</body>**. There can be only one **<body>** element per document. Common **<body>** attributes include **bgcolor** (background color); **background** (background image); **text** (body text color); and **link**, **alink**, and **vlink** (colors for links, active links, and visited links).

The **<body>** element may contain many other HTML elements. These fall into three distinct groups: block-level elements, text-level elements, and character entities.

Block-Level Elements

Block-level elements define structural content blocks like paragraphs or lists. If a document is written carefully in a block style, it may be possible to improve its machine readability. Block-level elements include paragraphs, divisions, headings, preformatted text, lists, tables, forms, and other elements. The basic idea of a block-structured document is illustrated in Figure 1-3.

Headings

The six different heading elements are used to create "headlines" in documents. These range in importance from **<h1>**, the most important, to **<h6>**, the least important. Most browsers display headings in a larger and/or bolder font than normal text. Text included in heading elements is displayed on a line of its own, and visual browsers generally insert an extra line after a heading. The heading elements also support the **align** attribute, with possible values of **left**, **right**, and **center**.

```
<h1>Heading 1</h1>
<h2 align="left">Heading 2</h2>
<h3 align="right">Heading 3</h3>
<h4 align="center">Heading 4</h4>
<h5>Heading 5</h5>
<h6>Heading 6</h6>
```

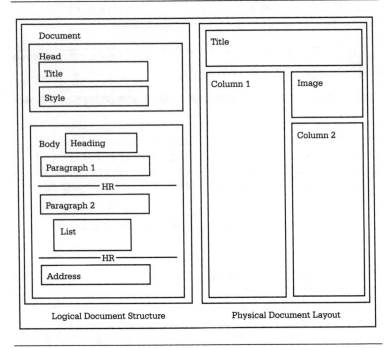

Figure 1-3. Outline of a block-structured document

This code will render like this:

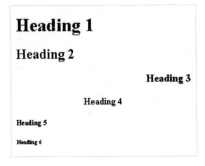

Paragraphs

Surrounding text with the **<p>** and **</p>** tags indicates that the text is a logical paragraph unit. Browsers usually place a blank line or two before the paragraph, but the exact rendering depends on the browser. Text within the **<p>** element is normally rendered flush left with a ragged right margin. The **align** attribute makes it possible to specify a left, right, center, or justified alignment. The closing tag for this element is optional.

```
This text is not formatted.

<p>This text is a new paragraph that goes on and
on for quite a while.</p>

<p align="center">This paragraph is centered.</p>
```

This code will render like this:

```
This text is not formatted.

This text is a new paragraph that goes on
and on for quite a while.

            This paragraph is centered.
```

Breaks

The **<p>** element is intended to define a paragraph as a logical unit of text. Multiple **<p>** elements without content will not produce additional line breaks; this should be done with the break element **
**, like this:

```
<p>This paragraph contains more than one line.<br><br>
The second line was created by using the break element.</p>
```

Here's how a browser will render this code:

```
This paragraph contains more than one line.

The second line was created by using the break element.
```

As an empty element, for XHTML compliance **
** would be written as **
**.

Divisions

The **<div>** element structures HTML documents into unique sections or divisions. Adding the **align** attribute makes it possible to align a portion of the document to the left, right, or center; under some browsers, it is also possible to justify the text with the attribute/value combination **align="justify"**. By default, content within the **<div>** element is left-aligned. In its most basic use, **<div>** produces a display similar to paragraphs. However, **<div>** can enclose multiple elements, including **<p>**, **<img>**, and additional **<div>** elements. Divisions are also useful when used in conjunction with style sheets or with scripts.

Centered Text

To center text or embedded objects such as images, simply enclose the content within **<center>** and **</center>**.

```
<center>This text is centered.</center>
```

While **<center>** is technically a shorthand for **<div align="center">**, its use is widespread and commonly accepted by browsers. It is interpreted as a block-level element, with an extra line above and below the centered content.

Block Quotes

The **<blockquote>** element encloses large block quotations within a document. Enclosing text within **<blockquote>** and **</blockquote>** usually indents the blocked information.

```
This is ordinary text.
<blockquote>This text has been
blockquoted.</blockquote>
This is some more ordinary text.
```

This code will generally render like this:

> This is ordinary text.
>
>   This text has been blockquoted.
>
> This is some more ordinary text.

Preformatted Text

The **<pre>** element can be used to surround text that should not
be formatted by the browser. The text enclosed within the **<pre>**
element retains all its spacing and returns, and does not reflow
when the browser is resized. Scroll bars and horizontal scrolling are
required if the lines are longer than the width of the window, so try
to avoid using **<pre>** to format large sections of text. The browser
generally renders the preformatted text in a monospaced font, such
as Courier.

```
<pre>The              extra    spaces    and line breaks in     this
          text are preserved       </pre>
but     the     extra spaces    in this text are    collapsed.
```

This code will render like this:

```
The                    extra     spaces      and line breaks in      this
            text are preserved

but the extra spaces in this text are collapsed.
```

Lists

There are three basic forms of lists in HTML: ordered lists (**<ol>**),
unordered lists (**<ul>**), and the less common definition lists (**<dl>**).
Two other rarely used list elements, **<menu>** and **<dir>**, are
sparsely supported and are usually treated as an unordered list.
Lists are block formatting elements that define a block structure.
They can be nested, and can contain other block-level structures,
such as paragraphs. In all cases, the list item element **<li>** is used
to define list items, and to mark them with a bullet or a number.
While HTML traditionally defines **<li>** as having no closing tag,
we use one to be future-proof with XHTML compliance in mind.

A simple unordered list is shown here:

```
<ul>
    <li>Item 1</li>
    <li>Item 2</li>
    <li>Item 3</li>
</ul>
```

A browser will generally render this code like this:

```
• Item 1
• Item 2
• Item 3
```

A simple ordered list is shown here:

```
<ol>
    <li>Item 1</li>
    <li>Item 2</li>
    <li>Item 3</li>
</ol>
```

A browser will generally display this ordered list like this:

```
1.  Item 1
2.  Item 2
3.  Item 3
```

The **type** attribute, which can be applied to **<ul>**, **<ol>**, or **<li>**, can be used to define the shape of the bullet for unordered lists, or the style of numbering for ordered lists, as shown in this table:

List Type Value	Meaning
<ul type="disc">	Assigns a disc, or dot, bullet to an unordered list item (default)
<ul type="circle">	Assigns an empty circle bullet to an unordered list item
<ul type="square">	Assigns a square bullet to an unordered list item
<ol type="1">	Assigns an Arabic (standard) numerical value to an ordered list item

List Type Value	Meaning
<ol type="a">	Assigns a lowercase Roman numerical value to an ordered list item
<ol type="A">	Assigns an uppercase Roman numerical value to an ordered list item
<ol type="i">	Assigns a lowercase alphabetical value to an ordered list item
<ol type="I">	Assigns an uppercase alphabetical value to an ordered list item

Horizontal Rules

A horizontal rule, indicated by the **<hr>** element, is a block-level element that can divide HTML documents into visually distinct regions. **<hr>** can have some logical meaning as a section break. Commonly used **<hr>** attributes include **align**, **noshade** (removes default shading effects), **size** (defines rule thickness in pixels), and **width** (defines width by pixels or percentage).

The following code creates a horizontal rule that is left aligned, 1 pixel thick, 300 pixels wide, and has no shading effects:

```
<hr align="left" size="1" width="300" noshade>
```

(Like other empty elements, to make **<hr>** XHTML friendly, you should always use a trailing slash with the element.)

Addresses

The **<address>** element is used to surround information such as the address of the organization the page is about. The HTML specification treats **<address>** as an idiosyncratic block-level element; browsers tend to render it as italicized text. It may enclose many lines of text (using the **
** element), formatting elements to change the font characteristics, and even images. It should not enclose other block-level elements.

```
Drop us a line some time!
<address>
   <b>Demo Company</b><br>
   2001 Demo Company Court<br>
   Demoville, CA 92101
</address>
```

This code will generally render like this:

> Drop us a line some time!
> *Demo Company*
> *2001 Demo Company Court*
> *Demoville, CA 92101*

Tables

Tables represent information in rows and columns. In its simplest form, a table places information inside the cells formed by dividing a rectangle into rows and columns. The syntax of tables is relatively complex and includes the ability to set individual table cell characteristics. The basic elements for creating tables are **<table>**, **<tr>**, **<th>**, and **<td>**.

This code shows a basic table using the **<table>**, **<tr>**, **<th>**, and **<td>** elements, and demonstrates the uses of several common attributes:

```
<table border="1" cellpadding="4" cellspacing="0"
width="375">
  <tr>
    <th width="125">Header 1</th>
    <th width="125">Header 2</th>
    <th width="125">Header 3</th>
  </tr>

  <tr>
    <td>Default alignment (left)</td>
    <td align="right">Right-aligned</td>
    <td valign="top">Top-aligned</td>
  </tr>

  <tr>
    <td colspan="3" align="center">This table data
    cell spans three columns and is center-
    aligned.</td>
  </tr>
</table>
```

Here the **<table>** element uses the **border, cellpadding, cellspacing,** and **width** attributes. Here's what they do:

border	Assigns thickness to the table border in pixels, from zero (no border) to any value desired
cellpadding	Assigns padding, in pixels, to table cells; in this example, **cellpadding="4"**, or four pixels
cellspacing	Defines the spaces between table cells in pixels; in this example, **cellspacing="0"**, or zero pixels
width	Defines the width of the table in pixels (375 pixels, in this example), or in percentages (50%, 100%, etc.); percentages will generally render in relation to the width of any enclosing elements

The **<tr>** element is used to define rows, which can contain table header cells (**<th>**) or table data cells (**<td>**). In the first and second rows, the **<th>** element defines table header cells; here the **width** attribute defines cell widths that should add up to the total width of the table. Table headers generally render in bold, center-aligned text.

In the third row, the **<td>** element is used to define three table data cells. The first **<td>** cell has no attributes, so its contents are left-aligned by default. The second **<td>** cell assigns a value of **right** to the **align** attribute. (The **align** attribute can be assigned a value of **left** as well; this attribute can also be used with **<th>**, but in that case the default alignment is to the center.) Here's what the table will look like in a browser:

Header 1	Header 2	Header 3
Default alignment (left)	Right-aligned	Top-aligned
This table data cell spans three columns and is center-aligned.		

Notice that the right-aligned table cell is vertically aligned to the middle of the cell. The next and final **<td>** cell in this row uses the **valign** attribute to set the vertical alignment to **top**. Other attributes for **valign** include **bottom**, and **middle**, which is the default.

The third row contains one **<td>** cell that stretches across the width of three cells. This is done by assigning a value of **3** to the **colspan** attribute.

This simple table example covers some basic aspects of HTML tables. Additional table elements defined by HTML 4, listed in the following table, can be found in Chapter 2.

Element	Description
<caption>	Defines a table caption
<thead>	Defines a table header
<tfoot>	Defines a table footer
<tbody>	Defines a table body
<col>	Defines a column within a table
<colgroup>	Creates column groups within a table

Forms

Forms are commonly used on the Web as a way to collect information from users. The **<form>** element and its associated elements allow for the creation of forms, ranging from simple text entry fields to more complex multiple-field forms. Here's a simple form as rendered by a browser:

What's your name? [   ]

What's your favorite color? (Check one)
○ Red
○ Blue
○ Green

Where do you live? [Western Hemisphere ▼]

How do you feel about this form?
[Type your answer here.   ]

[Submit] [Clear]

The entire form is enclosed between **<form>** and **</form>**. Attributes for this element include **name**, which names the form; **action**, which assigns its action, generally the URL of a program that will execute the form; and **method**, which can take a value of **GET** or **POST**. The opening <form> tag for this example might look like this:

```
<form action="../cgi-bin/formprocess.cgi"
 method="POST" name="sampleform">
```

For more about the **GET** and **POST** values, see the **<form>** entry in Chapter 2.

The form field for typing in a name is defined with the **<input>** element, as shown here:

```
<input type="text" size="20" maxlength="50"
 name="yourname">
```

The **type** attribute here defines this as a text input field, while **size** defines the width of the field in characters. The **maxlength** attribute defines the maximum number of characters that can be entered in the field. Finally, **name** assigns a name to the field; this is very important, as field names are crucial to helping programs or scripts to process a form. For XHTML compliance, **<input>** should be written as **<input />**.

The round "radio" buttons also use the **<input>** element, which is very versatile. Note that the **
** tag must be used to assign breaks here.

```
<input type="radio" name="color" value="red">Red<br>
<input type="radio" name="color" value="blue">Blue<br>
<input type="radio" name="color" value="red">Green<br>
```

Here, the input field type is defined as **radio**. All three radio buttons are grouped together by assigning them the same name, while **value** assigns their individual meanings. The user can only choose one radio button out of a named group. A similar input type, **checkbox**, creates checkboxes that allow users to choose multiple options from a named group.

The next question offers users a pull-down menu, which is created using the **<option>** and **<select>** elements.

```
<select name="home">
   <option>Western Hemisphere</option>
```

```
<option>Eastern Hemisphere</option>
   <option>North Pole</option>
</select>
```

It is important to assign a name to the **<select>** element, especially because a form may contain multiple menus. The closing tag for **<option>** is optional, but we have added it here for XHTML compliance.

Multiline text input fields can be created using the **<textarea>** element:

```
<textarea cols="30" rows="5" name="comments">
Type your answer here.</textarea>
```

The **cols** attribute defines the width of the text area in characters, while **rows** defines its height. Default text can be placed between the opening and closing tags, but is not required; users can remove this text when they type in their comments.

The **<input>** element shows up in yet another guise: the Submit button.

```
<input type="submit" value="Submit">
```

As usual, the **type** attribute defines the nature of the input field. The **value** attribute can be used to define the label that appears on the button; without it, the button will default to the phrase "Submit Query." It is also useful to provide a Reset button in case the user wants to clear the entire form:

```
<input type="Reset" value="Clear">
```

Again, **value** assigns the button label; without it, the Reset button will default to "Reset".

Other **type** values for **<input>** include **button**, **hidden**, **image**, and **password**. Additional form elements are listed in the following table.

Element	Description
<button>	Creates a clickable button associated with an **<input>** field
<fieldset>	Groups related elements within the **<form>** element; may include any of the elements listed in this table

Element	Description
<label>	Creates a label associated with an <input> field
<legend>	Creates a caption associated with a <fieldset> grouping

1

Text-Level Elements

While block elements are used to create groups or sections in a document, they usually contain content, typically text. The text within block elements can be formatted using text-level elements. There are two kinds of text-level elements in HTML: physical and logical. *Physical elements,* such as <b> for bold and <i> for italic, are used to specify how text should be rendered. *Logical elements,* such as <strong> and <em>, indicate what text is, but not necessarily how it should look. The rise of style sheets has led to a significant increase in the use of logical elements.

Physical Character-Formatting Elements

Common HTML supports a number of elements that can be used to influence physical formatting. The elements have no meaning other than to make text render a particular way. Any other meaning is assigned by the reader. The following table shows some common physical formatting elements.

Element	Description
<i>...</i>	Italic
<b>...</b>	Bold
<tt>...</tt>	Teletype (monospaced)
<u>...</u>	Underline
<strike>...</strike>	Strikethrough
<s>...</s>	Alternative form of strikethrough
_{...}	Subscript
^{...}	Superscript
<big>...</big>	Bigger font (one font size bigger)
<small>....</small>	Smaller font (one font size smaller)

Logical Elements

Logical elements indicate the type of content the elements enclose. The browser is then relatively free to determine the presentation of that content, although there are expected renderings for these

elements that are followed by nearly all browsers. The following
table illustrates the logical text-formatting elements generally
supported by browsers.

Element	Description
<cite>...**</cite>**	Citation
<code>...**</code>**	Source code
<dfn>...**</dfn>**	Definition
****...****	Emphasis
<kbd>...**</kbd>**	Keystrokes
<samp>...**</samp>**	Sample (example information)
****...****	Strong emphasis
<var>...**</var>**	Programming variable

Links

Linking between documents, or between sections of the same
document, is one of the most important aspects of HTML. Links can
employ complete URLs (Uniform Resource Locators) to connect to
any HTML document anywhere on the Web. They can also use
"relative" links that define a path to another document on the
same system as the referring document. The anchor element <a> is
used with text or images to create clickable hyperlinks in the body
of an HTML document. The **href** attribute defines the URL or path
of the document or object being linked.

```
Visit <a href="http://www.democompany.com">Demo
Company</a> online and win no prizes!
```

When using a complete URL in a link, always be sure to include
the prefix **http://** so that browsers will not try to find the linked
document on a user's local system.

Images

Images in GIF or JPEG format are commonly used in Web pages.
More recent browsers may also support PNG or other formats. To
place an image in an HTML document, use the **<img>** element.
The **src** attribute specifies the source of the image using a URL or
relative path, so

```
<img src="images/picture.gif">
```

is allowed as well as

```
<img src="http://www.notarealsite.com/images/picture.gif">.
```

As with other empty elements, a trailing slash should be added for XHTML compliance.

```
<img src="images/picture.gif" />
```

Other attributes are used to modify the properties of the included object. The **alt** attribute is perhaps the most important because it provides alternate text (**<img src="art.jpg" alt="This is not a Picasso.">**) that displays while the image is loading or when a browser's image display is turned off. In recent browsers, **alt** text also displays as a tool tip when the cursor passes over the image.

Setting the **height** and **width** attributes to the image's dimensions will allow the browser to reserve space for the image and preserve page layout during download. The **height** and **width** attributes can also be used to resize images, but this often leads to image distortion; it is better to resize images using a graphics manipulation program before you load them on the server. The **align** attribute determines an image's position relative to text flow and other content, as you can see in the illustration that follows this code.

```
<img src="images/picture.gif" align="right"
height="75" width="100">
This text should flow to the left of the image. This
text should flow to the left of the image. This text
should flow to the left of the image.
```

This text should flow to the left of the image. This text should flow to the left of the image. This text should flow to the left of the image.

The **hspace** and **vspace** attributes create horizontal and vertical space around the image.

```
<img src="images/picture.gif" height="75" width="100"
     hspace="10" vspace="10">
```

Images may also be used as background images for HTML documents by using the **background** attribute of the **<body>** element.

Linking Images

The **<img>** element can be placed within the **<a>** element to create graphic hyperlinks. A nonlinked image will not display a border unless the **border** attribute is set to the desired width; however, a linked image *will* display a one-pixel border by default, unless the image border is set to zero:

```
<a href="index.htm"><img src="picture.gif"
border="0"></a>
```

Image Maps

Images can also be used to create multiple links in a single image, or image maps. To define an image as an image map, use the **usemap** attribute:

```
<img src="images/picture.gif" usemap="#mainmap">
```

The **usemap** attribute's value is the name of a map, preceded by the # symbol. This references the **<map>** element, which can go anywhere in the body of the document; it is useful to place map information at the bottom of the page, after all other content, but before the closing </body> tag. The **<map>** element encloses one or more instance of the **<area>** element, which defines the shape and link for a given area.

```
<map name="mainmap">
    <area shape="rect" coords="123,7,329,110"
    href="index.htm">
</map>
```

This example would produce a single active link, or "hotspot," in the image. The **<map>** element must have its **name** attribute set to match the name in the **<image>** element's **usemap** attribute. There can be more than one **<img>** / **<map>** pairing in an HTML document, and the **<map>** element can enclose as many **<area>** elements as needed.

In the preceding code example, **<area>** has its **shape** attribute set to **rect**, which defines the hot spot's shape as a rectangle; other values include **circ** (circle) and **poly** (polygon). The **coords** attribute defines the area's coordinates, while **href** defines the file or URL it should link to. There are many tools, including MapEdit and DreamWeaver, that make creating image maps a simple process.

Fonts

The **<font>** element is used to define the fonts used in text display. The **face** attribute defines the font face or faces to be used.

```
<font face="Arial">This text has been formatted in
Arial.</font>
```

The **face** attribute also allows comma-separated lists of fonts; if a user's computer does not have the first font installed, it will attempt to display the second one, and so on. It also supports generic font names such as **serif**, **sans-serif**, and **monospace**. A browser interpreting the fragment shown here would first try Arial (a common PC font), then Helvetica (a common Mac font), and finally a generic sans-serif font before giving up and using whatever the current browser font is.

```
<font face="Arial, Helvetica, sans-serif">This
should be in a different font</font>
```

The **size** attribute defines the size of the text with numerical values. These values can be the numbers **1** through **7**, with **1** being the smallest, **3** the default, and **7** the largest. Sizes can also be defined relative to the default font size, using negative values (**-1** through **-6**) or positive values (**+1** through **+6**).

The font element also supports the color attribute:

```
<font face="Arial" color="red">Red text in the
sunset.</font>
```

More information on colors is presented in the next section.

Colors

HTML supports colors, which are defined in two basic ways: color names like **red**, **black**, and **green**, or hexadecimal codes equivalent to those colors (**FF0000**, **000000**, and **00FF00**, respectively). Green text could be defined with the opening tag,

```
<font color="green">
```

or

```
<font color="#00FF00">.
```

Note that the hexadecimal code must be preceded by the symbol #. When using color names, use only those defined by browser vendors or standards bodies. Chapter 4 lists all defined color names and their hexadecimal equivalents, and discusses such important issues as browser-safe colors as well. An online version of the color chart can be found at http://www.htmlref.com/reference/appE/colorchart.htm.

Color can also be applied to the background of certain elements using the **bgcolor** attribute. To define the background color of an entire document, use the code

```
<body bgcolor="#FFFFFF">.
```

The **bgcolor** attribute can also be used with various table elements, including **<table>**, **<tr>**, **<th>**, and **<td>**. Due to inconsistencies in browser support, it is best to use **bgcolor** only with **<th>** and **<td>**.

```
<table>
  <tr>
    <th bgcolor="gray" colspan="3">Header Bar</th>
  </tr>

  <tr>
    <td>Red Background</td>
    <td>White Background</td>
    <td>Red Background</td>
  </tr>
</table>
```

Style Sheets

Cascading style sheets, or simply CSS, are becoming more and more important to HTML documents, especially now that newer browsers support this technology fairly well. While not part of the HTML specification, CSS was designed to provide a much wider range of display options than HTML, and to eventually take display away from HTML completely, leaving HTML to provide structure as originally intended. This will be a brief review of some CSS basics, included here because CSS is key to formatting Web pages.

To understand style sheets and their relationship to HTML, consider the **<span>** element, an inline element used to enclose small sections of text:

```
<p>This paragraph is perfectly ordinary except for
<span>these three words</span>, and then it goes back
to normal.</p>
```

This HTML code, by itself, will not alter the display of the enclosed text. Add some style sheet information with the **style** attribute, however, and it can be very useful:

```
<p>This paragraph is perfectly ordinary except for
<span style="background-color: yellow">these three
words</span>, and then it goes back to normal.</p>
```

Now the spanned text will be highlighted in yellow when viewed in a browser that supports CSS. Style information can also be defined in the head of a document, using the **style** element. Style information is enclosed in brackets, with style properties separated by semicolons.

```
<style type="text/css">
<!--
p {background-color: yellow; padding: 10px}
.redtext {color: red}
-->
</style>
```

The bracketed information is preceded by an element name or a selector. The style information preceded by **p** will apply that style to all paragraphs in the document. The next line uses a class selector rather than an element name; this is an author-assigned class name preceded by a period. This would apply the associated style or styles with an element with its class **defined** as **redtext**. The following code placed in the body of the document would then be affected by the **<style>** element in the head.

```
<p>This paragraph has a yellow background and ten
pixels of padding, and <span class="redtext">this
text is red!</span>
</p>
```

Discussing CSS any further is beyond the range of this book; there are CSS properties for text display, margins, padding, borders, positioning, and many other display effects beyond the abilities of HTML. HTML documents can be linked to external style sheets, and style can be applied with several kinds of selectors. For a more comprehensive introduction to CSS, see Chapter 10 of *HTML: The Complete Reference* (http://www.htmlref.com/samples/chapt10/).

Character Entities

The last important topic in this overview of HTML is the use of special characters. Sometimes it is necessary to put characters within a document that may be difficult to input off your keyboard. These include accented letters, the copyright symbol, or even the angle brackets used to enclose HTML elements. To use such characters in an HTML document, they must be "escaped" using a special code. All character codes take the form **&code;** where *code* is a word or numeric code indicating the actual character you want to put on the screen. For example, the code **©** places the copyright symbol (©) in an HTML document. The character set currently supported by HTML is the ISO Latin-1 character set. Many of its characters, such as accents and special symbols, must be entered into HTML documents using the appropriate code. A complete list of the character entities and their browser support is presented in Chapter 3.

Chapter 2
HTML Element Reference

This chapter provides a complete reference for the HTML 4.01 specification elements and the elements commonly supported by Internet Explorer, Netscape, and WebTV. Some elements presented here might be nonstandard or deprecated, but are included because browser vendors continue to support them or they are still in common use. The HTML 4.01 specification is largely the same as HTML 4.0, but corrects a number of errors in the earlier version. The standard used in this text is the final version of HTML 4.01 as defined on December 24, 1999, and available at http://www.w3.org/TR/html4/.

XHTML Compatibility

One of the World Wide Web Consortium's latest activities is the development of XHTML, which stands for Extensible Hypertext Markup Language. XHTML essentially is a reformulation of HTML 4.01 intended to bring it into compliance with XML and XML-based browsers. Although such user agents are not in common use, the XHTML 1.0 (http://www.w3.org/TR/xhtml1/) specification is designed, among other purposes, to provide a relatively painless transition to XML-compliant HTML coding. Rather than wait until XML-based browsers begin to hit the market, developers are encouraged to implement some simple changes to their HTML coding, changes that will not adversely affect the way their HTML documents are displayed in the current array of HTML 4–based browsers, but will remove the need to reformulate those documents at a later date.

New Rules for XHTML Compatibility

To bring new or existing HTML documents into agreement with the XHTML specification, all authors need to do is follow a few simple rules as discussed in Chapter 1. If done properly, these coding practices should be backward-compatible with browsers that are not XHTML-compliant.

Well-Formed Documents Are Now Mandatory

Although this concept is nothing new to conscientious coders, XHTML makes proper nesting of elements mandatory. XHTML-compliant browsers will no longer tolerate poorly nested elements like

```
<p><i><b>How bold it feels to be italic</i></p></b>
```

but will rigorously require properly nested code such as this:

```
<p><i><b>How bold it feels to be italic</b></i></p>
```

All Element and Attribute Names Must Be Lowercased

XHTML is a subset of XML. XML is case-sensitive. HTML to date has not been case-sensitive, leaving coders the choice of using uppercase or lowercase tags. In order for an HTML document to be XHTML-compliant, all elements and attribute names must always be lowercased exclusively. Whereas previous editions of *HTML: The Complete Reference* employed uppercased HTML elements and attributes in order to favor readability, all HTML code in this edition is lowercased.

No More Optional End Tags for Non-Empty Elements

To date, HTML specifications and permissive Web browsers have allowed the closing tags for certain elements, such as **<p>** and **<li>**, to be left off. Under XHTML, these closing tags cease to be optional. Whereas current browsers still allow the omission of these closing tags, future XHTML-compliant browsers will be strict about this. Under XHTML, the following code will no longer be correct:

```
<ul>
    <li>List Item 1
    <li>List Item 1
    <li>List Item 1
 </ul>
```

To be correct under XHTML, this code must be revised as follows:

```
<ul>
    <li>List Item 1</li>
    <li>List Item 1</li>
    <li>List Item 1</li>
 </ul>
```

This change affects the following elements:

<body>	<html>	<td>
<colgroup>	<li>	<tfoot>
<dd>	<option>	<th>
<dt>	<p>	<thead>
<head>	<tbody>	<tr>

Empty Elements Must Be Closed

Under XHTML, *all* elements must be closed, including empty elements such as **
** and **<img>**. The XHTML specification offers two ways to do this. One way is to simply provide a closing tag, like so:

```
<br></br>
```

Because of uncertain browser interpretation of this code, however, the specification recommends the other method, which involves adding a trailing slash in the element tag itself:

```
<br />
```

To ensure compliance with pre-XHTML browsers, be certain to leave a space between the element name (in this case, **br**) and the trailing slash (/). This way, older browsers should simply read the slash as an unknown attribute, and ignore it.

This change affects the following elements:

<area>	<frame>	<link>
<base>	<hr>	<meta>
<basefont>	<img>	<param>
 	<input>	
<col>	<isindex>	

All Attribute Values Must Be Enclosed in Quotes

Although browsers to date have allowed attribute values without quoting—at least when attribute values do not contain any whitespace—XHTML makes quoting mandatory for all attribute values. So whereas the code

```
<img src="image.gif" width=200 height=20 border=0>
```

might still be valid under most current browsers, to be correct under XHTML it must have all attributes quoted:

```
<img src="image.gif" width="200" height="20" border="0" />
```

All Attributes Must Have Defined Values

To date, certain HTML elements have employed what is called "attribute minimization." One example is the **<ul>** element, which uses the **compact** attribute. The code

```
<ul compact>
```

actually is shorthand for the code

```
<ul compact="compact">
```

Since the only value defined for **compact** is **compact**, the reason for this minimization is obvious. However, attribute minimization is not allowed under XHTML, which makes

```
<ul compact="compact">
```

the only correct way to implement this code.

XHTML: Other Flavors

The XHTML-based changes discussed so far are based on the XHTML 1.0 specification (http://www.w3.org/TR/xhtml1/), a W3C recommendation issued on January 26, 2000. XHTML 1.0 retains a number of deprecated, presentational elements still present in the HTML specifications.

XHTML 1.1 is a stricter specification that, as defined by the W3C, is "a markup language that is rich in structural functionality, but that relies upon style sheets for presentation." XHTML 1.1's other focus is on modularization of XHTML. The XHTML 1.1 specification can be found online at http://www.w3.org/TR/xhtml11/. A pared-down version of XHTML 1.1, called XHTML Basic (http://www.w3.org/TR/xhtml-basic/), is geared toward mobile applications. For immediate HTML coding purposes, XHTML 1.0 should be sufficient for most developers. Developers interested in the future directions of XHTML are encouraged to read the W3C's working draft "Modularization of XHTML" online at http://www.w3.org/TR/xhtml-modularization/.

Core Attributes Reference

The HTML 4.01 specification provides four main attributes, which are common to nearly all elements and have much the same meaning for all elements. These elements are **class**, **id**, **style**, and **title**.

class

This attribute is used to indicate the class or classes that a particular element belongs to. A class name might be used by a style sheet to associate style rules to multiple elements at once. For example, it might be desirable to associate a special class name called "important" with all elements that should be rendered with a yellow background. Because class values are not unique to a particular element, **<b class="important">** could be used as well as **<p class="important">** in the same document. It also is possible to have multiple values for the **class** attribute separated by white space; **<strong class="important special-font">** would define two classes with the particular **<strong>** element. Currently, most browsers recognize only one class name for this attribute.

id

This attribute specifies a unique alphanumeric identifier to be associated with an element. Naming an element is important to being able to access it with a style sheet, a link, or a scripting language. Names should be unique to a document and should be meaningful, so although **id="x1"** is perfectly valid, **id="Paragraph1"** might be better. Values for the **id** attribute must begin with a letter (A-Z and a-z) and may be followed by any number of letters, digits, hyphens, and periods.

One potential problem with the **id** attribute is that for some elements, particularly form controls and images, the **name** attribute already serves its function. Values for **name** should not collide with values for **id**, as they share the same naming space. For example, the following would not be allowed:

```
<b id="elementX">This is a test.</b>
<img name="elementX" src="image.gif" />
```

There is some uncertainty about what to do to ensure backward compatibility with browsers that understand **name** but not **id**. Some experts suggest that the following is illegal:

```
<img name="image1" id="image1" src="image.gif" />
```

Because **name** and **id** are naming the same item, there should be no problem; the common browsers do not have an issue with such markup. Complex scripting used to deal with two different names for the image, such as

```
<img name="image1name" id="image1id" src="image.gif" />
```

is possible, but might not be necessary.

Page designers are encouraged to pick a naming strategy and use it consistently. Once elements are named, they should be easy to manipulate with a scripting language.

Like the **class** attribute, the **id** attribute also is used by style sheets for accessing a particular element. For example, an element named **Paragraph1** can be referenced by a style rule in a document-wide style using a fragment identifier:

```
#Paragraph1    {color: blue}
```

Once an element is named using **id**, it also is a potential destination for an anchor. In the past an **<a>** element was used to set a destination; now any element can be a destination. For example,

```
<a href="#firstbolditem">Go to first bold element.</a>
<b id="firstbolditem">This is important.</b>
```

style

This attribute specifies an inline style (as opposed to an external style sheet) associated with the element. The style information is used to determine the rendering of the affected element. Because the **style** attribute allows style rules to be used directly with the element, it gives up much of the benefit of style sheets that divide the presentation of an HTML document from its structure. An example of this attribute's use is shown here:

```
<strong style="font-family: Arial;
font-size: 18pt">Important text</strong>
```

title

This attribute supplies advisory text for the element that can be rendered as a tool tip when the mouse is over the element. (Internet Explorer has supported this tool tip display for some time, but Netscape browsers prior to version 6 do not.) A title also might simply provide information that alerts future document maintainers to the meaning of the element and its enclosed content. In some cases, such as the **<a>** element, the **title** attribute can provide additional help in bookmarking. Like the title for the document itself, **title** attribute values as advisory information should be short, yet useful. For example, **<p title="paragraph1">** provides little information of value, whereas **<p title="HTML Programmer's Reference Chapter 2 Paragraph 10">** provides much more detail. When combined with scripting, it can provide facilities for automatic index generation.

Language Reference

One of the main goals of the HTML 4.01 specification is better support for other languages besides English. The use of other languages in a Web page might require that text direction be changed from left to right or right to left. Furthermore, once supporting non-ASCII languages becomes easier, it might be more common to see documents in mixed languages. Thus, there must be a way to indicate the language in use.

lang

This attribute indicates the language being used for the enclosed content. The language is identified using the ISO standard language abbreviation such as *fr* for French, *en* for English, and so on. RFC 1766 (http://www.ietf.org/rfc/rfc1766.txt?number=1766) describes these codes and their formats.

dir

This attribute sets the text direction as related to the **lang** attribute. The accepted values under the HTML 4.01 specification are **ltr** (left to right) and **rtl** (right to left). It should be possible to override whatever direction a user agent sets by using this attribute with the **<bdo>** element:

```
<bdo dir="rtl">Napoleon never really said "Able
was I ere I saw Elba."</bdo>
```

Internet Explorer 5.5 supports **dir** for the **<bdo>** element, but Netscape 6 does not. If used with other block-level elements such as **<p>** and **<div>**, the **dir** attribute might produce right-aligned text, but will not change the actual direction of the text flow.

Events Reference

In preparation for a more dynamic Web, the W3C (World Wide Web Consortium) has defined a set of core events that are associated with nearly every HTML element. Most of these events cover simple user interaction such as the click of a mouse button or a key being pressed. A few elements, such as form controls, have some special events associated with them, signaling that the field has received focus from the user or that the form was submitted. Intrinsic events such as a document loading and unloading also are described. The core events are summarized in the following table. Note that in the table, Internet Explorer 4, 5, and 5.5 and Netscape 4, 4.5, and 4.7 are abbreviated to IE4, IE5, IE5.5, N4, N4.5, and N4.7, respectively. Due to the incomplete nature of the Netscape 6 beta (Preview Version 2) available at the time of this edition, Netscape 6 has not been included in this list.

Event Attribute	Event Description	Allowed Elements Under HTML 4
onblur	Occurs when an element loses focus, meaning that the user has moved focus to another element, typically either by clicking the mouse on it or tabbing to it.	<a>, <area>, <button>, <input>, <label>, <select>, <textarea> Also <applet>, <area>, <div>, <embed>, <hr>, <img>, <marquee>, <object>, <span>, <table>, <td>, <tr> (Internet Explorer 4, 5, 5.5); <body> (IE 4, 5, and 5.5, N 4–4.7); <frameset>, <ilayer>, <layer> (N 4–4.7)

Event Attribute	Event Description	Allowed Elements Under HTML 4
onchange	Signals that the form control has lost user focus and its value has been modified during its last access.	<input>, <select>, <textarea>
onclick	Indicates that the element has been clicked.	Most display elements* Also <applet>, <font> (IE 4, 5, 5.5)
ondblclick	Indicates that the element has been double-clicked.	Most display elements* Also <applet>, <font> (IE 4, 5, 5.5)
onfocus	The focus event indicates when an element has received focus; namely it has been selected for manipulation or data entry.	<a>, <area>, <button>, <input>, <label>, <select>, <textarea> Also <applet>, <div>, <embed>, <hr>, <img>, <marquee>, <object>, <span>, <table>, <td>, <tr> (IE 4, 5, 5.5); <body> (N 4–4.7, IE 4, 5, 5.5); <frameset>, <ilayer>, <layer> (N 4–4.7)
onkeydown	Indicates that a key is being pressed down with focus on the element.	Most display elements* Also <applet>, <font> (IE 4, 5, 5.5)
onkeypress	Describes the event of a key being pressed and released with focus on the element.	Most display elements* Also <applet>, <font> (IE 4, 5, 5.5)
onkeyup	Indicates that a key is being released with focus on the element.	Most display elements* Also <applet>, <font> (IE 4, 5, 5.5)
onload	Indicates the event of a window or frame set finishing the loading of a document.	<body>, <frameset> Also <applet>, <embed>, <link>, <script>, <style> (IE 4, 5, 5.5); <ilayer>, <img>, <layer> (N 4–4.7, IE 4, 5, 5.5)
onmousedown	Indicates the press of a mouse button with focus on the element.	Most display elements* Also <applet>, <font> (IE 4, 5, 5.5)
onmousemove	Indicates that the mouse has moved while over the element.	Most display elements* Also <applet> and <font> (IE 4, 5, 5.5)

2

Event Attribute	Event Description	Allowed Elements Under HTML 4
onmouseout	Indicates that the mouse has moved away from an element.	Most display elements* Also \<applet>, \<font> (IE 4, 5, 5.5); \<ilayer>, \<layer> (N 4–4.7)
onmouseover	Indicates that the mouse has moved over an element.	Most display elements* Also \<applet>, \<font> (IE 4, 5, 5.5); \<ilayer>, \<layer> (N 4–4.7)
onmouseup	Indicates the release of a mouse button with focus on the element.	Most display elements* Also \<applet>, \<font> (IE 4, 5, 5.5)
onreset	Indicates that the form is being reset, possibly by the press of a reset button.	\<form>
onselect	Indicates the selection of text by the user, typically by highlighting the desired text.	\<input>, \<textarea>
onsubmit	Indicates a form submission, generally by pressing a submit button.	\<form>
onunload	Indicates that the browser is leaving the current document and unloading it from the window or frame.	\<body>, \<frameset>

NOTE: In the table, "most display elements" means all elements except \<applet>, \<base>, \<basefont>, \<bdo>, \
, \<font>, \<frame>, \<frameset>, \<head>, \<html>, \<iframe>, \<isindex>, \<meta>, \<param>, \<script>, \<style>, and \<title>.

This event model is far from complete, and it still is not fully supported by browsers. The event model should be considered a work in progress. It will certainly change as the Document Object Model (DOM) is more carefully defined. More information about the DOM can be found at http://www.w3.org/DOM/.

Extended Events

Browsers might support events other than those defined in the preliminary HTML 4.0 specification. Microsoft in particular has introduced a variety of events to capture more complex mouse actions such as dragging, element events such as the bouncing of **<marquee>** text, and data-binding events signaling the loading of data. (Mouse events might be bound to data in a database.) The events are described in more detail in the following table.

Event Attribute	Event Description	Associated Elements	Compatibility
onabort	Triggered by the user aborting the image load with a stop button or similar effect.	<img>	Netscape 3, 4–4.7 Internet Explorer 4, 5, 5.5
onafterprint	Fires after user prints document or previews document for printing.	<body>, <frameset>	Internet Explorer 5, 5.5
onafterupdate	Fires after the transfer of data from the element to a data provider, namely a data update.	<applet>, <body>, <button>, <caption>, <div>, <embed>, <img>, <input>, <marquee>, <object>, <select>, <table>, <td>, <textarea>, <tr>	Internet Explorer 4, 5, 5.5

2

Event Attribute	Event Description	Associated Elements	Compatibility
onbeforecopy	Fires just before selected content is copied and placed in the user's system clipboard.	\<a>, \<address>, \<area>, \<b>, \<bdo>, \<big>, \<blockquote>, \<caption>, \<center>, \<cite>, \<code>, \<custom>, \<dd>, \<dfn>, \<dir>, \<div>, \<dl>, \<dt>, \<em>, \<fieldset>, \<form>, \<h1> – \<h6>, \<i>, \<img>, \<label>, \<legend>, \<li>, \<listing>, \<menu>, \<nobr>, \<ol>, \<p>, \<plaintext>, \<pre>, \<s>, \<samp>, \<small>, \<span>, \<strike>, \<strong>, \<sub>, \<sup>, \<td>, \<textarea>, \<th>, \<tr>, \<tt>, \<u>, \<ul>	Internet Explorer 5, 5.5

Event Attribute	Event Description	Associated Elements	Compatibility
onbeforecut	Fires just before selected content is cut from document and added to the system clipboard.	`<a>`, `<address>`, `<applet>`, `<area>`, `<b>`, `<bdo>`, `<big>`, `<blockquote>`, `<body>`, `<button>`, `<caption>`, `<center>`, `<cite>`, `<code>`, `<custom>`, `<dd>`, `<dfn>`, `<dir>`, `<div>`, `<dl>`, `<dt>`, `<em>`, `<embed>`, `<fieldset>`, `<font>`, `<form>`, `<h1>` – `<h6>`, `<hr>`, `<i>`, `<img>`, `<input>`, `<kbd>`, `<label>`, `<legend>`, `<li>`, `<listing>`, `<map>`, `<marquee>`, `<menu>`, `<nobr>`, `<ol>`, `<p>`, `<plaintext>`, `<pre>`, `<rt>`, `<ruby>`, `<s>`, `<samp>`, `<select>`, `<small>`, `<span>`, `<strike>`, `<strong>`, `<sub>`, `<sup>`, `<table>`, `<tbody>`, `<td>`, `<textarea>`, `<tfoot>`, `<th>`, `<thead>`, `<tr>`, `<tt>`, `<u>`, `<ul>`, `<var>`, `<xmp>`	Internet Explorer 5, 5.5

2

Event Attribute	Event Description	Associated Elements	Compatibility
onbeforepaste	Fires before the selected content is pasted into document.	\<a>, \<address>, \<applet>, \<area>, \<b>, \<bdo>, \<big>, \<blockquote>, \<body>, \<button>, \<caption>, \<center>, \<cite>, \<code>, \<custom>, \<dd>, \<dfn>, \<dir>, \<div>, \<dl>, \<dt>, \<em>, \<embed>, \<fieldset>, \<font>, \<form>, \<h1> – \<h6>, \<hr>, \<i>, \<img>, \<input >, \<kbd>, \<label>, \<legend>, \<li>, \<listing>, \<map>, \<marquee>, \<menu>, \<nobr>, \<ol>, \<p>, \<plaintext>, \<pre>, \<rt>, \<ruby>, \<s>, \<samp>, \<select>, \<small>, \<span>, \<strike>, \<strong>, \<sub>, \<sup>, \<table>, \<tbody>, \<td>, \<textarea>, \<tfoot>, \<th>, \<thead>, \<tr>, \<tt>, \<u>, \<ul>, \<var>, \<xmp>	Internet Explorer 5, 5.5
onbeforeprint	Fires before user prints document or previews document for printing.	\<body>, \<frameset>	Internet Explorer 5, 5.5
onbeforeunload	Fires just prior to a document being unloaded from a window.	\<body>, \<frameset>	Internet Explorer 4, 5, 5.5

Event Attribute	Event Description	Associated Elements	Compatibility
onpaste	Fires when selected content is pasted into document.	<a>, <address>, <applet>, <area>, <b>, <bdo>, <big>, <blockquote>, <body>, <button>, <caption>, <center>, <cite>, <code>, <dd>, <dfn>, <dir>, <div>, <dl>, <dt>, <em>, <embed>, <fieldset>, <font>, <form>, <h1> – <h6>, <hr>, <i>, <img>, <input>, <kbd>, <label>, <legend>, <li>, <listing>, <map>, <marquee>, <menu>, <nobr>, <ol>, <p>, <plaintext>, <pre>, <rt>, <ruby>, <s>, <samp>, <select>, <small>, <span>, <strike>, <strong>, <sub>, <sup>, <table>, <tbody>, <td>, <textarea>, <tfoot>, <th>, <thead>, <tr>, <tt>, <u>, <ul>, <var>, <xmp>	Internet Explorer 5, 5.5
onreadystate change	Similar to onload. Fires whenever the ready state for an object has changed.	<applet>, <body>, <embed>, <frame>, <frameset>, <iframe>, <img>, <link>, <object>, <script>, <style>	Internet Explorer 4, 5, 5.5

2

Event Attribute	Event Description	Associated Elements	Compatibility
onresize	Triggered whenever an object is resized. Can only be bound to the window under Netscape as set via the <body> element.	<applet>, <body>, <button>, <caption>, <div>, <embed>, <frameset>, <hr>, <img>, <marquee>, <object>, <select>, <table>, <td>, <textarea>, <tr>	Netscape 4, 4.5 (supports <body> only); Internet Explorer 4–5.5
onrowenter	Indicates that a bound data row has changed and new data values are available.	<applet>, <body>, <button>, <caption>, <div>, <embed>, <hr>, <img>, <marquee>, <object>, <select>, <table>, <td>, <textarea>, <tr>	Internet Explorer 4, 5, 5.5
onrowexit	Fires just prior to a bound data source control changing the current row.	<applet>, <body >, <button>, <caption>, <div >, <embed>, <hr>, <img>, <marquee>, <object>, <select>, <table>, <td>, <textarea>, <tr>	Internet Explorer 4, 5, 5.5
onscroll	Fires when a scrolling element is repositioned.	<body>, <div>, <fieldset>, <img>, <marquee>, <span>, <textarea>	Internet Explorer 4, 5, 5.5
onselectstart	Fires when the user begins to select information by highlighting.	Nearly all elements	Internet Explorer 4, 5, 5.5
onstart	Fires when a looped marquee begins or starts over.	<marquee>	Internet Explorer 4, 5, 5.5

CAUTION: Documentation errors might exist. The event model changes rapidly and the browser vendors have not stopped innovating in this area. Events were tested by the author for accuracy, but for an accurate, up-to-date event model for these browsers, visit http://developer.netscape.com or http://msdn.microsoft.com/default.asp.

HTML Element Reference

This chapter lists all HTML 4 elements, as well as some proprietary elements defined by different browser vendors. The element entries include all or some of the following information:

- **Syntax**   HTML 4.01 syntax for the element, including attributes and event handlers defined by the W3C specification

- **XHTML Syntax**   Notes changes in element syntax that are required for element to be compatible with XHTML 1.0

- **Attributes/Events Defined by Browser**   Additional syntax defined by different browsers

- **Attributes**   Descriptions of all attributes associated with the element

- **Attribute and Event Support**   Browser support of attributes and events

- **Example**   A code example or examples using the element

- **XHTML Example**   Presents an example using XHTML syntax, if that varies from existing HTML syntax for the element under discussion

- **Compatibility**   The element's general compatibility with HTML/XHTML specifications and browser versions

- **Notes**   Additional information about the element

Listings of attributes and events defined by browser versions assume that these attributes and events generally remain associated with later versions of that browser; for example, attributes defined by Internet Explorer 4 are valid for Internet Explorer 5 and higher, and attributes defined for Netscape 4 remain valid for Netscape 4.5 and higher, up to Netscape 4.7x.

NOTE: Although the Netscape 6 browser is planned to be highly compliant with HTML standards, at the time of this edition it is still a work in progress. The latest beta version of the Netscape 6 browser available for this book was Preview Release 2. References in this text to Netscape 6 might not, therefore, reflect element or attribute support as it will be in the final version of the Netscape 6 browser. For this reason, it is unwise to assume that all elements or attributes supported by 4.x generation Netscape browsers will be supported by Netscape 6.

<!-- ... --> (Comment)

This construct is used to include text comments that will not be displayed by the browser.

Syntax

```
<!-- ... -->
```

Attributes

None

Event Handlers

None

Examples

```
<!-- This is an informational comment that can occur
     anywhere in an HTML document. The next example
     shows how style sheets and scripts are "commented out"
     to prevent older browsers from misinterpreting the
     content. -->
```

```
<style type="text/css">
<!--
 H1 {color: red; font-size: 40pt;}
-->
</style>

<script>
<!--
document.write("hello world");
// -->
</script>
```

Compatibility

> HTML 2, 3.2, 4, 4.01, XHTML 1.0
> Internet Explorer 2, 3, 4, 5, 5.5
> Netscape 1, 2, 3, 4–4.7, 6
> Opera 4
> WebTV

Notes

- Comments often are used to exclude content from older browsers, particularly those that do not understand client-side scripting or style sheets.

- Page developers should be careful when commenting HTML markup. Older browsers may or may not render the enclosed content.

<!DOCTYPE> (Document Type Definition)

This SGML construct specifies the document type definition corresponding to the document.

Syntax

```
<!DOCTYPE "DTD IDENTIFIER">
```

Attributes

None

Event Handlers

None

Examples

```
<!DOCTYPE HTML PUBLIC "-//W3C//DTD HTML 4.01 TRANSITIONAL//EN">

<!DOCTYPE HTML PUBLIC "-//W3C//DTD XHTML 1.0 TRANSITIONAL//EN">
```

Compatibility

HTML 2, 3.2, 4, 4.01, XHTML 1.0
Internet Explorer 2, 3, 4, 5, and 5.5
Netscape 1, 2, 3, 4–4.7, and 6
Opera 4
WebTV

Notes

- The <!DOCTYPE> element should be used as the first line of all HTML documents. Validation programs might use this construct when determining the correctness of an HTML document. Be certain to use the document type appropriate for the elements used in the document.

- Because the doctype declaration actually is an SGML statement, the lowercase rule for XHTML compatibility does not apply to **<!DOCTYPE>**.

<a> (Anchor)

This element indicates the portion of the document that is a hyperlink or the named target destination for a hyperlink.

Syntax

```
<a
     accesskey="key"
     charset="character code for language of linked
               resource"
     class="class name(s)"
     coords="comma-separated list of numbers"
     dir="ltr | rtl"
     href="url"
     hreflang="language code"
     id="unique alphanumeric identifier"
     lang="language code"
     name="name of target location"
     rel="comma-separated list of relationship values"
     rev="comma-separated list of relationship values"
     shape="default | circle | poly | rect"
     style="style information"
     tabindex="number"
     target="_blank | frame-name | _parent | _self | _top"
           (transitional)
     title="advisory text"
     type="content type of linked data"
     onblur="script" (transitional)
     onclick="script"
     ondblclick="script">
     onfocus="script"
     onhelp="script"
     onkeydown="script"
     onkeypress="script"
     onkeyup="script"
     onmousedown="script"
     onmousemove="script"
     onmouseout="script"
     onmouseover="script"
     onmouseup="script">

     Linked content

</a>
```

Attributes and Events Defined by Internet Explorer 4

```
datafield="name of column supplying bound data"
datasrc="ID of data source object supplying data"
language="javascript | jscript | vbs | vbscript"
methods="http-method"
ondragstart="script"
onselectstart="script"
```

2

Attributes and Events Defined by Internet Explorer 5.5

```
contenteditable="false | true | inherit"
hidefocus="true | false"
```

Attributes Defined by WebTV

```
NOCOLOR
SELECTED
```

Attributes

accesskey   This attribute specifies a keyboard navigation accelerator for the element. Pressing ALT or a similar key (depending on the browser and operating system) in association with the specified key selects the anchor element correlated with that key.

charset   This attribute defines the character encoding of the linked resource. The value is a space- and/or comma-delimited list of character sets as defined in RFC 2045. The default value is **ISO-8859-1**.

class   See "Core Attributes Reference," earlier in this chapter.

contenteditable   This proprietary Microsoft attribute allows users to edit content rendered in the Internet Explorer 5.5 browser. Values are **false**, **true**, and **inherit**. A value of **false** will prevent content from being edited by users; **true** will allow editing. The default value, **inherit**, applies the value of the affected element's parent element.

coords   For use with object shapes, this attribute uses a comma-separated list of numbers to define the coordinates of the object on the page.

datafld   This attribute specifies the column name from the data source object that supplies the bound data. This attribute is specific to Microsoft's Data Binding in Internet Explorer 4.

datasrc   This attribute indicates the **id** of the data source object that supplies the data that is bound to this element. This attribute is specific to Microsoft's Data Binding in Internet Explorer 4.

dir   See "Language Reference," earlier in this chapter.

hidefocus   This proprietary element, introduced with Internet Explorer 5.5, hides focus on an element's content. Focus must be applied to the element using the **tabindex** attribute.

href   This is the single required attribute for anchors defining a hypertext source link. It indicates the link target, either a URL or a URL fragment, that is a name preceded by a hash mark (#), which specifies an internal target location within the current document. URLs are not restricted to Web (http)-based documents. URLs might use any protocol supported by the browser. For example, file, ftp, and mailto work in most user agents.

hreflang   This attribute is used to indicate the language of the linked resource. See "Language Reference," earlier in this chapter for information on allowed values.

id   See "Core Attributes Reference," earlier in this chapter.

lang   See "Language Reference," earlier in this chapter.

language   This attribute specifies the language the current script is written in and invokes the proper scripting engine. The default value is **javascript**. **Javascript** and **jscript** represent that the scripting language is written in JavaScript. **vbs** and **vbscript** represent that the scripting language is written in VBScript. It also might be possible to use extended names, such as **JavaScript1.1**, to hide code from JavaScript-aware browsers that don't conform to a particular version of the language.

methods   The value of this attribute provides information about the functions that might be performed on an object. The values generally are given by the HTTP protocol when it is used, but it might (for similar reasons as for the **title** attribute) be useful to include advisory information in advance in the link. For example, the browser might choose a different rendering of a link as a function of the methods specified; something that is searchable might get a different icon, or an outside link might render with an indication of leaving the current site. This element is not well understood nor supported, even by the defining browser, Internet Explorer 4.

name   This attribute is required in an anchor defining a target location within a page. A value for **name** is similar to a value for the **id** core attribute and should be an alphanumeric identifier unique to the document. Under the HTML 4.01 specification, **id** and **name** both can be used with the **<a>** element as long as they have identical values.

nocolor   Supported only by WebTV, this attribute overrides the **link** color set in the **body** element and prevents the link from changing color.

rel   For anchors containing the **href** attribute, this attribute specifies the relationship of the target object to the link object. The value is a comma-separated list of relationship values. The values and their semantics will be registered by some authority that might have meaning to the document author. The default relationship, if no other is given, is **void**. The **rel** attribute should be used only when the **href** attribute is present.

rev   This attribute specifies a reverse link, the inverse relationship of the **rel** attribute. It is useful for indicating where an object came from, such as the author of a document.

selected   Supported only in WebTV, this attribute selects the anchor with a yellow highlight box.

shape   This attribute is used to define a selectable region for hypertext source links associated with a figure to create an image map. The values for the attribute are **circle**, **default**, **polygon**, and **rect**. The format of the **coords** attribute depends on the value of **shape**. For **circle**, the value is x,y,r where x and y are the pixel coordinates for the center of the circle and r is the radius value in pixels. For **rect**, the **coords** attribute should be x,y,w,h. The x,y values define the upper-left-hand corner of the rectangle, while w and h define the width and height respectively. A value of **polygon** for **shape** requires $x1,y1,x2,y2,\ldots$ values for **coords**. Each of the x,y pairs define a point in the polygon, with successive points being joined by straight lines and the last point joined to the first. The value **default** for **shape** requires that the entire enclosed area, typically an image, be used.

NOTE: Today because of browser support it is advisable to use the **usemap** attribute for the **<img>** element and the associated **<map>** element to define hotspots.

style   See "Core Attributes Reference," earlier in this chapter.

tabindex   This attribute uses a number to identify the object's position in the tabbing order for keyboard navigation using the TAB key.

target   This attribute specifies the target window for a hypertext source link referencing frames. The information linked to it will be displayed in the named window. Frames must be named to be targeted. There are, however, special name values. These include **_blank**, which indicates a new window; **_parent**, which indicates the parent frame set containing the source link; **_self**, which indicates the frame containing the source link; and **_top**, which indicates the full browser window.

title   See "Core Attributes Reference," earlier in this chapter.

type   This attribute specifies the media type in the form of a MIME type for the link target. Generally, this is provided strictly as advisory information; however, in the future a browser might add a small icon for multimedia types. For example, a browser might add a small speaker icon when **type** was set to audio/wav. For a complete list of recognized MIME types, see http://www.w3.org/TR/html4/references.html#ref-MIMETYPES.

Attribute and Event Support

Netscape 4   href, name, target, onclick, onmouseout, and onmouseover. (class, id, lang, and style are implied.)

Internet Explorer 4   accesskey, class, href, id, lang, name, rel, rev, style, target, title, onblur, onclick, ondblclick, onfocus, onhelp, onkeydown, onkeypress, onkeyup, onmousedown, onmousemove, onmouseout, onmouseover, onmouseup, and all attributes and events defined by Internet Explorer 4.

Internet Explorer 5.5   Same as IE 4, plus contenteditable and hidefocus.

WebTV   href, id, name, nocolor, selected, onclick, onmouseout, and onmouseover.

2

Event Handlers

See "Events Reference," earlier in this chapter.

Examples

```
<!-- anchor linking to external file -->
<a href="http://www.democompany.com/">External Link</a>

<!-- anchor linking to file on local filesystem -->
<a href="file:/c:\html\index.htm">local file link</a>

<!-- anchor invoking anonymous FTP -->
<a href="ftp://ftp.democompany.com/freestuff">Anonymous FTP
link</a>

<!-- anchor invoking FTP with password -->
<a href="ftp://joeuser:secretpassword@democompany.com/path/file">
FTP with password</a>

<!-- anchor invoking mail -->
<a href="mailto:fakeid@democompany.com">Send mail</a>

<!-- anchor used to define target destination within document -->
<a name="jump">Jump target</a>

<!-- anchor linking internally to previous target anchor -->
<a href="#jump">Local jump within document</a>

<!-- anchor linking externally to previous target anchor -->
<a href="http://www.democompany.com/document#jump">
Remote jump within document</a>
```

Compatibility

HTML 2, 3.2, 4, 4.01, and XHTML 1.0
Internet Explorer 2, 3, 4, 5, and 5.5
Netscape 1, 2, 3, 4–4.7, and 6
Opera 4
WebTV

Notes

- The following are reserved browser key bindings for the two major browsers and should not be used as values to **accesskey**: **a**, **c**, **e**, **f**, **g**, **h**, **v**, left arrow, and right arrow.

- HTML 3.2 defines only **name**, **href**, **rel**, **rev**, and **title**.

- The **target** attribute is not defined in browsers that do not support frames, such as Netscape 1 generation browsers.
- The **dir** attribute for **<a>** is not yet supported by any browsers.

<abbr> (Abbreviation)

This element allows authors to clearly indicate a sequence of characters that compose an acronym or abbreviation for a word (XML, WWW, and so on). See **<acronym>**, which is similar in use.

Syntax

```
<abbr
     class="class name(s)"
     dir="ltr | rtl"
     id="unique alphanumeric identifier"
     lang="language code"
     style="style information"
     title="advisory text"
     onclick="script"
     ondblclick="script"
     onkeydown="script"
     onkeypress="script"
     onkeyup="script"
     onmousedown="script"
     onmousemove="script"
     onmouseout="script"
     onmouseover="script"
     onmouseup="script">

</abbr>
```

Attributes

class   See "Core Attributes Reference," earlier in this chapter.

dir   See "Language Reference," earlier in this chapter.

id   See "Core Attributes Reference," earlier in this chapter.

lang   See "Language Reference," earlier in this chapter.

style   See "Core Attributes Reference," earlier in this chapter.

title   See "Core Attributes Reference," earlier in this chapter.

Attribute and Event Support

The support in Netscape 6 of attributes and events for this element remain unclear, but Preview Release Version 2 clearly supports the **title** attribute, and displays its contents as a tool tip.

2

Event Handlers

See "Events Reference," earlier in this chapter.

Examples

```
<abbr title="Dynamic Hypertext Markup Language">DHTML
</abbr>

<abbr lang="fr" title="World Wrestling Federation">WWF
</abbr>
```

Compatibility

> HTML 4, 4.01, XHTML 1.0
> Netscape 6

Notes

- **<abbr>** is a new element that is not defined under HTML 2 or 3.2. At present, only Netscape 6 appears to support the **<abbr>** element. **<acronym>** serves a similar function but is only supported by Internet Explorer 4 and later. Because there is no HTML-oriented presentation for this element so far, it is primarily used in conjunction with style sheets and scripts.

<acronym> (Acronym)

This element allows authors to clearly indicate a sequence of characters that compose an acronym or abbreviation for a word (XML, WWW, and so on).

Syntax

```
<acronym
      class="class name(s)"
      dir="ltr | rtl"
      id="unique alphanumeric identifier"
      lang="language code"
      style="style information"
      title="advisory text"
      onclick="script"
```

```
    ondblclick="script"
    onkeydown="script"
    onkeypress="script"
    onkeyup="script"
    onmousedown="script"
    onmousemove="script"
    onmouseout="script"
    onmouseover="script"
    onmouseup="script">

</acronym>
```

Attributes and Events Defined by Internet Explorer 4

```
    language="javascript | jscript | vbs | vbscript"
    ondragstart="script"
    onhelp="script"
    onselectstart="script"
```

Attributes and Events Defined by Internet Explorer 5.5

```
    accesskey="key"
    contenteditable="false | true | inherit"
    hidefocus="true | false"
    tabindex="number"
```

Attributes

accesskey   This attribute specifies a keyboard navigation accelerator for the element. Pressing ALT or a similar key (depending on the browser and operating system) in association with the specified key selects the anchor element correlated with that key.

class   See "Core Attributes Reference," earlier in this chapter.

contenteditable   This proprietary Microsoft attribute allows users to edit content rendered in the Internet Explorer 5.5 browser. Values are **false**, **true**, and **inherit**. A value of **false** will prevent content from being edited by users; **true** will allow editing. The default value, **inherit**, applies the value of the affected element's parent element.

dir   See "Language Reference," earlier in this chapter.

hidefocus   This proprietary element, introduced with Internet Explorer 5.5, hides focus on an element's content. Focus must be applied to the element using the **tabindex** attribute.

id   See "Core Attributes Reference," earlier in this chapter.

lang   See "Language Reference," earlier in this chapter.

language   This attribute specifies the language the current script is written in and invokes the proper scripting engine. The default value is **javascript. Javascript** and **jscript** represent that the script is written in JavaScript. **vbs** and **vbscript** represent that the script is written in VBScript. It may also be possible to use extended names, such as **JavaScript1.1**, to hide code from JavaScript-aware browsers that don't conform to a particular version of the language.

style   See "Core Attributes Reference," earlier in this chapter.

tabindex   This attribute uses a number to identify the object's position in the tabbing order for keyboard navigation using the TAB key. Internet Explorer 5.5 applies this attribute to the **acronym** element; under IE 5.5, this focus can be disabled with the **hidefocus** attribute.

title   See "Core Attributes Reference," earlier in this chapter.

Attribute and Event Support

Internet Explorer 4   All attributes.

Internet Explorer 5.5   All attributes, plus **contenteditable**, **hidefocus**, and **tabindex**.

Netscape 6   Netscape 6's support for attributes and events for this element remain unclear, but Preview Release Version 2 clearly supports the **title** attribute, and displays its contents as a tool tip.

Event Handlers

See "Events Reference," earlier in this chapter.

Examples

```
<acronym title="Extensible Markup Language">XML</acronym>

<acronym lang="fr" title="oci&eacute;t&eacute; Nationale de
Chemins de Fer">SNCF</acronym>
```

Compatibility

HTML 4, 4.01, XHTML 1.0
Internet Explorer 4, 5, and 5.5
Netscape 6

Notes

- **<acronym>** is a new element that is not defined under HTML 2 or 3.2. Under Internet Explorer 4 and above, the **title** attribute renders as a tool tip that can be used to define the meaning of the acronym.

<address> (Address)

This element marks up text indicating authorship or ownership of information. It generally occurs at the beginning or end of a document.

Syntax

```
<address
    class="class name(s)"
    dir="ltr | rtl"
    id="unique alphanumeric identifier"
    lang="language code"
    style="style information"
    title="advisory text"
    onclick="script"
    ondblclick="script"
    onkeydown="script"
    onkeypress="script"
    onkeyup="script"
    onmousedown="script"
    onmousemove="script"
    onmouseout="script"
    onmouseover="script"
    onmouseup="script">

</address>
```

Attributes and Events Defined by Internet Explorer 4

```
language="javascript | jscript | vbs | sbscript"
ondragstart="script"
onhelp="script"
onselectstart="script"
```

Attributes and Events Defined by Internet Explorer 5.5

```
accesskey="key"
contenteditable="inherit | false | true"
hidefocus="true | false"
tabindex="number"
unselectable="off | on"
```

Attributes

accesskey   This attribute specifies a keyboard navigation accelerator for the element. Pressing ALT or a similar key (depending on the browser and operating system) in association with the specified key selects the anchor element correlated with that key.

class   See "Core Attributes Reference," earlier in this chapter.

contenteditable   This proprietary Microsoft attribute allows users to edit content rendered in the Internet Explorer 5.5 browser. Values are **false**, **true**, and **inherit**. A value of **false** will prevent content from being edited by users; **true** will allow editing. The default value, **inherit**, applies the value of the affected element's parent element.

dir   See "Language Reference," earlier in this chapter.

hidefocus   This proprietary element, introduced with Internet Explorer 5.5, hides focus on an element's content. Focus must be applied to the element using the **tabindex** attribute.

id   See "Core Attributes Reference," earlier in this chapter.

lang   See "Language Reference," earlier in this chapter.

language   This attribute specifies the language the current script is written in and invokes the proper scripting engine. The default value is **javascript**. **Javascript** and **jscript** represent that the scripting language is written in JavaScript. **vbs** and **vbscript**

represent that the scripting language is written in VBScript. It may also be possible to use extended names, such as **JavaScript1.1**, to hide code from JavaScript-aware browsers that don't conform to a particular version of the language.

style   See "Core Attributes Reference," earlier in this chapter.

tabindex   This attribute uses a number to identify the object's position in the tabbing order for keyboard navigation using the TAB key. Internet Explorer 5.5 applies this attribute to the **address** element; under IE 5.5, this focus can be disabled with the **hidefocus** attribute.

title   See "Core Attributes Reference," earlier in this chapter.

unselectable   This proprietary Microsoft element can be used to prevent content displayed in Internet Explorer 5.5 from being selected. Testing suggests that this might not work consistently. Values are **off** (selection permitted) and **on** (selection not allowed).

Attribute and Event Support

Netscape 4   class, id, lang, and style.

Internet Explorer 4   class, id, lang, language, style, title, onclick, ondblclick, ondragstart, onhelp, onkeydown, onkeypress, onkeyup, onmousedown, onmousemove, onmouseout, onmouseover, onmouseup, and onselectstart.

Internet Explorer 5.5   Adds support for **dir**, **tabindex**, plus IE 5.5 attributes **contenteditable**, **hidefocus**, **tabindex**, and **unselectable**.

WebTV   No attributes.

Event Handlers
See "Events Reference," earlier in this chapter.

Example
```
<address>Big Company, Inc.<br>2105 Demo Street<br>
San Diego, CA U.S.A.</address>
```

Compatibility

HTML 2, 3.2, 4, 4.01, and XHTML 1.0
Internet Explorer 2, 3, 4, 5, and 5.5
Netscape 1, 2, 3, 4–4.7, and 6
Opera 4
WebTV

Notes

- Under HTML 2.0, 3.2, and WebTV there are no attributes for **<address>**.

<applet> (Java Applet)

This element identifies the inclusion of a Java applet. The strict HTML 4.01 definition does not include this element; it has been deprecated in favor of **<object>**.

Syntax (HTML 4.01 Transitional Only)

```
<applet
     align="bottom | left | middle | right | top"
     alt="alternative text"
     archive="URL of archive file"
     class="class name(s)"
     code="URL of Java class file"
     codebase="URL for base referencing"
     height="pixels"
     hspace="pixels"
     id="unique alphanumeric identifier"
     name="unique name for scripting reference"
     object="filename"
     style="style information"
     title="advisory text"
     vspace="pixels"
     width="pixels">

     <param> elements

     Alternative content

</applet>
```

Attributes and Events Defined by Internet Explorer 4

```
     align="absbottom | absmiddle | baseline | bottom |
          left | middle | right | texttop"
     datafld="name of column supplying bound data"
     datasrc="ID of data source object supplying data"
     src="URL"
     onafterupdate="script"
     onbeforeupdate="script"
     onblur="script"
     onclick="script"
     ondataavailable="script"
     ondatasetchanged="script"
```

```
ondatasetcomplete="script"
ondblclick="script"
ondragstart="script"
onerrorupdate="script"
onfocus="script"
onhelp="script"
onkeydown="script"
onkeypress="script"
onkeyup="script"
onmousedown="script"
onmousemove="script"
onmouseout="script"
onmouseover="script"
onmouseup="script"
onreadystatechange="script"
onresize="script"
onrowenter="script"
onrowexit="script"
```

Attributes and Events Defined by Internet Explorer 5.5

```
accesskey="key"
hidefocus="true | false"
tabindex="number"
```

Attributes Defined by Netscape 4

```
align="absbottom | absmiddle | baseline | center | texttop"
mayscript
```

Attributes

accesskey   This attribute specifies a keyboard navigation accelerator for the element. Pressing ALT or a similar key (depending on the browser and operating system) in association with the specified key selects the anchor element correlated with that key.

align   This attribute is used to position the applet on the page relative to content that might flow around it. The HTML 4.01 specification defines values of **bottom**, **left**, **middle**, **right**, and **top**, whereas Microsoft and Netscape also might support **absbottom**, **absmiddle**, **baseline**, **center**, and **texttop**.

alt   This attribute causes a descriptive text alternate to be displayed on browsers that do not support Java. Page designers should also remember that content enclosed within the **<applet>** element may also be rendered as alternative text.

archive   This attribute refers to an archived or compressed version of the applet and its associated class files, which might help reduce download time.

class   See "Core Attributes Reference," earlier in this chapter.

2

code   This attribute specifies the URL of the applet's class file to be loaded and executed. Applet filenames are identified by a .class filename extension. The URL specified by **code** might be relative to the **codebase** attribute.

codebase   This attribute gives the absolute or relative URL of the directory where applets' .class files referenced by the **code** attribute are stored.

datafld   This attribute, supported by Internet Explorer 4 and higher, specifies the column name from the data source object that supplies the bound data. This attribute might be used to specify the various **<param>** elements passed to the Java applet.

datasrc   Like **datafld**, this attribute is used for data binding under Internet Explorer 4. It indicates the **id** of the data source object that supplies the data that is bound to the **<param>** elements associated with the applet.

height   This attribute specifies the height, in pixels, that the applet needs.

hidefocus   This proprietary element, introduced with Internet Explorer 5.5, hides focus on an element's content. Focus must be applied to the element using the **tabindex** attribute.

hspace   This attribute specifies additional horizontal space, in pixels, to be reserved on either side of the applet.

id   See "Core Attributes Reference," earlier in this chapter.

mayscript   In the Netscape implementation, this attribute allows access to an applet by programs in a scripting language embedded in the document.

name   This attribute assigns a name to the applet so that it can be identified by other resources, particularly scripts.

object   This attribute specifies the URL of a serialized representation of an applet.

src As defined for Internet Explorer 4 and higher, this attribute specifies a URL for an associated file for the applet. The meaning and use is unclear and not part of the HTML standard.

style See "Core Attributes Reference," earlier in this chapter.

tabindex This attribute uses a number to identify the object's position in the tabbing order for keyboard navigation using the TAB key. Internet Explorer 5.5 applies this attribute to the **applet** element; under IE 5.5, this focus can be disabled with the **hidefocus** attribute.

title See "Core Attributes Reference," earlier in this chapter.

vspace This attribute specifies additional vertical space, in pixels, to be reserved above and below the applet.

width This attribute specifies in pixels the width that the applet needs.

Attribute and Event Support

Netscape 4 **align, alt, archive, code, codebase, hspace, mayscript, name, vspace,** and **width.** (**class, id,** and **style** are implied.)

Internet Explorer 4 **alt, class, code, codebase, height, hspace, id, name, style, title, vspace, width,** and all attributes and events defined by Internet Explorer 4.

Internet Explorer 5.5 Same as IE 4, plus **hidefocus** and **tabindex.**

Event Handlers
None.

Example

```
<applet code="game.class"
        align="left"
        archive="game.zip"
        height="250" width="350">

<param name="difficulty"  value="easy">

<b>Sorry, you need Java to play this game.</b>

</applet>
```

Compatibility

HTML 2, 3.2, 4, 4.01, and XHTML 1.0
Internet Explorer 2, 3, 4, 5, and 5.5
Netscape 1, 2, 3, 4–4.7, and 6
WebTV

Notes

- The HTML 4.01 specification does not encourage the use of **<applet>** and prefers the use of the **<object>** element. Under the strict definition of HTML 4.01, this element is deprecated.

- The **<applet>** element replaces the original **<app>** element. Parameter values can be passed to applets using the **<param>** element in the applet's content area.

- WebTV's current implementation does not support Java applets.

- Java applets were first supported under Netscape 2–level browsers and Internet Explorer 3–level browsers.

<area> (Image Map Area)

<area> is an empty element used within the content model of the **<p>** element to implement client-side image maps. It defines a hot-spot region on the map and associates it with a hypertext link.

Syntax

```
<area
    accesskey="character"
    alt="alternative text"
    class="class name(s)"
    coords="comma separated list of values"
    dir="ltr | rtl"
    href="url"
    id="unique alphanumeric identifier"
    lang="language code"
    nohref
    shape="circle | default | poly | rect"
    style="style information"
    tabindex="number"
    target="_blank | frame-name | _parent | _self |
            _top" (transitional)
    title="advisory text"
    onblur="script"
    onclick="script"
    ondblclick="script"
```

```
onfocus="script"
onkeydown="script"
onkeypress="script"
onkeyup="script"
onmousedown="script"
onmousemove="script"
onmouseout="script"
onmouseover="script"
onmouseup="script">
```

XHTML Syntax

Because **<area>** is an empty element, a closing forward slash is required before the closing bracket of the tag, as in the following:

```
<area />
```

Attributes and Events Defined by Internet Explorer 4

```
language="javascript | jscript | vbs | vbscipt"
shape="circ | circle | poly | polygon | rect |
       rectangle"
ondragstart="script"
onhelp="script"
onselectstart="script"
```

Attributes and Events Defined by Internet Explorer 5.5

```
hidefocus="true | false"
```

Attributes Defined by Netscape 4

```
name="filename"
shape="circle | default | poly | polygon | rect"
```

Attributes Defined by WebTV

```
notab
```

Attributes

accesskey   This attribute specifies a keyboard navigation accelerator for the element. Pressing ALT or a similar key in association with the specified character selects the form control correlated with that key sequence. Page designers are forewarned to avoid key sequences already bound to browsers.

alt   This attribute contains a text string alternative to display on browsers that cannot display images.

class   See "Core Attributes Reference," earlier in this chapter.

coords   This attribute contains a set of values specifying the coordinates of the hot-spot region. The number and meaning of the values depend upon the value specified for the **shape** attribute. For a **rect** or **rectangle** shape, the **coords** value is two *x,y* pairs: **left, top, right**, and **bottom**. For a **circ** or **circle** shape, **coords** value is *x,y,r* where *x,y* is a pair specifying the center of the circle and *r* is a value for the radius. For a **poly** or **polygon** shape, the **coords** value is a set of *x,y* pairs for each point in the polygon: *x1,y1,x2,y2,x3,y3*, and so on.

dir   See "Language Reference," earlier in this chapter.

hidefocus   This proprietary element, introduced with Internet Explorer 5.5, hides focus on an element's content. Focus must be applied to the element using the **tabindex** attribute.

href   This attribute specifies the hyperlink target for the area. Its value is a valid URL. Either this attribute or the **nohref** attribute must be present in the element.

id   See "Core Attributes Reference," earlier in this chapter.

lang   See "Language Reference," earlier in this chapter.

language   This attribute specifies the language the current script is written in and invokes the proper scripting engine. The default value is **javascript. Javascript** and **jscript** represent that the scripting language is written in JavaScript. **vbs** and **vbscript** represent that the scripting language is written in VBScript. It also might be possible to use extended names, such as **JavaScript1.1**, to hide code from JavaScript-aware browsers that don't conform to a particular version of the language.

name   This attribute is used to define a name for the clickable area so that it can be scripted by older browsers.

nohref   This attribute indicates that no hyperlink exists for the associated area. Either this attribute or the **href** attribute must be present in the element.

notab   Supported by WebTV, this attribute keeps the element from appearing in the tabbing order.

shape   This attribute defines the shape of the associated hot spot. HTML 4 defines the values **rect**, which defines a rectangular region; **circle**, which defines a circular region; **poly**, which defines a polygon; and **default**, which indicates the entire region beyond any defined shapes. Many browsers, notably Internet Explorer 4 and higher, support **circ**, **polygon**, and **rectangle** as valid values for **shape**.

style   See "Core Attributes Reference," earlier in this chapter.

tabindex   This attribute represents a numeric value specifying the position of the defined area in the browser tabbing order.

target   This attribute specifies the target window for hyperlink referencing frames. The value is a frame name or one of several special names. A value of **_blank** indicates a new window. A value of **_parent** indicates the parent frame set containing the source link. A value of **_self** indicates the frame containing the source link. A value of **_top** indicates the full browser window.

title   See "Core Attributes Reference," earlier in this chapter.

Attribute and Event Support

Netscape 4   coords, href, nohref, shape, target, onmouseout, and onmouseover. (class, id, lang, and style are implied but not listed for this element in Netscape documentation.)

Internet Explorer 4   alt, class, coords, href, id, lang, language, nohref, shape, style, tabindex, target, title, all W3C-defined events, and all attributes and events defined by Internet Explorer 4.

Internet Explorer 5.5   Same as IE 4, plus **dir** and **hidefocus**.

WebTV   coords, href, id, name, notab, shape, target, onmouseout, and onmouseover.

Event Handlers
See "Events Reference," earlier in this chapter.

Example
```
<map name="primary">
  <area shape="circle" coords="200,250,25" href="another.htm">
  <area shape="default" nohref>
</map>
```

XHTML Example

```
<map name="primary">
  <area shape="circle" coords="200,250,25" href="another.htm" />
  <area shape="default" nohref />
</map>
```

Compatibility

> HTML 2, 3.2, 4, 4.01, and XHTML 1.0
> Internet Explorer 2, 3, 4, 5, and 5.5
> Netscape 1, 2, 3, 4–4.7, and 6
> Opera 4
> WebTV

Notes

- By the HTML 3.2 and 4.0 specifications, the closing tag
  </area> is forbidden.

- The XHTML 1.0 specification requires a trailing slash: **<area />**

- The **id**, **class**, and **style** attributes have the same meaning as
  the core attributes defined in the HTML 4 specification, but
  only Netscape and Microsoft define them.

- Netscape 1–level browsers do not understand the **target**
  attribute as it relates to frames.

- HTML 3.2 defines only **alt**, **coords**, **href**, **nohref**, and **shape**.

<audioscope> (Sound Amplitude Display)

This WebTV-specific element displays an audioscope for a sound
resource that displays a dynamic, graphical display of a sound's
amplitude.

Syntax (Defined by WebTV)

```
<audioscope
     align="absbottom | absmiddle | baseline | bottom |
            left | middle | right | texttop | top"
     border="pixels"
     gain="number"
     height="pixels"
     leftcolor="color name | #RRGGBB"
     leftoffset="number"
     maxlevel="true | false"
     rightcolor="name | #RRGGBB"
     rightoffset="number"
     width="pixels">
```

Attributes

align   This attribute positions the audioscope object on the page relative to text or other content that might flow around it.

border   This attribute sets the width of the audioscope border in pixels. The default value is **1**.

gain   This attribute takes a numeric value, which is a multiplier for the amplitude display. The default value is **1**.

height   This attribute sets the height of the audioscope in pixels. The default value is **80** pixels.

leftcolor   This attribute sets the color of the line displaying the left audio channel in the audioscope. Values can be given either as named colors or in the numeric *#RRGGBB* format. The default value is **#8ECE10**.

leftoffset   This attribute sets the vertical offset for the display of the left audio channel with positive and negative values relative to the center of the audioscope. The default value is **0**.

maxlevel   This Boolean attribute specifies whether the audioscope should clip sound according to the specified gain. The default value is **false**.

rightcolor   This attribute sets the color of the line displaying the right audio channel in the audioscope. Values can be given either as named colors or in the numeric *#RRGGBB* format. The default value is **#8ECE10**.

rightoffset   This attribute sets the vertical offset for the display of the right audio channel with positive and negative values relative to the center of the audioscope. The default value is **1**.

width   This attribute sets the width of the audioscope in pixels. The default width is **100** pixels.

Attribute and Event Support

WebTV   All attributes.

Event Handlers
None.

Example

```
<audioscope border="1" height="16" width="240" gain="3"
         maxlevel="false">
```

Compatibility

WebTV

Notes

- **<audioscope>** is supported only by WebTV. As such it is not subject to the XHTML 1.0 specification, and does not require a trailing slash /.

<b> (Bold)

This element indicates that the enclosed text should be displayed in boldface.

Syntax

```
<b
    class="class name(s)"
    dir="ltr | rtl"
    id="unique alphanumeric identifier"
    lang="language code"
    style="style information"
    title="advisory text"
    onclick="script"
    ondblclick="script"
    onkeydown="script"
    onkeypress="script"
    onkeyup="script"
    onmousedown="script"
    onmousemove="script"
    onmouseout="script"
    onmouseover="script"
    onmouseup="script">

</b>
```

Attributes and Events Defined by Internet Explorer 4

```
    language="javascript | jscript | vbs | vbscript"
    ondragstart="script"
    onhelp="script"
    onselectstart="script"
```

Attributes and Events Defined by Internet Explorer 5.5

```
accesskey="key"
contenteditable="false | true | inherit"
hidefocus="true | false"
tabindex=="n"
```

Attributes

accesskey   This attribute specifies a keyboard navigation accelerator for the element. Pressing ALT or a similar key (depending on the browser and operating system) in association with the specified key selects the anchor element correlated with that key.

class   See "Core Attributes Reference," earlier in this chapter.

contenteditable   This proprietary Microsoft attribute allows users to edit content rendered in the Internet Explorer 5.5 browser. Values are **false**, **true**, and **inherit**. A value of **false** will prevent content from being edited by users; **true** will allow editing. The default value, **inherit**, applies the value of the affected element's parent element.

dir   See "Language Reference," earlier in this chapter.

hidefocus   This proprietary element, introduced with Internet Explorer 5.5, hides focus on an element's content. Focus must be applied to the element using the **tabindex** attribute.

id   See "Core Attributes Reference," earlier in this chapter.

lang   See "Language Reference," earlier in this chapter.

language   This attribute specifies the language the current script is written in and invokes the proper scripting engine. The default value is **javascript**. **Javascript** and **jscript** represent that the scripting language is written in JavaScript. **vbs** and **vbscript** represent that the scripting language is written in VBScript. It also might be possible to use extended names, such as **JavaScript1.1**, to hide code from JavaScript-aware browsers that don't conform to a particular version of the language.

style   See "Core Attributes Reference," earlier in this chapter.

tabindex   This attribute uses a number to identify the object's position in the tabbing order for keyboard navigation using the TAB key. Internet Explorer 5.5 applies this attribute to the **b** element; under IE 5.5, this focus can be disabled with the **hidefocus** attribute.

title   See "Core Attributes Reference," earlier in this chapter.

2

Attribute and Event Support

Netscape 4   class, **id**, **lang**, and **style** are implied but not explicitly listed for this element.

Internet Explorer 4   All W3C-defined attributes and events except **dir**, and attributes and events defined by Internet Explorer 4.

Internet Explorer 5.5   Same as IE 4, plus **contenteditable**, **dir**, **hidefocus**, and **tabindex**.

Event Handlers

See "Events Reference," earlier in this chapter.

Example

```
This text is <b>bold</b> for emphasis.
```

Compatibility

```
HTML 2, 3.2, 4, 4.01, and XHTML 1.0
Internet Explorer 2, 3, 4, 5, and 5.5
Netscape 1, 2, 3, 4–4.7, and 6
Opera 4
WebTV
```

Notes

- HTML 2 and 3.2 do not define any attributes for this element.

<base> (Base URL)

This element specifies the base URL to use for all relative URLs contained within a document. It occurs only in the scope of a **<HEAD>** element.

Syntax

```
<base
    href="url"
    target="_blank | frame-name | _parent | _self |
          _top" (transitional)>
```

XHTML Syntax

Because this is an empty element, a closing forward slash is required before the closing bracket on the tag:

```
<base />
```

Syntax Defined by Internet Explorer 5.0/5.5

```
    id="string"
```

Attributes

href   This attribute specifies the base URL to be used throughout the document for relative URL addresses.

target   For documents containing frames, this attribute specifies the default target window for every link that does not have an explicit target reference. Aside from named frames, several special values exist. A value of **_blank** indicates a new window. A value of **_parent** indicates the parent frame set containing the source link. A value of **_self** indicates the frame containing the source link. A value of **_top** indicates the full browser window.

Attribute and Event Support

Netscape 4   href and target

Internet Explorer 4   href and target

Internet Explorer 5.5   href, id and target

WebTV   href and target

Event Handlers

None.

Examples

```
<base href="http://www.democompany.com/">

<base target="_blank" href="http://www.democompany.com/">
```

XHTML Examples

```
<base href="http://www.democompany.com/" />

<base target="_blank" href="http://www.democompany.com/" />
```

Compatibility

> HTML 2, 3.2, 4, 4.01, and XHTML 1.0
> Internet Explorer 2, 3, 4, 5, and 5.5
> Netscape 1, 2, 3, 4–4.7, and 6
> Opera 4
> WebTV

Notes

- HTML 2.0 and 3.2 define only the **href** attribute.
- XHTML 1.0 requires a trailing slash: **<base />**

<basefont> (Base Font)

This element establishes a default font size for a document. Font size then can be varied relative to the base font size using the **<font>** element. The **<basefont>** element must be placed near the beginning of the body part of the page.

Syntax (Transitional Only)

```
<basefont
    color="color name | #RRGGBB"
    face="font name(s)"
    id="unique alphanumeric identifier"
    size="1-7 | +/-int">
```

XHTML Syntax

Because this is an empty element, a closing forward slash is required before the closing bracket on the tag:

```
<basefont />
```

Attributes Defined by Internet Explorer 4

```
class="class name(s)"
lang="language code"
```

Attributes

class Internet Explorer 4 documentation indicates that the **class** can be set for the **<basefont>** element; however, this probably is a mistake in the documentation.

color This attribute sets the text color using either a named color or a color specified in the hexadecimal *#RRGGBB* format.

face This attribute contains a list of one or more font names. The document text in the default style is rendered in the first font face that the client's browser supports. If no font listed is installed on the local system, the browser typically defaults to the proportional or fixed-width font for that system.

id See "Core Attributes Reference," earlier in this chapter.

lang Internet Explorer 4 documentation also mentions use of the **lang** attribute to indicate the language used. Meaning with this element is not well defined.

size This attribute specifies the font size as either a numeric or relative value. Numeric values range from **1** to **7** with **1** being the smallest and **3** the default.

Attribute and Event Support

Netscape 4 **id** (implied) and **size**

Internet Explorer 4 All attributes

WebTV **size**

Event Handlers
None.

Example
```
<basefont color="#FF0000" face="Helvetica" size="+2">
```

XHTML Example
```
<basefont color="#FF0000" face="Helvetica" size="+2" />
```

Compatibility

HTML 2, 3.2, 4, 4.01, and XHTML 1.0
Internet Explorer 2, 3, 4, 5, and 5.5

Netscape 1, 2, 3, 4–4.7
WebTV

Notes

- HTML 3.2 supports the **<basefont>** element and the **size** attribute. HTML 4.0 transitional specification added support for **color** and **face** as well.

- The HTML 4.01 strict specification does not support this element.

- The font sizes indicated by numeric values are browser dependent and not absolute.

- At the time of this writing, Netscape 6 (Preview Release 2) does not support this element.

- XHTML 1.0 requires a trailing slash for this element: **<basefont />**.

<bdo> (Bidirectional Override)

This element is used to override the current directionality of text.

Syntax

```
<bdo>
      class="class name(s)"
      dir="ltr | rtl"
      id="unique alphanumeric identifier"
      lang="language code"
      style="style information"
      title="advisory text">

</bdo>
```

Attributes and Events Defined by Internet Explorer 5.5

```
accesskey="key"
contenteditable="inherit | false | true"
hidefocus="true | false"
language="javascript | jscript | vbs | vbscript | xml"
tabindex="number"
unselectable="off | on"
```

Attributes

accesskey   This attribute specifies a keyboard navigation accelerator for the element. Pressing ALT or a similar key (depending on the browser and operating system) in association with the specified key selects the anchor element correlated with that key.

class   See "Core Attributes Reference," earlier in this chapter.

contenteditable   This proprietary Microsoft attribute allows users to edit content rendered in the Internet Explorer 5.5 browser. Values are **false**, **true**, and **inherit**. A value of **false** will prevent content from being edited by users; **true** will allow editing. The default value, **inherit**, applies the value of the affected element's parent element.

dir   This attribute is required for the **<bdo>** element. It sets the text direction either left to right (**ltr**) or right to left (**rtl**).

hidefocus   This proprietary element, introduced with Internet Explorer 5.5, hides focus on an element's content. Focus must be applied to the element using the **tabindex** attribute.

id   See "Core Attributes Reference," earlier in this chapter.

lang   See "Language Reference," earlier in this chapter.

language   This attribute, applied to this element by Internet Explorer 5.5, specifies the language the current script is written in and invokes the proper scripting engine. The default value is **javascript**. **Javascript** and **jscript** represent that the scripting language is written in JavaScript. **vbs** and **vbscript** represent that the scripting language is written in VBScript. It also might be possible to use extended names, such as **JavaScript1.1**, to hide code from JavaScript-aware browsers that don't conform to a particular version of the language.

style   See "Core Attributes Reference," earlier in this chapter.

tabindex   This attribute uses a number to identify the object's position in the tabbing order for keyboard navigation using the TAB key. Internet Explorer 5.5 applies this attribute to the **bdo** element; under IE 5.5, this focus can be disabled with the **hidefocus** attribute.

title   See "Core Attributes Reference," earlier in this chapter.

unselectable   This proprietary Microsoft element can be used to prevent content displayed in Internet Explorer 5.5 from being selected. Testing suggests that this might not work consistently. Values are **off** (selection permitted) and **on** (selection not allowed).

Attribute and Event Support

Internet Explorer 5.5   IE documentation adds support for all attributes, plus **contenteditable**, **hidefocus**, **language**, **tabindex**, and **unselectable**.

Event Handlers
None.

Example
```
<!-- Switch text direction -->
<bdo dir="rtl">This text will go right to left if you can
find a browser that supports this element.
</bdo>
```

Compatibility

HTML 4, 4.01, XHTML 1.0
Internet Explorer 5, 5.5

Notes

- Internet Explorer 5 was the first browser to support this element; to date, **<bdo>** is the only element with which the **dir** attribute works.

<bgsound> (Background Sound)

This Internet Explorer and WebTV element associates a background sound with a page.

Syntax (Defined by Internet Explorer 4)
```
<bgsound
     balance="number"
     class="class name(s)"
     id="unique alphanumeric identifier"
     lang="language code"
     loop=number
     src="url of sound file"
     title="advisory text"
     volume="number">
```

Attributes

balance   This attribute defines a number between −10,000 and +10,000 that determines how the volume will be divided between the speakers.

class   See "Core Attributes Reference," earlier in this chapter.

id   See "Core Attributes Reference," earlier in this chapter.

lang   See "Language Reference," earlier in this chapter.

loop   This attribute indicates the number of times a sound is to be played and either has a numeric value or the keyword **infinite**.

src   This attribute specifies the URL of the sound file to be played, which must be one of the following types: .wav, .au, or .mid.

title   See "Core Attributes Reference," earlier in this chapter.

volume   This attribute defines a number between -10,000 and 0 that determines the loudness of a page's background sound.

Attribute and Event Support

Internet Explorer 4   All attributes

WebTV   **loop** and **src**

Event Handlers
None.

Examples
```
<bgsound src="sound1.mid">

<bgsound src="sound2.au" loop="infinite">
```

Compatibility

Internet Explorer 2, 3, 4, 5, and 5.5
WebTV

Notes

- Similar functionality can be achieved in Netscape using the **<embed>** element to invoke LiveAudio.

<big> (Big Font)

This element indicates that the enclosed text should be displayed in a larger font relative to the current font.

2

Syntax

```
<big
     class="class name(s)"
     dir="ltr | rtl"
     id="unique alphanumeric identifier"
     lang="language code"
     style="style information"
     title="advisory text"
     onclick="script"
     ondblclick="script"
     onkeydown="script"
     onkeypress="script"
     onkeyup="script"
     onmousedown="script"
     onmousemove="script"
     onmouseout="script"
     onmouseover="script"
     onmouseup="script">

</big>
```

Attributes and Events Defined by Internet Explorer 4

```
     language="javascript | jscript | vbs | vbsript"
     ondragstart="script"
     onhelp="script"
     onselectstart="script"
```

Attributes and Events Defined by Internet Explorer 5.5

```
     accesskey="key"
     contenteditable="false | true | inherit"
     hidefocus="true | false"
     tabindex="number"
```

Attributes

accesskey   This attribute specifies a keyboard navigation accelerator for the element. Pressing ALT or a similar key (depending on the browser and operating system) in association with the specified key selects the anchor element correlated with that key.

class See "Core Attributes Reference," earlier in this chapter.

contenteditable This proprietary Microsoft attribute allows users to edit content rendered in the Internet Explorer 5.5 browser. Values are **false, true,** and **inherit.** A value of **false** will prevent content from being edited by users; **true** will allow editing. The default value, **inherit,** applies the value of the affected element's parent element.

dir See "Language Reference," earlier in this chapter.

hidefocus This proprietary element, introduced with Internet Explorer 5.5, hides focus on an element's content. Focus must be applied to the element using the **tabindex** attribute.

id See "Core Attributes Reference," earlier in this chapter.

lang See "Language Reference," earlier in this chapter.

language This attribute specifies the language the current script is written in and invokes the proper scripting engine. The default value is **javascript. Javascript** and **jscript** represent that the scripting language is written in JavaScript. **vbs** and **vbscript** represent that the scripting language is written in VBScript.

style See "Core Attributes Reference," earlier in this chapter.

tabindex This attribute uses a number to identify the object's position in the tabbing order for keyboard navigation using the TAB key. Internet Explorer 5.5 applies this attribute to the **big** element; under IE 5.5, this focus can be disabled with the **hidefocus** attribute.

title See "Core Attributes Reference," earlier in this chapter.

Attribute and Event Support

Netscape 4 **class, id, lang,** and **style** are implied.

Internet Explorer 4 All attributes and events except **dir.**

Internet Explorer 5.5 Same as IE 4, plus **contenteditable, dir, hidefocus,** and **tabindex.**

Event Handlers

See "Events Reference," earlier in this chapter.

Example

```
This text is regular size. <big>This text is
larger.</big>
```

Compatibility

2

HTML 2, 3.2, 4, 4.01, and XHTML 1.0
Internet Explorer 2, 3, 4, 5, and 5.5
Netscape 1, 2, 3, 4–4.7, and 6
Opera 4
WebTV

Notes

- HTML 3.2 does not support any attributes for this element.

<blackface> (Blackface Font)

This WebTV element renders the enclosed text in a double-weight boldface font. It is used for headings and other terms needing special emphasis.

Syntax

```
<blackface>  Text  </blackface>
```

Attributes
None

Event Handlers
None

Example

```
<blackface>Buy now!</blackface> This offer expires
in five minutes.
```

Compatibility

WebTV

Notes

- This element is supported only by WebTV.

<blink> (Blinking Text Display)

This Netscape-specific element causes the enclosed text to flash slowly.

Syntax (Defined by Netscape)

```
<blink
     class="class name(s)"
     id="unique alphanumeric identifier"
     lang="language code"
     style="style information">

</blink>
```

Attributes

class   See "Core Attributes Reference," earlier in this chapter.

id   See "Core Attributes Reference," earlier in this chapter.

lang   See "Language Reference," earlier in this chapter.

style   See "Core Attributes Reference," earlier in this chapter.

Attribute and Event Support

Netscape 4   All attributes

Event Handlers

None

Example

```
<blink>Annoying, isn't it?</blink>
```

Compatibility

Netscape 1, 2, 3, 4–4.7, 6

Notes

- Although not explicitly defined in Netscape documentation, the **class**, **id**, **lang**, and **style** attributes are indicated to be universal to all elements under Netscape 4 and higher, and might have meaning here.

<blockquote> (Block Quote)

This block element indicates that the enclosed text is an extended quotation. Usually this is rendered visually by indentation.

Syntax

```
<blockquote
     cite="url of source information"
     class="class name(s)"
     dir="ltr | rtl"
     id="unique alphanumeric identifier"
     lang="language code"
     style="style information"
     title="advisory text"
     onclick="script"
     ondblclick="script"
     onkeydown="script"
     onkeypress="script"
     onkeyup="script"
     onmousedown="script"
     onmousemove="script"
     onmouseout="script"
     onmouseover="script"
     onmouseup="script">

</blockquote>
```

Attributes and Events Defined by Internet Explorer 4

```
     language="javascript | jscript | vbs | vbscript"
     ondragstart="script"
     onhelp="script"
     onselectstart="script"
```

Attributes and Events Defined by Internet Explorer 5.5

```
     accesskey="key"
     contenteditable="false | true | inherit"
     hidefocus="true | false"
     tabindex="number"
```

Attributes

accesskey   This attribute specifies a keyboard navigation accelerator for the element. Pressing ALT or a similar key (depending on the browser and operating system) in association with the specified key selects the anchor element correlated with that key.

cite   The value of this attribute should be a URL of the document in which the information cited can be found.

class   See "Core Attributes Reference," earlier in this chapter.

contenteditable   This proprietary Microsoft attribute allows users to edit content rendered in the Internet Explorer 5.5 browser. Values are **false, true,** and **inherit**. A value of **false** will prevent content from being edited by users; **true** will allow editing. The default value, **inherit**, applies the value of the affected element's parent element.

dir   See "Language Reference," earlier in this chapter.

hidefocus   This proprietary element, introduced with Internet Explorer 5.5, hides focus on an element's content. Focus must be applied to the element using the **tabindex** attribute.

id   See "Core Attributes Reference," earlier in this chapter.

lang   See "Language Reference," earlier in this chapter.

language   This attribute specifies the language the current script is written in and invokes the proper scripting engine. The default value is **javascript**. **Javascript** and **jscript** represent that the scripting language is written in JavaScript. **vbs** and **vbscript** represent that the scripting language is written in VBScript.

style   See "Core Attributes Reference," earlier in this chapter.

tabindex   This attribute uses a number to identify the object's position in the tabbing order for keyboard navigation using the TAB key. Internet Explorer 5.5 applies this attribute to the **blockquote** element; under IE 5.5, this focus can be disabled with the **hidefocus** attribute.

title   See "Core Attributes Reference," earlier in this chapter.

Attribute and Event Support

Netscape 4   class, id, lang, and **style**.

Internet Explorer 4   All attributes and events except **cite** and **dir**.

Internet Explorer 5.5   Same as IE 4, plus **contenteditable, dir, hidefocus,** and **tabindex**.

Event Handlers

See "Events Reference," earlier in this chapter.

Example

```
The following paragraph is taken from our March report:
<blockquote cite="marchreport.htm"> ... text ...
</blockquote>
```

2

Compatibility

> HTML 2, 3.2, 4, 4.01, and XHTML 1.0
> Internet Explorer 2, 3, 4, 5, and 5.5
> Netscape 1, 2, 3, 4–4.7, and 6
> Opera 4
> WebTV

Notes

- HTML 2.0 and 3.2 do not support any attributes for this element.
- WebTV only indents the left margin of text enclosed in the <blockquote> element.
- Some browsers understand the <bq> shorthand notation.

<body> (Document Body)

This element encloses a document's displayable content, in contrast to the descriptive and informational content contained in the <head> element.

Syntax

```
<body
    alink="color name | #RRGGBB" (transitional)
    background="url of background image" (transitional)
    bgcolor="color name | #RRGGBB" (transitional)
    class="class name(s)"
    dir="ltr | rtl"
    id="unique alphanumeric identifier"
    lang="language code"
    link="color name | #RRGGBB" (transitional)
    style="style information"
    text="color name | #RRGGBB" (transitional)
    title="advisory text"
    vlink="color name | #RRGGBB" (transitional)
    onclick="script"
```

```
    ondblclick="script"
    onkeydown="script"
    onkeypress="script"
    onkeyup="script"
    onload="script"
    onmousedown="script"
    onmousemove="script"
    onmouseout="script"
    onmouseover="script"
    onmouseup="script"
    onunload="script">

</body>
```

XHTML Syntax Notes

Under XHTML 1.0, the closing **</body>** tag no longer can be considered optional.

Attributes and Events Defined by Internet Explorer 4

```
    bgproperties="fixed"
    bottommargin="pixels"
    language="javascript | jscript | vbs | vbscript"
    leftmargin="pixels"
    rightmargin="pixels"
    scroll="no | yes"
    topmargin="pixels"
    onafterupdate="script"
    onbeforeunload="script"
    onbeforeupdate="script"
    ondragstart="script"
    onhelp="script"
    onrowenter="script"
    onrowexit="script"
    onscroll="script"
    onselect="script"
    onselectstart="script"
```

Attributes and Events Defined by Internet Explorer 5.5

```
    accesskey="key"
    contenteditable="false | true | inherit"
    hidefocus="true | false"
    tabindex="number"
```

Events Defined by Netscape 4

```
onblur="script"
onfocus="script"
marginheight="pixels"
marginwidth="pixels"
```

2

Attributes Defined by WebTV

```
credits="url"
instructions="url"
logo="url"
```

Attributes

accesskey   This attribute specifies a keyboard navigation accelerator for the element. Pressing ALT or a similar key (depending on the browser and operating system) in association with the specified key selects the anchor element correlated with that key.

alink   This attribute sets the color for active links within the document. Active links represent the state of a link as it is being pressed. The value of the attribute can be either a browser-dependent named color or a color specified in the hexadecimal *#RRGGBB* format.

background   This attribute contains a URL for an image file, which will be tiled to provide the document background.

bgcolor   This attribute sets the background color for the document. Its value can be either a browser-dependent named color or a color specified using the hexadecimal *#RRGGBB* format.

bgproperties   This attribute, first introduced in Internet Explorer 2, has one value, **fixed**, which causes the background image to act as a fixed watermark and not to scroll.

bottommargin   This attribute specifies the bottom margin for the entire body of the page and overrides the default margin. When set to **0** or "", the bottom margin is the bottom edge of the window or frame the content is displayed in.

class   See "Core Attributes Reference," earlier in this chapter.

contenteditable   This proprietary Microsoft attribute allows users to edit content rendered in the Internet Explorer 5.5 browser. Values are **false**, **true**, and **inherit**. A value of **false** will prevent content from being edited by users; **true** will allow editing. The default value, **inherit**, applies the value of the affected element's parent element.

credits   In the WebTV implementation, this attribute contains the URL of the document to retrieve when the viewer presses the credits button on the Info Panel.

dir   See "Language Reference," earlier in this chapter.

hidefocus   This proprietary element, introduced with Internet Explorer 5.5, hides focus on an element's content. Focus must be applied to the element using the **tabindex** attribute.

id   See "Core Attributes Reference," earlier in this chapter.

instructions   In the WebTV implementation, this attribute contains the URL of the document to retrieve when the viewer presses the instructions button on the Info Panel.

lang   See "Language Reference," earlier in this chapter.

language   This attribute specifies the language the current script is written in and invokes the proper scripting engine. The default value is **javascript**. **Javascript** and **jscript** represent that the scripting language is written in JavaScript. **vbs** and **vbscript** represent that the scripting language is written in VBScript.

leftmargin   This Internet Explorer–specific attribute sets the left margin for the page in pixels, overriding the default margin. When set to **0** or "", the left margin is the left edge of the window or the frame.

link   This attribute sets the color for hyperlinks within the document that have not yet been visited. Its value can be either a browser-dependent named color or a color specified using the hexadecimal *#RRGGBB* format.

logo   In the WebTV implementation, this attribute contains the URL of a 70 × 52–pixel thumbnail image for the page, which is used in the history and bookmarks for WebTV.

marginheight   This Netscape–specific attribute sets the top margin for the document in pixels. If set to **0** or "", the top margin will be exactly on the top edge of the window or frame. It is equivalent to combining the Internet Explorer attributes **bottommargin** and **topmargin**.

2

marginwidth   This Netscape-specific attribute sets the left and right margins for the page in pixels, overriding the default margin. When set to **0** or "", the left margin is the left edge of the window or the frame. It is equivalent to combining the Internet Explorer attributes **leftmargin** and **rightmargin**.

rightmargin   This attribute, specific to Internet Explorer, sets the right margin for the page in pixels, overriding the default margin. When set to **0** or "", the right margin is the right edge of the window or the frame.

scroll   This attribute turns the scrollbars on or off. The default value is **YES**.

style   See "Core Attributes Reference," earlier in this chapter.

tabindex   This attribute uses a number to identify the object's position in the tabbing order for keyboard navigation using the TAB key. Internet Explorer 5.5 applies this attribute to the **body** element; the entire document will be selected when its tabbing order is reached. Under IE 5.5, this focus can be disabled with the **hidefocus** attribute.

text   This attribute sets the text color for the document. Its value can be either a browser-dependent named color or a color specified using the hexadecimal *#RRGGBB* format.

title   See "Core Attributes Reference," earlier in this chapter.

topmargin   This Internet Explorer–specific attribute sets the top margin for the document in pixels. If set to **0** or "", the top margin will be exactly on the top edge of the window or frame.

Attribute and Event Support

Netscape 4   alink, **background**, **bgcolor**, **link**, **text**, **vlink**, **onblur**, **onfocus**, **onload**, and **onunload**. (**class**, **id**, **lang**, and **style** are implied.)

Internet Explorer 4   All W3C-defined attributes and events except **dir**, all attributes and events defined by Internet Explorer 4, and **onblur** and **onfocus**.

Internet Explorer 5.5   Same as IE 4, plus **contenteditable**, **dir**, **hidefocus**, and **tabindex**.

WebTV background, bgcolor, credits, instructions, link, logo, text, vlink, onload, and onunload.

Event Handlers

See "Events Reference," earlier in this chapter.

Example

```
<body background="checkered.gif"
    bgcolor="white"
    alink="red"
    link="blue"
    vlink="red"
    text="black"> ... </body>

<!-- myLoadFunction defined in document head in <SCRIPT> element -->
<body onload="myLoadFunction()"> ... </body>
```

Compatibility

HTML 2, 3.2, 4, 4.01, and XHTML 1.0
Internet Explorer 2, 3, 4, 5, and 5.5
Netscape 1, 2, 3, 4–4.7, and 6
Opera 4
WebTV

Notes

- When defining text colors, it is important to be careful to specify both foreground and background explicitly so that they are not masked out by browser defaults set by the user.

- Under the HTML 4.01 strict definition, no color-setting attributes and background attributes are allowed. This includes the **alink**, **background**, **bgcolor**, **link**, **text**, and **vlink** attributes.

- This element must be present in all documents except those declaring a frame set.

- Under XHTML 1.0, the closing **</body>** tag is mandatory.

<bq> (Block Quote)

This obsolete element signifies that the enclosed text is an extended quotation. Although it has been defined in early HTML specifications, currently it is supported only by the WebTV browser as an alias for the **<blockquote>** element.

Syntax (Obsolete)

```
<bq>
</bq>
```

Attributes

None

Event Handlers

None

Example

```
<bq>The HTML Programmer's Reference says "Don't
use this element."</bq>
```

Compatibility

WebTV

Notes

- This element originated in the early days of HTML and is considered obsolete. It should not be used.

 (Line Break)

This empty element forces a line break.

Syntax

```
<br
    class="class name(s)"
    clear="all | left | none | right" (transitional)
    id="unique alphanumeric identifier"
    style="style information"
    title="advisory text">
```

XHTML 1.0 Syntax

Because this is an empty element, a closing forward slash is required before the closing bracket on the tag:

```
<br />
```

Attributes Defined by Internet Explorer 4

```
language="javascript | jscript | vbs | vbscript"
```

Attributes

class   See "Core Attributes Reference," earlier in this chapter.

clear   This attribute forces the insertion of vertical space so that the tagged text can be positioned with respect to images. A value of **left** clears text that flows around left-aligned images to the next full left margin, a value of **right** clears text that flows around right-aligned images to the next full right margin, and a value of **all** clears text until it can reach both full margins. The default value according to the HTML 4 transitional specification is **none**, but its meaning generally is supported as just introducing a return and nothing more.

id   See "Core Attributes Reference," earlier in this chapter.

language   This attribute specifies the language the current script is written in and invokes the proper scripting engine. The default value is **javascript**. **Javascript** and **jscript** represent that the scripting language is written in JavaScript. **vbs** and **vbscript** represent that the scripting language is written in VBScript.

style   See "Core Attributes Reference," earlier in this chapter.

title   See "Core Attributes Reference," earlier in this chapter.

Attribute and Event Support

Netscape 4   **clear**. (**class**, **id**, and **style** are implied by Netscape documentation.)

Internet Explorer 4   All attributes.

WebTV   **clear**

Event Handlers
None

Examples
```
This text will be broken here <br>and continued on a new line.

<img src="test.gif" align="right">
This is the image caption.<br clear="right">
```

XHTML Examples

This text will be broken here **
**and continued on a new line.

<img src="test.gif" align="right" />
This is the image caption.**<br clear="right" />**

Compatibility

> HTML 2, 3.2, 4, 4.01, and XHTML 1.0
> Internet Explorer 2, 3, 4, 5, and 5.5
> Netscape 1, 2, 3, 4–4.7, and 6
> Opera 4
> WebTV

Notes

- This is an empty element. A closing tag is illegal under all HTML specifications. For XHTML compatibility, a closing slash is required: **
**.

- Under the HTML 4.01 strict specification, the **clear** attribute is not valid. Style sheet rules provide the functionality of the **clear** attribute.

<button> (Form Button)

This element defines a nameable region known as a button, which can be used together with scripts.

Syntax

```
<button
    accesskey="key"
    class="class name(s)"
    dir="ltr | rtl"
    disabled
    id="unique alphanumeric identifier"
    lang="language code"
    name="button name"
    style="style information"
    tabindex="number"
    title="advisory text"
    type="button | reset | submit"
    value="button value"
    onblur="script"
    onclick="script"
    ondblclick="script"
```

```
onfocus="script"
onkeydown="script"
onkeypress="script"
onkeyup="script"
onmousedown="script"
onmousemove="script"
onmouseout="script"
onmouseover="script"
onmouseup="script">
```

```
</button>
```

Attributes and Events Defined by Internet Explorer 4

```
datafld="name of column supplying bound data"
dataformatas="html | text"
datasrc="id of data source object supplying data"
language="javascript | jscript | vbs | vbscript"
onafterupdate="script"
onbeforeupdate="script"
ondragstart="script"
onhelp="script"
onresize="script"
onrowenter="script"
onrowexit="script"
onselectstart="script"
```

Attributes and Events Defined by Internet Explorer 5.5

```
contenteditable="false | true | inherit"
hidefocus="true | false"
```

Attributes

accesskey   This attribute specifies a keyboard navigation accelerator for the element. Pressing ALT or a similar key in association with the specified key selects the anchor element correlated with that key.

class   See "Core Attributes Reference," earlier in this chapter.

contenteditable   This proprietary Microsoft attribute allows users to edit content rendered in the Internet Explorer 5.5 browser. Values are **false**, **true**, and **inherit**. A value of **false** will prevent content from being edited by users; **true** will allow editing. The default value, **inherit**, applies the value of the affected element's parent element.

datafld   This attribute specifies the column name from the data source object that supplies the bound data that defines the information for the **<button>** element's content.

dataformatas   This attribute indicates whether the bound data is plain text or HTML.

datasrc   This attribute indicates **id** of the data source object that supplies the data that is bound to the **<button>** element.

dir   See "Language Reference," earlier in this chapter.

disabled   This attribute is used to disable the button.

hidefocus   This proprietary element, introduced with Internet Explorer 5.5, hides focus on an element's content. Focus must be applied to the element using the **tabindex** attribute.

id   See "Core Attributes Reference," earlier in this chapter.

lang   See "Language Reference," earlier in this chapter.

language   This attribute specifies the language that the current script associated with the event handlers is written in and invokes the proper scripting engine. The default value is **javascript**. **Javascript** and **jscript** represent that the scripting language is written in JavaScript. **vbs** and **vbscript** represent that the scripting language is written in VBScript.

name   This attribute is used to define a name for the button so that it can be scripted by older browsers or used to provide a name for submit buttons when there is more than one in a page.

style   See "Core Attributes Reference," earlier in this chapter.

tabindex   This attribute uses a number to identify the object's position in the tabbing order.

title   See "Core Attributes Reference," earlier in this chapter.

type   Defines the type of button. According to the HTML 4.01 specification, by default the button is undefined. Possible values include **button, reset,** and **submit,** which are used to indicate the button is a plain button, reset button, or submit button respectively.

value   Defines the value that is sent to the server when the button is pressed. This might be useful when using multiple **submit** buttons that perform different actions to indicate which button was pressed to the handling CGI program.

Attribute and Event Support

Internet Explorer 4 All attributes and events except **dir**, **name**, **tabindex**, and **value**.

Internet Explorer 5.5 All attributes and events, plus **contenteditable**, **hidefocus**, and **tabindex**.

Event Handlers

See "Events Reference," earlier in this chapter.

Examples

```
<button name="Submit"
        value="Submit"
        type="Submit">Submit Request</button>

<button type="button"
        onclick="doSomething()">Click This Button</button>

<button type="button">
<img src="polkadot.gif" alt="Polkadot"></button>
```

Compatibility

HTML 4
Internet Explorer 4, 5, 4.5
Netscape 6

Notes

- It is illegal to associate an image map with an **<img>** that appears as the contents of a **button** element.
- The HTML 4.01 specification reserves the data-binding attributes **datafld**, **dataformatas**, and **datasrc** for future use.

<caption> (Figure or Table Caption)

This element is used within both the figure and table elements to define a caption.

Syntax

```
<caption
    align="bottom | left | right | top" (transitional)
    class="class name(s)"
```

```
dir="ltr | rtl"
id="unique alphanumeric identifier"
lang="language code"
style="style information"
title="advisory text"
onclick="script"
ondblclick="script"
onkeydown="script"
onkeypress="script"
onkeyup="script"
onmousedown="script"
onmousemove="script"
onmouseout="script"
onmouseover="script"
onmouseup="script">
```

```
</caption>
```

Attributes and Events Defined by Internet Explorer 4

```
language="javascript | jscript | vbs | vbscript"
valign="bottom | top"
onafterupdate="script"
onbeforeupdate="script"
onblur="script"
onchange="script"
ondragstart="script"
onfocus="script"
onhelp="script"
onresize="script"
onrowenter="script"
onrowexit="script"
onselect="script"
onselectstart="script"
```

Attributes and Events Defined by Internet Explorer 5.5

```
accesskey="key"
contenteditable="false | true | inherit"
hidefocus="true | false"
tabindex="number"
```

Attributes

accesskey   This attribute specifies a keyboard navigation accelerator for the element. Pressing ALT or a similar key (depending on the browser and operating system) in association with the specified key selects the anchor element correlated with that key.

align   This attribute specifies the alignment of the caption. HTML 4 defines **bottom**, **left**, **right**, and **top** as legal values. Internet Explorer and WebTV also support **center**. Because this does not provide the possibility to combine vertical and horizontal alignments, Microsoft has introduced the **valign** attribute for the **<caption>** element.

class   See "Core Attributes Reference," earlier in this chapter.

contenteditable   This proprietary Microsoft attribute allows users to edit content rendered in the Internet Explorer 5.5 browser. Values are **false**, **true**, and **inherit**. A value of **false** will prevent content from being edited by users; **true** will allow editing. The default value, **inherit**, applies the value of the affected element's parent element.

dir   See "Language Reference," earlier in this chapter.

hidefocus   This proprietary element, introduced with Internet Explorer 5.5, hides focus on an element's content. Focus must be applied to the element using the **tabindex** attribute.

id   See "Core Attributes Reference," earlier in this chapter.

lang   See "Language Reference," earlier in this chapter.

language   This attribute specifies the language the current script is written in and invokes the proper scripting engine. The default value is **javascript**. **Javascript** and **jscript** represent that the scripting language is written in JavaScript. **vbs** and **vbscript** represent that the scripting language is written in VBScript.

style   See "Core Attributes Reference," earlier in this chapter.

tabindex   This attribute uses a number to identify the object's position in the tabbing order for keyboard navigation using the TAB key. Internet Explorer 5.5 applies this attribute to the **caption** element; under IE 5.5, this focus can be disabled with the **hidefocus** attribute.

title   See "Core Attributes Reference," earlier in this chapter.

valign   This Internet Explorer–specific attribute specifies whether the table caption appears at the top or bottom.

Attribute and Event Support

Netscape 4   align. (**class**, **id**, **lang**, and **style** are implied.)

Internet Explorer 4   All attributes and events except **dir**.

Internet Explorer 5.5   Same as IE 4, plus **contenteditable**, **dir**, **hidefocus**, and **tabindex**.

WebTV   align (center | left | right).

Event Handlers

See "Events Reference," earlier in this chapter.

Example

```
<table>
    <caption align="top">Our High-Priced Menu</caption>
        <tr>
            <td>Escargot</td>
            <td>Filet Mignon</td>
            <td>Big Mac</td>
                </tr>
</table>
```

Compatibility

HTML 2, 3.2, 4, 4.01, and XHTML 1.0
Internet Explorer 2, 3, 4, 5, and 5.5
Netscape 1, 2, 3, 4–4.7, and 6
Opera 4
WebTV

Notes

- There should be only one caption per table.

- HTML 3.2 defines only the **align** attribute with values of **bottom** and **top**. No other attributes are defined prior to HTML 4. WebTV adds a **center** value to the **align** attribute.

<center> (Center Alignment)

This element causes the enclosed content to be centered within the margins currently in effect. Margins are either the default page margins or those imposed by overriding elements such as tables.

Syntax (Transitional Only)

```
<center
    class="class name(s)"
    dir="ltr | rtl"
    id="unique alphanumeric identifier"
    lang="language code"
    style="style information"
    title="advisory text"
    onclick="script"
    ondblclick="script"
    onkeydown="script"
    onkeypress="script"
    onkeyup="script"
    onmousedown="script"
    onmousemove="script"
    onmouseout="script"
    onmouseover="script"
    onmouseup="script">

</center>
```

Attributes and Events Defined by Internet Explorer 4

```
    language="javascript | jscript | vbs | vbscript"
    ondragstart="script"
    onhelp="script"
    onselectstart="script"
```

Attributes and Events Defined by Internet Explorer 5.5

```
    accesskey="key"
    contenteditable="false | true | inherit"
    hidefocus="true | false"
    tabindex="number"
```

Attributes

accesskey   This attribute specifies a keyboard navigation accelerator for the element. Pressing ALT or a similar key (depending on the browser and operating system) in association with the specified key selects the anchor element correlated with that key.

class   See "Core Attributes Reference," earlier in this chapter.

contenteditable   This proprietary Microsoft attribute allows users to edit content rendered in the Internet Explorer 5.5 browser.

Values are **false**, **true**, and **inherit**. A value of **false** will prevent content from being edited by users; **true** will allow editing. The default value, **inherit**, applies the value of the affected element's parent element.

dir   See "Language Reference," earlier in this chapter.

hidefocus   This proprietary element, introduced with Internet Explorer 5.5, hides focus on an element's content. Focus must be applied to the element using the **tabindex** attribute.

id   See "Core Attributes Reference," earlier in this chapter.

lang   See "Language Reference," earlier in this chapter.

language   This attribute specifies the language the current script is written in and invokes the proper scripting engine. The default value is **javascript. Javascript** and **jscript** represent that the scripting language is written in JavaScript. **vbs** and **vbscript** represent that the scripting language is written in VBScript.

style   See "Core Attributes Reference," earlier in this chapter.

tabindex   This attribute uses a number to identify the object's position in the tabbing order for keyboard navigation using the TAB key. Internet Explorer 5.5 applies this attribute to the **center** element; under IE 5.5, this focus can be disabled with the **hidefocus** attribute.

title   See "Core Attributes Reference," earlier in this chapter.

Attribute and Event Support

Netscape 4   **class**, **id**, **lang**, and **style** are implied.

Internet Explorer 4   All attributes and events except **dir**.

Internet Explorer 5.5   All attributes and events (including **dir**) plus **contenteditable**, **hidefocus**, and **tabindex**.

Event Handlers
See "Events Reference," earlier in this chapter.

Example
```
<center>This is in the center of the page.</center>
```

Compatibility

HTML 3.2 and 4 (transitional)
HTML 2, 3.2, 4, 4.01, and XHTML 1.0
Internet Explorer 2, 3, 4, 5, and 5.5
Netscape 1, 2, 3, 4–4.7, and 6
Opera 4
WebTV

Notes

- The **<center>** element defined by the W3C is a shorthand notation for **<div align="center">**. The strict version of HTML 4.01 does not include the **<center>** element.

- HTML 3.2 does not support any attributes for this element.

<cite> (Citation)

This element indicates a citation from a book or other published source and usually is rendered in italics by a browser.

Syntax

```
<cite
    class="class name(s)"
    dir="ltr | rtl"
    id="unique alphanumeric identifier"
    lang="language code"
    style="style information"
    title="advisory text"
    onclick="script"
    ondblclick="script"
    onkeydown="script"
    onkeypress="script"
    onkeyup="script"
    onmousedown="script"
    onmousemove="script"
    onmouseout="script"
    onmouseover="script"
    onmouseup="script">

</cite>
```

Attributes and Events Defined by Internet Explorer 4

```
language="javascript | jscript | vbs | vbscript"
ondragstart="script"
onhelp="script"
onselectstart="script"
```

2

Attributes and Events Defined by Internet Explorer 5.5

```
accesskey="key"
contenteditable="false | true | inherit"
hidefocus="true | false"
tabindex="number"
```

Attributes

accesskey   This attribute specifies a keyboard navigation accelerator for the element. Pressing ALT or a similar key (depending on the browser and operating system) in association with the specified key selects the anchor element correlated with that key.

class   See "Core Attributes Reference," earlier in this chapter.

contenteditable   This proprietary Microsoft attribute allows users to edit content rendered in the Internet Explorer 5.5 browser. Values are **false**, **true**, and **inherit**. A value of **false** will prevent content from being edited by users; **true** will allow editing. The default value, **inherit**, applies the value of the affected element's parent element.

dir   See "Language Reference," earlier in this chapter.

hidefocus   This proprietary element, introduced with Internet Explorer 5.5, hides focus on an element's content. Focus must be applied to the element using the **tabindex** attribute.

id   See "Core Attributes Reference," earlier in this chapter.

lang   See "Language Reference," earlier in this chapter.

language   This attribute specifies the language the current script is written in and invokes the proper scripting engine. The default value is **javascript**. **Javascipt** and **jscript** represent that the scripting language is written in JavaScript. **vbs** and **vbscript** represent that the scripting language is written in VBScript.

style   See "Core Attributes Reference," earlier in this chapter.

tabindex   This attribute uses a number to identify the object's position in the tabbing order for keyboard navigation using the TAB key. Internet Explorer 5.5 applies this attribute to the **cite** element; under IE 5.5, this focus can be disabled with the **hidefocus** attribute.

title   See "Core Attributes Reference," earlier in this chapter.

Attribute and Event Support

Netscape 4   **class**, **id**, **lang**, and **style** are implied.

Internet Explorer 4   All events and attributes except **dir**.

Internet Explorer 5.5   All events and attributes (including **dir**), plus **contenteditable**, **hidefocus**, and **tabindex**.

Event Handlers
See "Events Reference," earlier in this chapter.

Example
```
This example is taken from <cite>The HTML Programmer's
Reference.</cite>
```

Compatibility

> HTML 2, 3.2, 4, 4.01, and XHTML 1.0
> Internet Explorer 2, 3, 4, 5, and 5.5
> Netscape 1, 2, 3, 4–4.7, and 6
> Opera 4
> WebTV

Notes

- HTML 2 and 3.2 do not indicate any attributes for this element.

<code> (Code Listing)

This element indicates that the enclosed text is source code in a programming language. Usually it is rendered in a monospaced font.

Syntax
```
<code
    class="class name(s)"
    dir="ltr | rtl"
```

```
id="unique alphanumeric identifier"
lang="language code"
style="style information"
title="advisory text"
onclick="script"
ondblclick="script"
onkeydown="script"
onkeypress="script"
onkeyup="script"
onmousedown="script"
onmousemove="script"
onmouseout="script"
onmouseover="script"
onmouseup="script">
```

`</code>`

Attributes and Events Defined by Internet Explorer 4

```
language="javascript | jscript | vbs | vbscript"
ondragstart="script"
onhelp="script"
onselectstart="script"
```

Attributes Defined by Internet Explorer 5.5

```
contenteditable="false | true | inherit"
```

Attributes

class   See "Core Attributes Reference," earlier in this chapter.

contenteditable   This proprietary Microsoft attribute allows users to edit content rendered in the Internet Explorer 5.5 browser. Values are **false**, **true**, and **inherit**. A value of **false** will prevent content from being edited by users; **true** will allow editing. The default value, **inherit**, applies the value of the affected element's parent element.

dir   See "Language Reference," earlier in this chapter.

id   See "Core Attributes Reference," earlier in this chapter.

lang   See "Language Reference," earlier in this chapter.

language   This attribute specifies the language the current script is written in and invokes the proper scripting engine. The default value is **javascript**. **Javascript** and **jscript** represent that the scripting language is written in JavaScript. **vbs** and **vbscript** represent that the scripting language is written in VBScript.

style   See "Core Attributes Reference," earlier in this chapter.

title   See "Core Attributes Reference," earlier in this chapter.

Attribute and Event Support

Netscape 4   **class**, **id**, **lang**, and **style** are implied.

Internet Explorer 4   All attributes and events except **dir**.

Internet Explorer 5.5   All attributes and events, plus **contenteditable** and **dir**.

Event Handlers

See "Events Reference," earlier in this chapter.

Example

To increment a variable called *count,* use
```
<code> count++ </code>
```

Compatibility

HTML 2, 3.2, 4, 4.01, and XHTML 1.0
Internet Explorer 2, 3, 4, 5, and 5.5
Netscape 1, 2, 3, 4–4.7, and 6
Opera 4
WebTV

Notes

- This element is best for short code fragments because it does not preserve special indentation.

- HTML 2.0 and 3.2 do not support any attributes for this element.

<col> (Column)

This element defines a column within a table and is used for grouping and alignment purposes. It generally is found within a **<colgroup>** element.

Syntax

```
<col
    align="center | char | justify | left | right"
```

```
char="character"
charoff="number"
class="class name(s)"
dir="ltr | rtl"
id="unique alphanumeric identifier"
lang="language code"
span="number"
style="style information"
title="advisory text"
valign="baseline | bottom | middle | top"
width="column width specification"
onclick="script"
ondblclick="script"
onkeydown="script"
onkeypress="script"
onkeyup="script"
onmousedown="script"
onmousemove="script"
onmouseout="script"
onmouseover="script"
onmouseup="script">
```

XHTML Syntax

Because this is an empty element, a closing forward slash is required before the closing bracket on the tag:

```
<col />
```

Syntax Defined by Internet Explorer 5.5

```
bgcolor="color name | #RRGGBB"
```

Attributes

align   This attribute specifies horizontal alignment of a cell's contents.

bgcolor   Applies a background color to all cells in the column (IE 5.5 only).

char   This attribute is used to set the character to align the cells in a column on. Typical values for this include a period (.) when attempting to align numbers or monetary values.

charoff   This attribute is used to indicate the number of characters to offset the column data from the alignment characters specified by the **char** value.

class   See "Core Attributes Reference," earlier in this chapter.

dir   See "Language Reference," earlier in this chapter.

id   See "Core Attributes Reference," earlier in this chapter.

lang   See "Language Reference," earlier in this chapter.

span   When present, this attribute applies the attributes of the
<col> element to additional consecutive columns.

style   See "Core Attributes Reference," earlier in this chapter.

title   See "Core Attributes Reference," earlier in this chapter.

valign   This attribute specifies the vertical alignment of the text
within the cell. Possible values for this attribute are **baseline**,
bottom, **middle**, and **top**.

width   This attribute specifies a default width for each column
in the current column group. In addition to the standard pixel and
percentage values, this attribute might take the special form **0***,
which means that the width of each column in the group should
be the minimum width necessary to hold the column's contents.
Relative widths such as 0.5* also can be used.

Attribute and Event Support

Internet Explorer 4   align (center | left | right), **class**, **id**, **span**,
style, **title**, **valign**, and **width**.

Internet Explorer 5.5   Adds **bgcolor**, **dir**, and **lang**.

Event Handlers
See "Events Reference," earlier in this chapter.

Example
```
<table border="1" width="400">
<colgroup>
<col align="center" width="150"><col align="right">
</colgroup>
  <td>This column is aligned to the center.</td>
  <td>This one is aligned to the right.</td>
</td>

<tr><td>!</td><td>?</td></tr>

<tr><td>!</td><td>?</td></tr>
</table>
```

XHTML Example

```
<table border="1" width="400">
<colgroup>
<col align="center" width="150" /><col align="right" />
</colgroup>
  <td>This column is aligned to the center.</td>
  <td>This one is aligned to the right.</td>
</td>

<tr><td>!</td><td>?</td></tr>

<tr><td>!</td><td>?</td></tr>
</table>
```

Compatibility

> HTML 4, 4.01, XHTML 1.0
> Internet Explorer 4, 5, 5.5

Notes

- As an empty element, **<col>** does not require a closing tag.

- Under XHTML 1.0, **<col>** requires a trailing slash: **<col />**.

- This element generally appears within a **<colgroup>** element; like that element, it is somewhat of a convenience feature used to set attributes with one or more table columns.

<colgroup> (Column Group)

This element creates an explicit column group to access a group of table columns for scripting or formatting.

Syntax

```
<colgroup
    align="center | char | justify | left | right"
    char="character"
    charoff="number"
    class="class name(s)"
    dir="ltr | rtl"
    id="unique alphanumeric identifier"
    lang="language code"
    span="number"
    style="style information"
    title="advisory text"
    valign="baseline | bottom | middle | top"
    width="column width specification"
```

```
onclick="script"
ondblclick="script"
onkeydown="script"
onkeypress="script"
onkeyup="script"
onmousedown="script"
onmousemove="script"
onmouseout="script"
onmouseover="script"
onmouseup="script">

    <col> elements

</colgroup>
```

XHTML 1.0 Syntax

Under XHTML 1.0, the closing tag **</colgroup>** no longer can be considered optional.

Attributes

align   This attribute specifies horizontal alignment of contents of the cells in the column group. The values of **center**, **left**, and **right** have obvious meanings. A value of **justify** for the attribute should attempt to justify all the column's contents. A value of **char** attempts to align the contents based on the value of the **char** attribute in conjunction with **charoff**.

char   This attribute is used to set the character to align the cells in a column on. Typical values for this include a period (.) when attempting to align numbers or monetary values.

charoff   This attribute is used to indicate the number of characters to offset the column data from the alignment characters specified by the **char** value.

class   See "Core Attributes Reference," earlier in this chapter.

dir   See "Language Reference," earlier in this chapter.

id   See "Core Attributes Reference," earlier in this chapter.

lang   See "Language Reference," earlier in this chapter.

span   When present, this attribute specifies the default number of columns in this group. Browsers should ignore this attribute if the current column group contains one or more **<col>** elements. The default value of this attribute is **1**.

style   See "Core Attributes Reference," earlier in this chapter.

title   See "Core Attributes Reference," earlier in this chapter.

valign   This attribute specifies the vertical alignment of the contents of the cells within the column group.

2

width   This attribute specifies a default width for each column and its cells in the current column group. In addition to the standard pixel and percentage values, this attribute might take the special form **0***, which means that the width of each column in the group should be the minimum width necessary to hold the column's contents.

Attribute and Event Support

Internet Explorer 4   align (center | left | right), class, id, span, style, title, valign, and width

Internet Explorer 5.5   align (center | justify | left | right), class, dir, id, lang, span, style, and valign

Event Handlers

See "Events Reference," earlier in this chapter.

Examples

```
<colgroup span="10" align="char" char=":" valign="center">

<colgroup style="{background: green}">
<col align="left">
<col align="center">
</colgroup>
```

Compatibility

HTML 4, 4.01, XHTML 1.0
Internet Explorer 4, 5, 5.5

Notes

- Each column group defined by a **<colgroup>** can contain zero or more **<col>** elements.
- Under XHTML 1.0, the closing **</colgroup>** tag is mandatory.

<comment> (Comment Information)

This nonstandard element treats enclosed text as nondisplaying comments while processing enclosed HTML. This element should not be used.

Syntax (Defined by Internet Explorer 4)

```
<comment
      id="unique alphanumeric identifier"
      lang="language code"
      title="advisory text">

      Commented information

</comment>
```

Attributes

id   See "Core Attributes Reference," earlier in this chapter.

lang   See "Language Reference," earlier in this chapter.

title   See "Core Attributes Reference," earlier in this chapter.

Attribute and Event Support

Internet Explorer 4   All attributes.

Event Handlers

None

Example

```
<comment>This is not the proper way to form
comments.</comment>
```

Compatibility

```
Internet Explorer 4, 5, and 5.5
WebTV
```

Notes

- It is better to use the <!--. . .--> element, an alternate comment element that does not process enclosed HTML in all specification-conforming browsers.

- Because the **<comment>** element is not supported by all browsers, commented text done in this fashion will appear in Netscape browsers. Although Internet Explorer still supports this element, IE documentation recommends use of the <!--. . .--> element.

- Although some notes indicate that the **<comment>** element will render HTML included within it, in practice this does not seem to be the case.

<dd> (Definition in a Definition List)

This element indicates the definition of a term within a list of defined terms (**<dt>**) enclosed by a definition list (**<dl>**).

Syntax

```
<dd  class="class name(s)"
     dir="ltr | rtl"
     id="unique alphanumeric identifier"
     lang="language code"
     style="style information"
     title="advisory text"
     onclick="script"
     ondblclick="script"
     onkeydown="script"
     onkeypress="script"
     onkeyup="script"
     onmousedown="script"
     onmousemove="script"
     onmouseout="script"
     onmouseover="script"
     onmouseup="script">

</dd>
```

XHTML Syntax

Under XHTML 1.0, the closing tag **</dd>** can no longer be considered optional.

Attributes and Events Defined by Internet Explorer 4

```
language="javascript | jscript | vbs | vbscript"
ondragstart="script"
onhelp="script"
onselectstart="script"
```

Attributes and Events Defined by Internet Explorer 5.5

```
accesskey="key"
contenteditable="false | true | inherit"
hidefocus="true | false"
tabindex="number"
```

Attributes

accesskey This attribute specifies a keyboard navigation accelerator for the element. Pressing ALT or a similar key (depending on the browser and operating system) in association with the specified key selects the anchor element correlated with that key.

class See "Core Attributes Reference," earlier in this chapter.

contenteditable This proprietary Microsoft attribute allows users to edit content rendered in the Internet Explorer 5.5 browser. Values are **false**, **true**, and **inherit**. A value of **false** will prevent content from being edited by users; **true** will allow editing. The default value, **inherit**, applies the value of the affected element's parent element.

dir See "Language Reference," earlier in this chapter.

id See "Core Attributes Reference," earlier in this chapter.

hidefocus This proprietary element, introduced with Internet Explorer 5.5, hides focus on an element's content. Focus must be applied to the element using the **tabindex** attribute.

lang See "Language Reference," earlier in this chapter.

language This attribute specifies the language the current script is written in and invokes the proper scripting engine. The default value is **javascript**. **Javascript** and **jscript** represent that the scripting language is written in JavaScript. **Vbs** and **vbscript** represent that the scripting language is written in VBScript.

style See "Core Attributes Reference," earlier in this chapter.

tabindex This attribute uses a number to identify the object's position in the tabbing order for keyboard navigation using the TAB key. Internet Explorer 5.5 applies this attribute to the **dd** element; under IE 5.5, this focus can be disabled with the **hidefocus** attribute.

title See "Core Attributes Reference," earlier in this chapter.

Attribute and Event Support

Netscape 4   class, id, **lang**, and **style**.

Internet Explorer 4   All attributes and events except **dir**.

Internet Explorer 5.5   All attributes and events, plus contenteditable, **dir**, **hidefocus**, and **tabindex**.

Event Handlers

See "Events Reference," earlier in this chapter.

Example

```
<dl>
    <dt>DOG</dt>
        <dd>A domesticated animal that craves attention all
            the time</dd>
    <dt>CAT</dt>
        <dd>An animal that would just as soon ignore you until it
            gets hungry</dd>
</dl>
```

Compatibility

HTML 2, 3.2, 4, 4.01, and XHTML 1.0
Internet Explorer 2, 3, 4, 5, and 5.5
Netscape 1, 2, 3, 4–4.7, and 6
Opera 4
WebTV

Notes

- Under HTML specifications, the closing tag for this element is optional, though encouraged when it will help make the list more understandable.

- Under XHTML 1.0, the closing **</dd>** tag is mandatory.

- This element occurs within a list of defined terms enclosed by the **<dl>** element. Typically associated with it is the term it defines, indicated by the **<dl>** element that precedes it.

- HTML 2 and 3.2 define no attributes for this element.

<del> (Deleted Text)

This element is used to indicate that text has been deleted from a document. A browser might render deleted text as strikethrough text.

Syntax

```
<del
    cite="url"
    class="class name(s)"
    datetime="date"
    dir="ltr | rtl"
    id="unique alphanumeric identifier"
    lang="language code"
    style="style information"
    title="advisory text"
    onclick="script"
    ondblclick="script"
    onkeydown="script"
    onkeypress="script"
    onkeyup="script"
    onmousedown="script"
    onmousemove="script"
    onmouseout="script"
    onmouseover="script"
    onmouseup="script"
    onselectstart="script">

</del>
```

Attributes and Events Defined by Internet Explorer 4

```
language="javascript | jscript | vbs | vbscript"
ondragstart="script"
onhelp="script"
```

Attributes Defined by Internet Explorer 5.5

```
accesskey="key"
contenteditable="false | true | inherit"
tabindex="number"
```

Attributes

accesskey   Applied to this element under Internet Explorer 5.5 only. This attribute specifies a keyboard navigation accelerator for the element. Pressing ALT or a similar key (depending on the browser and operating system) in association with the specified key selects the anchor element correlated with that key.

cite   The value of this attribute is a URL that designates a source document or message that might give a reason that the information was deleted.

class   See "Core Attributes Reference," earlier in this chapter.

contenteditable   This proprietary Microsoft attribute allows
users to edit content rendered in the Internet Explorer 5.5 browser.
Values are **false**, **true**, and **inherit**. A value of **false** will prevent
content from being edited by users; **true** will allow editing. The
default value, **inherit**, applies the value of the affected element's
parent element.

2

datetime   This attribute is used to indicate the date and time
the deletion was made. The value of the attribute is a date in a
special format as defined by ISO 8601. The basic date format is

```
YYYY-MM-DDThh:mm:ssTZD
```

where the following is true:

```
YYYY=four-digit year such as 1999
   MM=two-digit month (01=January, 02=February, and so on.)
   DD=two-digit day of the month (01 through 31)
   hh=two digit hour (00 to 23) (24-hour clock, not AM or PM)
   mm=two digit minute (00 through 59)
   ss=two digit second (00 through 59)
   TZD=time zone designator
```

The time zone designator is either **Z**, which indicates UTC
(Universal Time Coordinate, or coordinated universal time format),
or **+hh:mm**, which indicates that the time is a local time that is *hh*
hours and *mm* minutes ahead of UTC. Alternatively, the format for
the time zone designator could be **-hh:mm**, which indicates that the
local time is behind UTC. Note that the letter "T" actually appears in
the string, all digits must be used, and **00** values for minutes and
seconds might be required. An example value for the **datetime**
attribute might be **1999-10-6T09:15:00-05:00**, which corresponds to
October 6, 1999, 9:15 A.M., U.S. Eastern Standard Time.

dir   See "Language Reference," earlier in this chapter.

id   See "Core Attributes Reference," earlier in this chapter.

lang   See "Language Reference," earlier in this chapter.

language   In the Microsoft implementation, this attribute
specifies the scripting language to be used with an associated
script bound to the element, typically through an event handler
attribute. Possible values might include **javascript**, **jscript**, **vbs**,
and **vbscript**. Other values, which include the version of the
language used, such as **JavaScript1.1**, also might be possible.

style   See "Core Attributes Reference," earlier in this chapter.

tabindex   This attribute uses a number to identify the object's position in the tabbing order for keyboard navigation using the TAB key. Internet Explorer 5.5 applies this attribute to the **del** element.

title   See "Core Attributes Reference," earlier in this chapter.

Attribute and Event Support

Internet Explorer 4   All attributes and events except **cite**, **datetime**, and **dir**.

Internet Explorer 5.5   Same as IE 4, plus **contenteditable**, **dir**, and **tabindex**.

Event Handlers

See "Events Reference," earlier in this chapter.

Example

```
<del cite="http://www.bigcompany.com/changes/oct97.htm"
    datetime="1998-10-06T09:15:00-05:00">
The penalty clause applies to client lateness as well.
</del>
```

Compatibility

HTML 4, 4.01, XHTML 1.0
Internet Explorer 4, 5, and 5.5
Netscape 6

Notes

- Browsers can render deleted (**<del>**) text in a different style to show the changes that have been made to the document. Internet Explorer 4 renders the text as strikethrough text. Eventually, a browser could have a way to show a revision history on a document. User agents that do not understand **<del>** or **<ins>** will show the information anyway, so there is no harm in adding information—only in deleting it. Because of the fact that **<del>**-enclosed text might show up, it might be wise to comment it out within the element as shown here:

```
<del>
<!-- This is old information. -->
</del>
```

- The **<del>** element is not supported under the HTML 2.0 and 3.2 specifications.

<dfn> (Defining Instance of a Term)

This element encloses the defining instance of a term. It usually is rendered as bold or bold italic text.

Syntax

```
<dfn
      class="class name(s)"
      dir="ltr | rtl"
      id="unique alphanumeric identifier"
      lang="language code"
      style="style information"
      title="advisory text"
      onclick="script"
      ondblclick="script"
      onkeydown="script"
      onkeypress="script"
      onkeyup="script"
      onmousedown="script"
      onmousemove="script"
      onmouseout="script"
      onmouseover="script"
      onmouseup="script">

</dfn>
```

Attributes and Events Defined by Internet Explorer 4

```
      language="javascript | jscript | vbs | vbscript"
      ondragstart="script"
      onhelp="script"
      onselectstart="script"
```

Attributes and Events Defined by Internet Explorer 5.5

```
      accesskey="key"
      contenteditable="false | true | inherit"
      hidefocus="true | false"
      tabindex="number"
```

Attributes

accesskey This attribute specifies a keyboard navigation accelerator for the element. Pressing ALT or a similar key (depending on the browser and operating system) in association with the specified key selects the anchor element correlated with that key.

class See "Core Attributes Reference," earlier in this chapter.

contenteditable This proprietary Microsoft attribute allows users to edit content rendered in the Internet Explorer 5.5 browser. Values are **false**, **true**, and **inherit**. A value of **false** will prevent content from being edited by users; **true** will allow editing. The default value, **inherit**, applies the value of the affected element's parent element.

dir See "Language Reference," earlier in this chapter.

hidefocus This proprietary element, introduced with Internet Explorer 5.5, hides focus on an element's content. Focus must be applied to the element using the **tabindex** attribute.

id See "Core Attributes Reference," earlier in this chapter.

lang See "Language Reference," earlier in this chapter.

language This attribute specifies the language the current script is written in and invokes the proper scripting engine. The default value is **javascript**. **Javascript** and **jscript** represent that the scripting language is written in JavaScript. **Vbs** and **vbscript** represent that the scripting language is written in VBScript.

style See "Core Attributes Reference," earlier in this chapter.

tabindex This attribute uses a number to identify the object's position in the tabbing order for keyboard navigation using the TAB key. Internet Explorer 5.5 applies this attribute to the **dfn** element; under IE 5.5, this focus can be disabled with the **hidefocus** attribute.

title See "Core Attributes Reference," earlier in this chapter.

Attribute and Event Support

Internet Explorer 4 All attributes and events except **dir**.

Internet Explorer 5.5 All attributes and events, plus **accesskey**, **contenteditable**, **hidefocus**, and **tabindex**.

Event Handlers

See "Events Reference," earlier in this chapter.

Example

An **<dfn>**elephant**</dfn>** is too large to make a viable pet for anyone poorer than Bill Gates.

Compatibility

> HTML 2, 3.2, 4, and 4.01
> Internet Explorer 2, 3, 4, 5, 5.5
> Netscape 6
> Opera 4
> WebTV

Notes

- HTML 2 and 3.2 defined no attributes for this element.

<dir> (Directory List)

This element encloses a list of brief, unordered items, such as might occur in a menu or directory. The individual items are indicated by the **<ul>** element. Use of this element is not encouraged, as it is not part of the HTML 4.01 strict specification and provides little extra benefit over the **<ul>** element.

Syntax (Transitional Only)

```
<dir
     class="class name(s)"
     compact
     dir="ltr | rtl"
     id="unique alphanumeric identifier"
     lang="language code"
     style="style information"
     title="advisory text"
     onclick="script"
     ondblclick="script"
     onkeydown="script"
     onkeypress="script"
     onkeyup="script"
     onmousedown="script"
     onmousemove="script"
     onmouseout="script"
```

```
onmouseover="script"
onmouseup="script">

</dir>
```

XHTML Syntax

Due to XHTML 1.0's deprecation of attribute minimization, the **compact** attribute must have a quoted attribute when used:

```
<dir compact="compact"></dir>
```

Attributes and Events Defined by Internet Explorer 4

```
language="javascript | jscript | vbs | vbscript"
ondragstart="script"
onhelp="script"
onselectstart="script"
```

Attributes and Events Defined by Internet Explorer 5.5

```
accesskey="key"
contenteditable="false | true | inherit"
hidefocus="true | false"
tabindex="number"
```

Attributes

accesskey   This attribute specifies a keyboard navigation accelerator for the element. Pressing ALT or a similar key (depending on the browser and operating system) in association with the specified key selects the anchor element correlated with that key.

class   See "Core Attributes Reference," earlier in this chapter.

compact   This attribute reduces the white space between list items.

contenteditable   This proprietary Microsoft attribute allows users to edit content rendered in the Internet Explorer 5.5 browser. Values are **false**, **true**, and **inherit**. A value of **false** will prevent content from being edited by users; **true** will allow editing. The default value, **inherit**, applies the value of the affected element's parent element.

dir   See "Language Reference," earlier in this chapter.

hidefocus   This proprietary element, introduced with Internet Explorer 5.5, hides focus on an element's content. Focus must be applied to the element using the **tabindex** attribute.

id   See "Core Attributes Reference," earlier in this chapter.

lang   See "Language Reference," earlier in this chapter.

language   This attribute specifies the language the current script is written in and invokes the proper scripting engine. The default value is **javascript**. **Javascript** and **jscript** represent that the scripting language is written in JavaScript. **Vbs** and **vbscript** represent that the scripting language is written in VBScript.

style   See "Core Attributes Reference," earlier in this chapter.

tabindex   This attribute uses a number to identify the object's position in the tabbing order for keyboard navigation using the TAB key. Internet Explorer 5.5 applies this attribute to the **dir** element; under IE 5.5, this focus can be disabled with the **hidefocus** attribute.

title   See "Core Attributes Reference," earlier in this chapter.

Attribute and Event Support

Netscape 4   **class**, **id**, **lang**, and **style** are explicit.

Internet Explorer 4   All WC3 events and attributes except **compact** and **dir**, all IE 4-defined attributes and events.

Internet Explorer 5.5   All WC3 events and attributes except **compact**, all IE 4- and IE 5.5-defined attributes and events.

WebTV   No attributes. (Note: WebTV bolds text enclosed in the <**dir**> element.)

Event Handlers

See "Events Reference," earlier in this chapter.

Example

```
<dir>
  <li>Header Files
  <li>Code Files
  <li>Comment Files
</dir>
```

Compatibility

> HTML 2, 3.2, 4 (transitional), and 4.01 (transitional), XHTML 1.0
> Internet Explorer 2, 3, 4, 5, and 5.5
> Netscape 1, 2, 3, 4–4.7, 6
> Opera 4
> WebTV

Notes

- Because the **<dir>** element is supposed to be used with short lists, the items in the list should have a maximum width of 20 characters.

- The HTML 4.01 strict specification does not support this element.

- Many browsers will not render the **<dir>** element any differently from the **<ul>** element.

- Many browsers will not render the **compact** list style.

- HTML 2 and 3.2 support only the **compact** attribute.

- For XHTML compatibility, the **compact** attribute must be expanded: **<dir compact="compact">**.

<div> (Division)

This element indicates a block of document content, which should be treated as a logical unit.

Syntax

```
<div
    align="center | justify | left | right"
        (transitional)
    class="class name(s)"
    datafld="name of column supplying bound data"
        (reserved)
    dataformatas="html | text" (reserved)
    datasrc="id of data source object supplying data"
        (reserved)
    dir="ltr | rtl"
    id="unique alphanumeric identifier"
    lang="language code"
    style="style information"
    title="advisory text"
    onclick="script"
    ondblclick="script"
    onkeydown="script"
```

```
onkeypress="script"
onkeyup="script"
onmousedown="script"
onmousemove="script"
onmouseout="script"
onmouseover="script"
onmouseup="script">
```

`</div>`

Attributes and Events Defined by Internet Explorer 4

```
language="javascript | jscript | vbs | vbscript"
onafterupdate="script"
onbeforeupdate="script"
onblur="script"
ondragstart="script"
onfocus="script"
onhelp="script"
onresize="script"
onrowenter="script"
onrowexit="script"
onscroll="script"
onselectstart="script"
```

Attributes and Events Defined by Internet Explorer 5.5

```
accesskey="key"
contenteditable="false | true | inherit"
hidefocus="true | false"
tabindex="number"
```

Attributes

accesskey   This attribute specifies a keyboard navigation accelerator for the element. Pressing ALT or a similar key (depending on the browser and operating system) in association with the specified key selects the anchor element correlated with that key.

align   This attribute indicates how the tagged text should be horizontally aligned on the page. The default value is **left**. The **justify** value is supported only by the Microsoft implementation.

charset   This attribute defines the character encoding of the linked resource specified by the **HREF** attribute. The value is a space- and/or comma-delimited list of character sets as defined in RFC 2045. The default value is **ISO-8859-1**.

class   See "Core Attributes Reference," earlier in this chapter.

contenteditable   This proprietary Microsoft attribute allows users to edit content rendered in the Internet Explorer 5.5 browser. Values are **false**, **true**, and **inherit**. A value of **false** will prevent content from being edited by users; **true** will allow editing. The default value, **inherit**, applies the value of the affected element's parent element.

datafld   This attribute specifies the column name from the data source object that supplies the bound data.

dataformatas   This attribute indicates if the bound data is plain text or HTML.

datasrc   This attribute indicates the **id** of the data source object that supplies the data that is bound to this element.

dir   See "Language Reference," earlier in this chapter.

hidefocus   This proprietary element, introduced with Internet Explorer 5.5, hides focus on an element's content. Focus must be applied to the element using the **tabindex** attribute.

id   See "Core Attributes Reference," earlier in this chapter.

lang   See "Language Reference," earlier in this chapter.

language   This attribute specifies the language the current script is written in and invokes the proper scripting engine. The default value is **javascript**. **Javascript** and **jscript** represent that the scripting language is written in JavaScript. **Vbs** and **vbscript** represent that the scripting language is written in VBScript.

style   See "Core Attributes Reference," earlier in this chapter.

tabindex   This attribute uses a number to identify the object's position in the tabbing order for keyboard navigation using the TAB key. Internet Explorer 5.5 applies this attribute to the **div** element; under IE 5.5, this focus can be disabled with the **hidefocus** attribute.

title   See "Core Attributes Reference," earlier in this chapter.

Attribute and Event Support

Netscape 4   align, class, id, lang, and style.

Internet Explorer 4   All attributes and events except dir.

Internet Explorer 5.5   All events and attributes, plus accesskey, contenteditable, hidefocus, and tabindex.

WebTV   align (center | left | right).

Event Handlers

See "Events Reference," earlier in this chapter.

Examples

```
<div align="justify">
All text within this division will be justified (but only under
Netscape 4).
</div>

<div class="special" ID="div1" style="background: yellow">
Get ready to animate and stylize this.
</div>
```

Compatibility

> HTML 3.2, 4, 4.01, XHTML 1.0
> Internet Explorer 2, 3, 4, 5, and 5.5
> Netscape 2, 3, 4–4.7, and 6
> Opera 4
> WebTV

Notes

- Many users are confused by the proper use of the **<div>**
  element, because all it does is create a block element. It is very
  useful for binding scripts or styles to an arbitrary section of a
  document. In this sense, **<div>** complements **<span>**, which is
  used inline.

- The HTML 4.01 specification specifies that the **datafld**,
  dataformatas, and **datasrc** attributes are reserved for **<div>**
  and might be supported in the future. Internet Explorer 4
  already supports these reserved attributes.

- Under the HTML 4.01 strict specification, the **align** attribute is not supported.
- HTML 3.2 supports only the **align** attribute.

<dl> (Definition List)

This element encloses a list of terms and definition pairs. A common use for this element is to implement a glossary.

Syntax

```
<dl
    class="class name(s)"
    compact
    dir="ltr | rtl"
    id="unique alphanumeric identifier"
    lang="language code"
    style="style information"
    title="advisory text"
    onclick="script"
    ondblclick="script"
    onkeydown="script"
    onkeypress="script"
    onkeyup="script"
    onmousedown="script"
    onmousemove="script"
    onmouseout="script"
    onmouseover="script"
    onmouseup="script">

</dl>
```

XHTML Syntax

Because of XHTML 1.0's deprecation of attribute minimization, the **compact** attribute must have a quoted attribute when used:

```
<dl compact="compact"></dl>
```

Attributes and Events Defined by Internet Explorer 4

```
    language="javascript | jscript | vbs | vbscript"
    ondragstart="script"
    onhelp="script"
    onselectstart="script"
```

Attributes and Events Defined by Internet Explorer 5.5

```
accesskey="key"
contenteditable="false | true | inherit"
hidefocus="true | false"
tabindex="number"
```

Attributes

accesskey   This attribute specifies a keyboard navigation accelerator for the element. Pressing ALT or a similar key (depending on the browser and operating system) in association with the specified key selects the anchor element correlated with that key.

class   See "Core Attributes Reference," earlier in this chapter.

compact   This attribute reduces the white space between list items.

contenteditable   This proprietary Microsoft attribute allows users to edit content rendered in the Internet Explorer 5.5 browser. Values are **false**, **true**, and **inherit**. A value of **false** will prevent content from being edited by users; **true** will allow editing. The default value, **inherit**, applies the value of the affected element's parent element.

dir   See "Language Reference," earlier in this chapter.

hidefocus   This proprietary element, introduced with Internet Explorer 5.5, hides focus on an element's content. Focus must be applied to the element using the **tabindex** attribute.

id   See "Core Attributes Reference," earlier in this chapter.

lang   See "Language Reference," earlier in this chapter.

language   This attribute specifies the language the current script is written in and invokes the proper scripting engine. The default value is **javascript**. **Javascript** and **jscript** represent that the scripting language is written in JavaScript. **Vbs** and **vbscript** represent that the scripting language is written in VBScript.

style   See "Core Attributes Reference," earlier in this chapter.

tabindex   This attribute uses a number to identify the object's position in the tabbing order for keyboard navigation using the TAB key. Internet Explorer 5.5 applies this attribute to the **dl** element; under IE 5.5, this focus can be disabled with the **hidefocus** attribute.

title   See "Core Attributes Reference," earlier in this chapter.

Attribute and Event Support

Netscape 4   class, compact, id, lang, and style.

Internet Explorer 4   All attributes and events except **dir**.

Internet Explorer 5.5   All events and attributes, plus **accesskey**, **contenteditable**, **hidefocus**, and **tabindex**.

Event Handlers

See "Events Reference," earlier in this chapter.

Example

```
<dl>
    <dt>Cat
        <dd>A domestic animal that likes fish
    <dt>Skunk
        <dd>A wild animal that needs deodorant
</dl>
```

Compatibility

HTML 2, 3.2, 4, 4.01, XHTML 1.0
Internet Explorer 2, 3, 4, 5, and 5.5
Netscape 1, 2, 3, 4–4.7, 6
Opera 4
WebTV

Notes

- The items in the list comprise two parts: the term, indicated by the **<dt>** element, and its definition, indicated by the **<dd>** element.

- Some page designers might use the **<dl>** element or **<ul>** element to help create text indention. Although this is a common practice on the Web, it is not advisable because it confuses the meaning of the element by making it a physical layout device rather than a list.

- Under the HTML 4.01 strict definition, the **compact** attribute is not allowed.

- HTML 2 and 3.2 support only the **compact** attribute for this element.

- For XHTML compatibility, the **compact** attribute must be expanded: **<dl compact="compact"></dl>**.

<dt> (Term in a Definition List)

This element identifies a definition list term in a definition list term-definition pair.

Syntax

```
<dt
     class="class name(s)"
     dir="ltr | rtl"
     id="unique alphanumeric identifier"
     lang="language code"
     style="style information"
     title="advisory text"
     onclick="script"
     ondblclick="script"
     onkeydown="script"
     onkeypress="script"
     onkeyup="script"
     onmousedown="script"
     onmousemove="script"
     onmouseout="script"
     onmouseover="script"
     onmouseup="script">
```

XHTML Syntax

Under XHTML 1.0, the **<dt>** element now requires a closing tag:

```
<dt></dt>
```

Attributes and Events Defined by Internet Explorer 4

```
     language="javascript | jscript | vbs | vbscript"
     ondragstart="script"
     onhelp="script"
     onselectstart="script"
```

Attributes and Events Defined by Internet Explorer 5.5

```
accesskey="key"
contenteditable="false | true | inherit"
hidefocus="true | false"
nowrap="true | false"
tabindex="number"
```

Attributes

accesskey   This attribute specifies a keyboard navigation accelerator for the element. Pressing ALT or a similar key (depending on the browser and operating system) in association with the specified key selects the anchor element correlated with that key.

class   See "Core Attributes Reference," earlier in this chapter.

contenteditable   This proprietary Microsoft attribute allows users to edit content rendered in the Internet Explorer 5.5 browser. Values are **false**, **true**, and **inherit**. A value of **false** will prevent content from being edited by users; **true** will allow editing. The default value, **inherit**, applies the value of the affected element's parent element.

dir   See "Language Reference," earlier in this chapter.

hidefocus   This proprietary element, introduced with Internet Explorer 5.5, hides focus on an element's content. Focus must be applied to the element using the **tabindex** attribute.

id   See "Core Attributes Reference," earlier in this chapter.

lang   See "Language Reference," earlier in this chapter.

language   This attribute specifies the language the current script is written in and invokes the proper scripting engine. The default value is **javascript**. **Javascript** and **jscript** represent that the scripting language is written in JavaScript. **Vbs** and **vbscript** represent that the scripting language is written in VBScript.

nowrap   This attribute specifies whether the browser performs wordwrap. A value of **true** means that it will not wrap; a value of **false** means that it can wrap.

style   See "Core Attributes Reference," earlier in this chapter.

tabindex This attribute uses a number to identify the object's position in the tabbing order for keyboard navigation using the TAB key. Internet Explorer 5.5 applies this attribute to the **dt** element; under IE 5.5, this focus can be disabled with the **hidefocus** attribute.

2

title See "Core Attributes Reference," earlier in this chapter.

Attribute and Event Support

Netscape 4 **class**, **id**, **lang**, and **style**.

Internet Explorer 4 All attributes and events except **dir**.

Internet Explorer 5.5 All events and attributes, plus **accesskey**, **contenteditable**, **hidefocus**, **nowrap**, and **tabindex**.

Event Handlers

See "Events Reference," earlier in this chapter.

Example

```
<dl>
    <dt>Rake
    <dd>A garden tool used to gather leaves and rubbish
    <dt>Trowel
    <dd>A small garden tool used to shovel earth
</dl>
```

XHTML Example

```
<dl>
    <dt>Vole</dt>
    <dd>Small creature related to the weasel</dd>
    <dt>Weasel</dt>
    <dd>Small creature related to the vole</dd>
</dl>
```

Compatibility

> HTML 2, 3.2, 4, 4.01, XHTML 1.0
> Internet Explorer 2, 3, 4, 5, and 6
> Netscape 1, 2, 3, 4–4.7, 6
> Opera 4
> WebTV

Notes

- This element occurs within a list of defined terms enclosed by the **<dl>** element. It generally is used in conjunction with the **<dd>** element, which indicates its definition. However, **<dt>** elements do not require a one-to-one correspondence with **<dd>** elements.

- The close tag for the element is optional but suggested when it will make things more clear, particularly with multiple-line definitions.

- Under XHTML 1.0, the closing **</dt>** tag is mandatory.

- HTML 2 and 3.2 support no attributes for this element.

<em> (Emphasis)

This element indicates emphasized text, which many browsers will display as italic text.

Syntax

```
<em
        class="class name(s)"
        dir="ltr | rtl"
        id="unique alphanumeric identifier"
        lang="language code"
        style="style information"
        title="advisory text"
        onclick="script"
        ondblclick="script"
        onkeydown="script"
        onkeypress="script"
        onkeyup="script"
        onmousedown="script"
        onmousemove="script"
        onmouseout="script"
        onmouseover="script"
        onmouseup="script">

</em>
```

Attributes and Events Defined by Internet Explorer 4

```
language="javascript | jscript | vbs | vbscript"
ondragstart="script"
onhelp="script"
onselectstart="script"
```

Attributes and Events Defined by Internet Explorer 5.5

```
accesskey="key"
contenteditable="false | true | inherit"
hidefocus="true | false"
tabindex="number"
```

Attributes

accesskey   This attribute specifies a keyboard navigation accelerator for the element. Pressing ALT or a similar key (depending on the browser and operating system) in association with the specified key selects the anchor element correlated with that key.

class   See "Core Attributes Reference," earlier in this chapter.

contenteditable   This proprietary Microsoft attribute allows users to edit content rendered in the Internet Explorer 5.5 browser. Values are **false**, **true**, and **inherit**. A value of **false** will prevent content from being edited by users; **true** will allow editing. The default value, **inherit**, applies the value of the affected element's parent element.

dir   See "Language Reference," earlier in this chapter.

hidefocus   This proprietary element, introduced with Internet Explorer 5.5, hides focus on an element's content. Focus must be applied to the element using the **tabindex** attribute.

id   See "Core Attributes Reference," earlier in this chapter.

lang   See "Language Reference," earlier in this chapter.

language   This attribute specifies the language the current script is written in and invokes the proper scripting engine. The default value is **javascript**. **Javascript** and **jscript** represent that the scripting language is written in JavaScript. **Vbs** and **vbscript** represent that the scripting language is written in VBScript.

style See "Core Attributes Reference," earlier in this chapter.

tabindex This attribute uses a number to identify the object's position in the tabbing order for keyboard navigation using the TAB key. Internet Explorer 5.5 applies this attribute to the **em** element; under IE 5.5, this focus can be disabled with the **hidefocus** attribute.

title See "Core Attributes Reference," earlier in this chapter.

Attribute and Event Support

Netscape 4 **class**, **id**, **lang**, and **style** are implied.

Internet Explorer 4 All attributes and events except **dir**.

Internet Explorer 5.5 All events and attributes, plus **accesskey**, **contenteditable**, **hidefocus**, and **tabindex**.

Event Handlers

See "Events Reference," earlier in this chapter.

Example

```
This is an <em>important point</em> to consider.
```

Compatibility

```
HTML 2, 3.2, 4, 4.01, XHTML 1.0
Internet Explorer 2, 3, 4, 5, and 5.5
Netscape 1, 2, 3, 4–4.7, and 6
Opera 4
WebTV
```

Notes

- As a logical element, <em> is a prime candidate to bind style information to. For example, to define emphasis to mean a larger font size in the Impact font, you might use a CSS rule like the following in a document-wide style sheet:

```
em {font-size: larger; font-family: Impact;}
```

- HTML 2 and 3.2 support no attributes for this element.

`<embed>` (Embedded Object)

This widely supported but nonstandard element specifies an
object, typically a multimedia element, to be embedded in an
HTML document.

Syntax (Defined by Internet Explorer 4)

```
<embed
    align="absbottom | absmiddle | baseline | bottom |
            left | middle | right | texttop | top"
    alt="alternative text"
    class="class name(s)"
    code="filename"
    codebase="url"
    height="pixels"
    hspace="pixels"
    id="unique alphanumeric identifier"
    name="string"
    src="url"
    style="style information"
    title="advisory text"
    vspace="pixels"
    width="pixels">

</embed>
```

Attributes and Events Defined by Internet Explorer 5.5

```
    accesskey="key"
    language="javascript | jscript | vbs | vbscript | xml"
```

Attributes Defined by Netscape 4

```
    border="pixels"
    hidden="true | false"
    palette="background | foreground"
    pluginspage="url"
    type="mime type"
    units="en | pixels"
```

Attributes

accesskey This attribute specifies a keyboard navigation
accelerator for the element. Pressing ALT or a similar key
(depending on the browser and operating system) in association
with the specified key selects the anchor element correlated with
that key.

align   This attribute controls the alignment of adjacent text with respect to the embedded object. The default value is **left**.

alt   This attribute indicates the text to be displayed if the applet cannot be executed.

border   This attribute specifies the size in pixels of the border around the embedded object.

class   See "Core Attributes Reference," earlier in this chapter.

code   This attribute specifies the name of the file containing the compiled Java class if the **<embed>** element is used to include a Java applet. This is a strange alternate form of Java inclusion documented by Microsoft.

codebase   This specifies the base URL for the plug-in or potential applet in the case of the alternative form under Internet Explorer.

height   This attribute sets the height in pixels of the embedded object.

hidden   If this attribute is set to the value **true**, the embedded object is not visible on the page and implicitly has a size of zero.

hspace   This attribute specifies in pixels the size of the left and right margins between the embedded object and surrounding text.

language   This attribute specifies the language the current script is written in and invokes the proper scripting engine. The default value is **javascript**. **Javascript** and **jscript** represent that the scripting language is written in JavaScript. **Vbs** and **vbscript** represent that the scripting language is written in VBScript. It also might be possible to use extended names, such as **JavaScript1.1**, to hide code from JavaScript-aware browsers that don't conform to a particular version of the language. Internet Explorer adds support for XML as well.

id   See "Core Attributes Reference," earlier in this chapter.

name   This attribute specifies a name for the embedded object, which can be referenced by client-side programs in an embedded scripting language.

palette   This attribute is used only on Windows systems to select the color palette used for the plug-in and might be set to **background** or **foreground**. The default is **background**.

pluginspage   This attribute contains the URL of instructions for installing the plug-in required to render the embedded object.

src   This attribute specifies the URL of source content for the embedded object.

style   See "Core Attributes Reference," earlier in this chapter.

title   See "Core Attributes Reference," earlier in this chapter.

type   This attribute specifies the MIME type of the embedded object. It is used by the browser to determine an appropriate plug-in for rendering the object. It can be used instead of the **src** attribute for plug-ins that have no content or that fetch it dynamically.

units   This Netscape-specific attribute is used to set the units for measurement for the embedded object either in **en** or in the default, **pixels**.

vspace   This attribute specifies in pixels the size of the top and bottom margins between the embedded object and surrounding text.

width   This attribute sets the width in pixels of the embedded object.

Attribute and Event Support

Netscape 4   align (**bottom** | **left** | **right** | **top**), **height**, **src**, **width**, and all Netscape-defined attributes. (**class**, **id**, **lang**, and **style** are implied.)

Internet Explorer 4   All Microsoft-defined attributes and events.

Internet Explorer 5.5   Same as IE 4, plus **accesskey** and **language**.

WebTV   align (**bottom** | **left** | **right** | **top**), **border**, **height**, **hidden**, **hspace**, **name**, **src**, **vspace**, and **width**.

Event Handlers

See "Events Reference," earlier in this chapter.

Examples

```
<!-- embed without a close tag -->
<embed src="testmovie.mov" height="150" width="150">
<noembed>
  <img src="testgif.gif" height="150" width="150" alt="Test Image">
</noembed>

<!- embed with a close tag ->
<embed src="testmovie.mov" height="150" width="150">
<noembed>
  <img src="testgif.gif" height="150" width="150" alt="Test Image">
</noembed>
</embed>
```

Compatibility

> Internet Explorer 3, 4, 5, and 5.5
> Netscape 2, 3, 4–4.7
> WebTV

Notes

- It is unclear whether or not the close tag for **<embed>** is required. Many sites tend not to use it, and documentation is not consistent. Some people claim that a close tag is required and should surround any alternative content in a **<noembed>** element; others do not use a close tag. Because eventually this element should be phased out in favor of **<object>**, this might be a moot issue.

- While WebTV might support the **<embed>** element, it can deal only with media types the equipment knows how to handle, such as Macromedia Flash or certain standard audio files. Other plug-ins cannot be added to the system.

- The **<embed>** element is not favored by the W3C and is not part of any official HTML specification; however, it is very common. The HTML specification says to use the **<object>** element, which can be used in conjunction with the **<embed>** element to provide backward compatibility.

- Embedded objects are multimedia content files of arbitrary type, which are rendered by browser plug-ins. The **type** attribute uses a file's MIME type to determine an appropriate browser plug-in. Any attributes not defined are treated as object-specific parameters and passed through to the embedded object. Consult the plug-in or object documentation to determine these. The standard parameters supported by the Microsoft implementation are **height**, **name**, **palette**, **src**, **units**, and **width**.

<fieldset> (Form Field Set)

This element allows form designers to group thematically related controls together.

Syntax

```
<fieldset
    class="class name(s)"
    dir="ltr | rtl"
    id="unique alphanumeric identifier"
    lang="language code"
    style="style information"
    title="advisory text"
    onclick="script"
    ondblclick="script"
    onkeydown="script"
    onkeypress="script"
    onkeyup="script"
    onmousedown="script"
    onmousemove="script"
    onmouseout="script"
    onmouseover="script"
    onmouseup="script">

</fieldset>
```

Attributes and Events Defined by Internet Explorer 4

```
    align="center | left | right"
    language="javascript | jscript | vbs | vbscript"
    onblur="script"
    onchange="script"
    ondragstart="script"
    onfilterchange="script"
    onfocus="script"
    onhelp="script"
    onresize="script"
    onscroll="script"
    onselect="script"
    onselectstart="script"
```

Attributes and Events Defined by Internet Explorer 5.5

```
accesskey="key"
contenteditable="false | true | inherit"
hidefocus="true | false"
tabindex="number"
```

Attributes

accesskey   This attribute specifies a keyboard navigation accelerator for the element. Pressing ALT or a similar key (depending on the browser and operating system) in association with the specified key selects the anchor element correlated with that key.

align   Internet Explorer defines the **align** attribute, which sets how the element and its contents are positioned in a table or the window.

class   See "Core Attributes Reference," earlier in this chapter.

contenteditable   This proprietary Microsoft attribute allows users to edit content rendered in the Internet Explorer 5.5 browser. Values are **false**, **true**, and **inherit**. A value of **false** will prevent content from being edited by users; **true** will allow editing. The default value, **inherit**, applies the value of the affected element's parent element.

dir   See "Language Reference," earlier in this chapter.

hidefocus   This proprietary element, introduced with Internet Explorer 5.5, hides focus on an element's content. Focus must be applied to the element using the **tabindex** attribute.

id   See "Core Attributes Reference," earlier in this chapter.

lang   See "Language Reference," earlier in this chapter.

language   This attribute specifies the language the current script is written in and invokes the proper scripting engine. The default value is **javascript**. **Javascript** and **jscript** represent that the scripting language is written in JavaScript. **Vbs** and **vbscript** represent that the scripting language is written in VBScript.

style   See "Core Attributes Reference," earlier in this chapter.

tabindex   This attribute uses a number to identify the object's position in the tabbing order for keyboard navigation using the TAB key. Internet Explorer 5.5 applies this attribute to the **fieldset** element; under IE 5.5, this focus can be disabled with the **hidefocus** attribute.

title   See "Core Attributes Reference," earlier in this chapter.

Attribute and Event Support

Internet Explorer 4   All attributes and events except **dir**.

Internet Explorer 5.5   All events and attributes, plus **accesskey**, **contenteditable**, **hidefocus**, and **tabindex**.

Event Handlers

See "Events Reference," earlier in this chapter.

Example

```
<fieldset>
<legend>Customer Identification</legend>
<br>
<label>Customer Name:
<input type="text" id="CustName" SIZE="25">
</fieldset>
```

Compatibility

HTML 4, 4.01, XHTML 1.0
Internet Explorer 4, 5, and 5.5
Opera 4
Netscape 6

Notes

- Grouping controls makes it easier for users to understand the purposes of the controls while simultaneously facilitating tabbing navigation for visual user agents and speech navigation for speech-oriented user agents. The proper use of this element makes documents more accessible to people with disabilities.

- The caption for this element is defined by the **<legend>** element within the **<fieldset>** element.

\<fn\> (Footnote)

This WebTV-specific element indicates either a reference to a
footnote or the footnote itself.

Syntax (Defined by WebTV)

```
<fn
    href="url"
    id="unique alphanumeric identifier">

</fn>
```

Attributes

href   This attribute contains a URL that references the footnote.
Typically the URL is a fragment in the form of the pound sign (#)
followed by the name of the footnote anchor. It indicates that the
tagged text is a reference to a footnote.

id   This attribute contains the name of the footnote anchor.
It indicates that the tagged text is a footnote.

Attribute and Event Support

WebTV   **href** and **id**

Event Handlers

None

Example

```
This wonderful idea came from <fn href="#smith">Smith.</fn>

<fn id="smith">Smith, Fred, Journal of Really Good Ideas</fn>
```

Compatibility

WebTV

Notes

- Footnotes are implemented as internal links within a
  document. Use the **href** attribute to indicate a reference to a
  footnote. Use the **id** attribute to indicate the footnote itself.
- Footnotes are not to be used outside the WebTV environment.
  They are a leftover of the failed HTML 3 proposal.

<font> (Font Definition)

This element allows specification of the size, color, and font of the text it encloses. Use of this element is not encouraged, as it is not part of the HTML 4.01 strict specification. Style sheets provide a cleaner way of providing the same functionality when they are supported.

Syntax (Transitional Only)

```
<font
     class="class name(s)"
     color="color name | #RRGGBB"
     dir="ltr | rtl"
     face="font name"
     id="unique alphanumeric identifier"
     lang="language code"
     size="1 to 7 | +1 to +6 | -1 to -6"
     style="style information"
     title="advisory text">

</font>
```

Attributes and Events Defined by Internet Explorer 4

```
     language="javascript | jscript | vbs | vbscript"
     onclick="script"
     ondblclick="script"
     ondragstart="script"
     onhelp="script"
     onkeydown="script"
     onkeypress="script"
     onkeyup="script"
     onmousedown="script"
     onmousemove="script"
     onmouseout="script"
     onmouseover="script"
     onmouseup="script"
     onselectstart="script"
```

Attributes and Events Defined by Internet Explorer 5.5

```
     accesskey="key"
     contenteditable="false | true | inherit"
     hidefocus="true | false"
     tabindex="number"
```

Attributes Defined by Netscape 4

```
point-size="point size for font"
weight="100 | 200 | 300 | 400 | 500 | 600 | 700 |
        800 | 900"
```

Attributes Defined by WebTV

```
effect="emboss | relief | shadow"
ran="number (0-100)"
```

Attributes

accesskey   This attribute specifies a keyboard navigation accelerator for the element. Pressing ALT or a similar key (depending on the browser and operating system) in association with the specified key selects the anchor element correlated with that key.

class   See "Core Attributes Reference," earlier in this chapter.

color   This attribute sets the text color using either a browser-dependent named color or a color specified in the hexadecimal #RRGGBB format.

contenteditable   This proprietary Microsoft attribute allows users to edit content rendered in the Internet Explorer 5.5 browser. Values are **false**, **true**, and **inherit**. A value of **false** will prevent content from being edited by users; **true** will allow editing. The default value, **inherit**, applies the value of the affected element's parent element.

dir   See "Language Reference," earlier in this chapter.

effect   In the WebTV implementation, this attribute renders the tagged text in a special way. The **relief** value causes the text to appear to be raised off the page. The **emboss** value causes the text to appear embossed into the page.

face   This attribute contains a list of one or more font names separated by commas. The user agent looks through the specified font names and renders the text in the first font that is supported.

hidefocus   This proprietary element, introduced with Internet Explorer 5.5, hides focus on an element's content. Focus must be applied to the element using the **tabindex** attribute.

id   See "Core Attributes Reference," earlier in this chapter.

lang   See "Language Reference," earlier in this chapter.

language   This attribute specifies the language the current script is written in and invokes the proper scripting engine. The default value is **javascript. Javascript** and **jscript** represent that the scripting language is written in JavaScript. **Vbs** and **vbscript** represent that the scripting language is written in VBScript.

point-size   This Netscape 4–specific attribute specifies the point size of text and is used with downloadable fonts.

size   This attribute specifies the font size as either a numeric or relative value. Numeric values range from **1** to **7** with **1** being the smallest and **3** the default. The relative values, + and –, increment or decrement the font size relative to the current size. The value for increment or decrement should range only from **+1** to **+ 6** or **–1** to **–6**.

style   See "Core Attributes Reference," earlier in this chapter.

tabindex   This attribute uses a number to identify the object's position in the tabbing order for keyboard navigation using the TAB key. Internet Explorer 5.5 applies this attribute to the **font** element; under IE 5.5, this focus can be disabled with the **hidefocus** attribute.

title   See "Core Attributes Reference," earlier in this chapter.

transparency   WebTV's proprietary **transparency** attribute is used to set the transparency level of the text. A value of **0** indicates the text is opaque; a value of **100** indicates text is fully transparent, allowing the background to show through. The default value for this attribute is **0**.

weight   Under Netscape 4, this attribute specifies the weight of the font, with a value of **100** being lightest and **900** being heaviest.

Attribute and Event Support

Netscape 4   color, **point-size, size,** and **weight.** (**class, id, lang,** and **style** are implied.)

(At the time of this writing, Netscape 6 did not appear to support **point-size.**)

Internet Explorer 4   All W3C-defined attributes and events except **dir**, and all attributes and events defined by Internet Explorer 4.

Internet Explorer 5.5   All events and attributes, plus **accesskey, contenteditable, hidefocus,** and **tabindex.**

WebTV   **color, effect, size** and **transparency.**

Event Handlers

See "Events Reference," earlier in this chapter.

Example

```
<font color="#FF0000" face="Helvetica, Times Roman" size="+1">
Relatively large red text in Helvetica or Times.
</font>
```

Compatibility

HTML 3.2, 4, 4.01, XHTML 1.0
Internet Explorer 2, 3, 4, 5, and 5.5
Netscape 1.1, 2, 3, 4–4.7, 6
Opera 4
WebTV

Notes

- The default text size for a document can be set using the **size** attribute of the **<basefont>** element.

- The HTML 3.2 specification supports only the **color** and **size** attributes for this element.

- The HTML 4.01 transitional specification supports the **class, color, dir, face, id, lang, size, style,** and **title** attributes.

- The HTML 4.01 strict specification does not support the **<font>** element at all.

<form> (Form for User Input)

The element defines a fill-in form to contain labels and form controls, such as menus and text entry boxes that might be filled in by a user.

Syntax

```
<form
    accept-charset="list of supported character sets"
```

```
action="url"
class="class name(s)"
dir="ltr | rtl"
enctype="application/x-www-form-urlencoded |
         multipart/form-data | text/plain |
         Media Type as per RFC 2045"
id="unique alphanumeric identifier"
lang="language code"
method="get | post"
style="style information"
target="_blank | frame name | _parent | _self |
        _top" (transitional)
title="advisory text"
onclick="script"
ondblclick="script"
onkeydown="script"
onkeypress="script"
onkeyup="script"
onmousedown="script"
onmousemove="script"
onmouseout="script"
onmouseover="script"
onmouseup="script"
onreset="script"
onsubmit="script">
```

```
</form>
```

Attributes and Events Defined by Internet Explorer 4

```
language="javascript | jscript | vbs | vbscript"
name="string"
ondragstart="script"
onhelp="script"
onselectstart="script"
```

Attributes and Events Defined by Internet Explorer 5.0

```
autocomplete="yes | no"
```

Attributes and Events Defined by Internet Explorer 5.5

```
contenteditable="false | true | inherit"
hidefocus="true | false"
tabindex="number"
```

Attributes

accept-charset   This attribute specifies the list of character encodings for input data that must be accepted by the server processing form. The value is a space- or comma-delimited list of character sets as defined in RFC 2045. The default value for this attribute is the reserved value **unknown**.

action   This attribute contains the URL of the server program, which will process the contents of the form. Some browsers also might support a mailto URL, which can mail the results to the specified address.

autocomplete   This Microsoft proprietary attribute, introduced in Internet Explorer 5.0, will automatically finish filling in information that the user has previously input into an input field, and which has been encrypted and stored by the browser.

class   See "Core Attributes Reference," earlier in this chapter.

contenteditable   This proprietary Microsoft attribute allows users to edit content rendered in the Internet Explorer 5.5 browser. Values are **false**, **true**, and **inherit**. A value of **false** will prevent content from being edited by users; **true** will allow editing. The default value, **inherit**, applies the value of the affected element's parent element.

dir   See "Language Reference," earlier in this chapter.

enctype   This attribute indicates how form data should be encoded before being sent to the server. The default is **application/x-www-form-urlencoded**. This encoding replaces blank characters in the data with a + and all other nonprinting characters with a % followed by the character's ASCII HEX representation. The multipart/form-data option does not perform character conversion and transfers the information as a compound MIME document. This must be used when using **<input-type="file">**. It also might be possible to use another encoding such as text/plain to avoid any form of hex encoding which might be useful with mailed forms.

hidefocus   This proprietary element, introduced with Internet Explorer 5.5, hides focus on an element's content. Focus must be applied to the element using the **tabindex** attribute.

id   See "Core Attributes Reference," earlier in this chapter.

lang   See "Language Reference," earlier in this chapter.

language   This attribute specifies the language the current script is written in and invokes the proper scripting engine. The default value is **javascript**. **Javascript** and **jscript** represent that the scripting language is written in JavaScript. **Vbs** and **vbscript** represent that the scripting language is written in VBScript.

2

method   This attribute indicates how form information should be transferred to the server. The **get** option appends data to the URL specified by the **action** attribute. This approach gives the best performance, but imposes a size limitation determined by the command line length supported by the server. The **post** option transfers data using a HTTP post transaction. This approach is more secure and imposes no data size limitation.

name   This attribute specifies a name for the form and can be used by client-side programs to reference form data.

style   See "Core Attributes Reference," earlier in this chapter.

tabindex   This attribute uses a number to identify the object's position in the tabbing order for keyboard navigation using the TAB key. Internet Explorer 5.5 applies this attribute to the **form** element; under IE 5.5, this focus can be disabled with the **hidefocus** attribute.

target   In documents containing frames, this attribute specifies the target frame to display the results of a form submission. In addition to named frames, several special values exist. The **_blank** value indicates a new window. The **_parent** value indicates the parent frame set containing the source link. The **_self** value indicates the frame containing the source link. The **_top** value indicates the full browser window.

title   See "Core Attributes Reference," earlier in this chapter.

Attribute and Event Support

Netscape 4   **action**, **enctype**, **method**, **name**, **target**, **onreset**, and **onsubmit**. (**class**, **id**, **lang**, and **style** are implied.)

Internet Explorer 4   All attributes and events except **accept-charset** and **dir**.

Internet Explorer 5.0   All events and attributes except **accept-charset**, plus **autocomplete**.

Internet Explorer 5.5   All events and attributes, plus autocomplete, contenteditable, **hidefocus**, and **tabindex**.

WebTV   action, method, target, onreset, and **onsubmit**.

Event Handlers

See "Events Reference," earlier in this chapter.

Example

```
<form action="http://www.bigcompany.com/cgi-bin/
processit.exe" method="post" name="testform" onsubmit="validate()">
Enter your comments here:<BR>
<textarea name="comments" COLS="30" ROWS="8"></textarea>
<br>
<input type="submit">
<input type="reset">
</form>
```

Compatibility

HTML 2, 3.2, 4, 4.01, XHTML 1.0
Internet Explorer 2, 3, 4, 5, and 5.5
Netscape 1, 2, 3, 4–4.7, and 6
WebTV

Notes

- Form content is defined using the **<button>**, **<input>**, **<select>**, and **<textarea>** elements as well as other HTML formatting and structuring elements. Special grouping elements such as **<fieldset>**, **<label>**, and **<legend>** have been introduced to provide better structuring for forms, but other HTML elements such as **<div>** and **<table>** also can be used to improve form layout.

- HTML 2 and 3.2 support only the **action, enctype**, and **method** attributes for the **<form>** element.

<frame> (Window Region)

This element defines a nameable window region, known as a frame, that can independently display its own content.

Syntax (Transitional Only)

```
<frame
    class="class name(s)"
    frameborder="0 | 1"
    id="unique alphanumeric identifier"
    longdesc="url of description"
    marginheight="pixels"
    marginwidth="pixels"
    name="string"
    noresize
    scrolling="auto | no | yes"
    src="url" of frame contents"
    style="style information"
    title="advisory text">
```

2

XHTML Syntax

As an empty element, the **<frame>** element must have a trailing slash to be compliant with the XHTML 1.0 specification:

```
<frame />
```

Attributes and Events Defined by Internet Explorer 4

```
bordercolor="color name | #RRGGBB"
datafld="name of column supplying bound data"
datasrc="id of data source object supplying data"
frameborder="no | yes | 0 | 1"
height="pixels"
lang="language code"
language="javascript | jscript | vbs | vbscript"
width="pixels"
onreadystatechange="script"
```

Attributes and Events Defined by Internet Explorer 5.5

```
hidefocus="true | false"
tabindex="number"
```

Attributes Defined by WebTV

```
align="bottom | center | left | right | top"
```

Attributes

bordercolor   This attribute sets the color of the frame's border using either a named color or a color specified in the hexadecimal *#RRGGBB* format.

class   See "Core Attributes Reference," earlier in this chapter.

datafld   This Internet Explorer attribute specifies the column name from the data source object that supplies the bound data.

datasrc   This Internet Explorer attribute indicates the **id** of the data source object that supplies the data that is bound to this element.

frameborder   This attribute determines whether the frame is surrounded by an outlined three-dimensional border. The HTML specification prefers the use of **1** for the frame border on and **0** for off; most browsers also acknowledge the use of **no** and **yes**.

hidefocus   This proprietary element, introduced with Internet Explorer 5.5, hides focus on an element's content. Focus must be applied to the element using the **tabindex** attribute.

id   See "Core Attributes Reference," earlier in this chapter.

lang   See "Language Reference," earlier in this chapter.

language   This attribute specifies the language the current script is written in and invokes the proper scripting engine. The default value is **javascript**. **Javascript** and **jscript** represent that the scripting language is written in JavaScript. **Vbs** and **vbscript** represent that the scripting language is written in VBScript.

longdesc   This attribute specifies a URL of a document that contains a long description of the frame's content. This attribute should be used in conjunction with the **<title>** element.

marginheight   This attribute sets the height in pixels between the frame's contents and its top and bottom borders.

marginwidth   This attribute sets the width in pixels between the frame's contents and its left and right borders.

name   This attribute assigns the frame a name so that it can be the target destination of hyperlinks as well as being a possible candidate for manipulation via a script.

noresize   This attribute overrides the default ability to resize frames and gives the frame a fixed size.

scrolling   This attribute determines if the frame has scroll bars. A **yes** value forces scroll bars, a **no** value prohibits them, and an **auto** value lets the browser decide. When not specified, the default value of **auto** is used. Authors are recommended to leave the value as **auto**. If you turn off scrolling and the contents end up being too large for the frame (due to rendering differences, window size, and so forth), the user will not be able to scroll to see the rest of the contents. If you turn scrolling on and the contents all fit in the frame, the scroll bars will needlessly consume screen space. With the **auto** value, scroll bars appear only when needed.

src   This attribute contains the URL of the contents to be displayed in the frame. If absent, nothing will be loaded in the frame.

style   See "Core Attributes Reference," earlier in this chapter.

tabindex   This attribute uses a number to identify the object's position in the tabbing order for keyboard navigation using the TAB key. Internet Explorer 5.5 applies this attribute to the **frame** element; under IE 5.5, this focus can be disabled with the **hidefocus** attribute.

title   See "Core Attributes Reference," earlier in this chapter.

Attribute and Event Support

Netscape 4   **bordercolor, frameborder, marginheight, marginwidth, name, noresize, scrolling,** and **src.** (**class, id, lang,** and **style** are implied.)

Internet Explorer 4   All W3C-defined attributes except **longdesc** and **style,** and all attributes and events defined by Internet Explorer 4. (Note: Internet Explorer 4 supports the values **noresize** and **resize.**)

Internet Explorer 5.5   All W3C-defined attributes except **longdesc** and **style,** and all attributes and events defined by Internet Explorer 4, plus **hidefocus,** and **tabindex.**

WebTV   **align, frameborder (0 I 1), marginheight, marginwidth, name,** and **src.**

Event Handlers
See "Events Reference," earlier in this chapter.

Example

```
<frameset rows="20%,80%">
  <frame src="controls.htm" name="controls" noresize scrolling="no">
  <frame src="content.htm">
</frameset>
```

XHTML Example

```
<frameset rows="20%,80%">
  <frame src="controls.htm" name="controls" noresize
    scrolling="no" />
  <frame src="content.htm" />
</frameset>
```

Compatibility

> HTML 4, 4.01, XHTML 1.0
> Internet Explorer 2, 3, 4, 5, and 5.5
> Netscape 2, 3, 4–4.7. 6
> Opera 4
> WebTV

Notes

- A frame must be declared as part of a frame set as set by the **<frameset>** element, which specifies the frame's relationship to other frames on a page. A frame set occurs in a special HTML document in which the **<frameset>** element replaces the **<body>** element. Another form of frames called *independent frames,* or *floating frames,* also is supported by Microsoft as well as the HTML 4.01 transitional specification. Floating frames can be directly embedded in a document without belonging to a frameset. These are defined with the **<iframe>** element.

- Many browsers do not support frames and require the use of the **<noframes>** element.

- Frames introduce potential navigation difficulties; their use should be limited to instances in which they can be shown to help navigation rather than hinder it.

- XHMTL 1.0 requires a trailing slash for this element: **<frame />**.

<frameset> (Frameset Definition)

This element is used to define the organization of a set of independent window regions known as *frames* as defined by the **<frame>** element. This element replaces the **<body>** element in framing documents.

Syntax (Transitional Only)

```
<frameset
    class="class name(s)"
    cols="list of columns"
    id="unique alphanumeric identifier"
    rows="list of rows"
    style="style information"
    title="advisory text"
    onload="script"
    onunload="script">

    <frame> elements and <noframes>

</frameset>
```

Attributes and Events Defined by Internet Explorer 4

```
    border="pixels"
    bordercolor="color name | #RRGGBB"
    frameborder="NO | YES | 0 | 1"
    framespacing="pixels"
    lang="language code"
    language="javascript | jscript | vbs | vbscript"
```

Attributes and Events Defined by Netscape 4

```
    border="pixels"
    bordercolor="color name | #RRGGBB"
    frameborder="no | yes | 0 | 1"
    lang="language code"
    onblur="script"
    onfocus="script"
```

Attributes and Events Defined by Internet Explorer 5.5

```
    hidefocus="true | false"
    tabindex="number"
```

Attributes Defined by WebTV

```
    border="pixels"
    frameborder="0 | 1"
```

Attributes

border This attribute sets the width in pixels of frame borders within the frame set. Setting **border="0"** eliminates all frame borders. This attribute is not defined in the HTML specification but is widely supported.

bordercolor   This attribute sets the color for frame borders within the frame set using either a named color or a color specified in the hexadecimal *#RRGGBB* format.

class   See "Core Attributes Reference," earlier in this chapter.

cols   This attribute contains a comma-delimited list, which specifies the number and size of columns contained within a set of frames. List items indicate columns from left to right. Column size is specified in three formats, which might be mixed. A column can be assigned a fixed width in pixels. It also can be assigned a percentage of the available width, such as 50 percent. Finally, a column can be set to expand to fill the available space by setting the value to *, which acts as a wildcard.

frameborder   This attribute controls whether or not frame borders should be displayed. Netscape supports **no** and **yes** values. Microsoft uses **1** and **0** as well as **no** and **yes**.

framespacing   This attribute indicates the space between frames in pixels.

hidefocus   This proprietary element, introduced with Internet Explorer 5.5, hides focus on an element's content. Focus must be applied to the element using the **tabindex** attribute.

id   See "Core Attributes Reference," earlier in this chapter.

lang   See "Language Reference," earlier in this chapter.

language   This attribute specifies the language the current script is written in and invokes the proper scripting engine. The default value is **javascript**. **Javascript** and **jscript** represent that the scripting language is written in JavaScript. **Vbs** and **vbscript** represent that the scripting language is written in VBScript.

rows   This attribute contains a comma-delimited list, which specifies the number and size of rows contained within a set of frames. The number of entries in the list indicates the number of rows. Row size is specified with the same formats used for columns.

style   See "Core Attributes Reference," earlier in this chapter.

tabindex   This attribute uses a number to identify the object's position in the tabbing order for keyboard navigation using the TAB key. Internet Explorer 5.5 applies this attribute to the **frameset** element; under IE 5.5, this focus can be disabled with the **hidefocus** attribute.

title See "Core Attributes Reference," earlier in this chapter.

Attribute and Event Support

Netscape 4 border, bordercolor, cols, frameborder, rows, onblur, onfocus, onload, and onunload. (class, id, lang, and style are implied.)

Internet Explorer 4 border, bordercolor, class, cols, frameborder, id, lang, language, rows, and title.

Internet Explorer 5.5 All HTML events and attributes except style, all IE 4 events and attributes, plus hidefocus, and tabindex.

WebTV border, cols, frameborder (0 | 1), framespacing, rows, onload, and onunload.

Event Handlers

See "Events Reference," earlier in this chapter.

Examples

```
<!-- This example defines a frame set of three columns. The
middle column is 50 pixels wide. The first and last columns
fill the remaining space.
The last column takes twice as much space as the first. -->

<frameset COLS="*,50,*">
  <frame src="column1.htm">
  <frame src="column2.htm">
  <frame src="column3.htm">
</frameset>

<!-- This example defines a frame set of two columns, one of
which is 20% of the screen, and the other, 80%. -->

<frameset cols="20%, 80%">
  <frame src="controls.htm">
  <frame src="display.htm">
</frameset>

<!-- This example defines two rows, one of which is 10% of
the screen, and the other, whatever space is left. -->

<frameset rows="10%, *">
  <frame src="adbanner.htm" name="ad_frame">
  <frame src="contents.htm" name="content_frame">
</frameset>
```

Compatibility

HTML 4 and 4.01 (frameset), XHTML 1.0
Internet Explorer 2, 3, 4, 5, and 5.5
Netscape 2, 3, 4–4.7, 6
Opera 4
WebTV

Notes

- The **<frameset>** element contains one or more **<frame>** elements, which are used to indicate the framed contents. The **<frameset>** element also might contain a **<noframes>** element whose contents will be displayed on browsers that do not support frames.

- The **<frameset>** element replaces the **<body>** element in a framing document as shown here:

```
<html>
<head>
<title>Collection of Frames</title>
</head>

<frameset cols="*,50,*">
   <frame src="column1.htm" NAME="col1">
   <frame src="column2.htm" NAME="col2">
   <frame src="column3.htm" NAME="col3">
<noframes>
Please visit our <a href"noframes.htm">no frames</a>
site.
</frameset>

</html>
```

<h1> Through <h6> (Headings)

These tags implement six levels of document headings; **<h1>** is the most prominent, and **<h6>** is the least prominent.

Syntax

```
<h1
    align="center | justify | left | right"
         (transitional)
    class="class name(s)"
    dir="ltr | rtl"
    id="unique alphanumeric identifier"
    lang="language code"
```

```
style="style information"
title="advisory text"
onclick="script"
ondblclick="script"
onkeydown="script"
onkeypress="script"
onkeyup="script"
onmousedown="script"
onmousemove="script"
onmouseout="script"
onmouseover="script"
onmouseup="script">
```

```
</h1>
```

Attributes and Events Defined by Internet Explorer 4

```
language="javascript | jscript | vbs | vbscript"
ondragstart="script"
onhelp="script"
onselectstart="script"
```

Attributes and Events Defined by Internet Explorer 5.5

```
accesskey="key"
contenteditable="false | true | inherit"
hidefocus="true | false"
tabindex="number"
```

Attributes

accesskey   This attribute specifies a keyboard navigation accelerator for the element. Pressing ALT or a similar key (depending on the browser and operating system) in association with the specified key selects the anchor element correlated with that key.

align   This attribute controls the horizontal alignment of the heading with respect to the page. The default value is **left**.

class   See "Core Attributes Reference," earlier in this chapter.

contenteditable   This proprietary Microsoft attribute allows users to edit content rendered in the Internet Explorer 5.5 browser. Values are **false, true**, and **inherit**. A value of **false** will prevent content from being edited by users; **true** will allow editing. The default value, **inherit**, applies the value of the affected element's parent element.

dir   See "Language Reference," earlier in this chapter.

hidefocus   This proprietary element, introduced with Internet Explorer 5.5, hides focus on an element's content. Focus must be applied to the element using the **tabindex** attribute.

id   See "Core Attributes Reference," earlier in this chapter.

lang   See "Language Reference," earlier in this chapter.

language   This attribute specifies the language the current script is written in and invokes the proper scripting engine. The default value is **javascript. Javascript** and **jscript** represent that the scripting language is written in JavaScript. **Vbs** and **vbscript** represent that the scripting language is written in VBScript.

style   See "Core Attributes Reference," earlier in this chapter.

tabindex   This attribute uses a number to identify the object's position in the tabbing order for keyboard navigation using the TAB key. Internet Explorer 5.5 applies this attribute to the header elements; under IE 5.5, this focus can be disabled with the **hidefocus** attribute.

title   See "Core Attributes Reference," earlier in this chapter.

Attribute and Event Support

Netscape 4   **align**. (**class**, **id**, **lang**, and **style** are implied.)

Internet Explorer 4   All attributes and events except **dir**. (Note: The **justify** value for **align** is not supported.)

Internet Explorer 5.5   All events and attributes, plus **accesskey**, **contenteditable**, **hidefocus**, and **tabindex**.

WebTV   **align** (center | left | right).

Event Handlers
See "Events Reference," earlier in this chapter.

Example
```
<h1>This is a Major Document Heading</h1>
<h2 align="center=">Second heading, aligned to the center</h2>
<h3 align="right">Third heading, aligned to the right</h3>
<h4>Fourth heading</h4>
<h5 style="{font-size: 20pt}">Fifth heading with style information</h5>
<h6>The smallest heading</h6>
```

Compatibility

HTML 2, 3.2, 4, 4.01, XHTML 1.0
Internet Explorer 2, 3, 4, 5, and 5.5
Netscape 1, 2, 3, 4–4.7, 6
Opera 4
WebTV

2

Notes

- In most implementations, heading numbers correspond inversely with the six font sizes supported by the **<font>** element. For example, **<h1>** corresponds to **<font size="6">**. The default font size is **3**. However, this approach to layout is not encouraged and page designers should consider using styles to set even relative sizes.

- HTML 3.2 supports only the **align** attribute. HTML 2 does not support any attributes for headings.

- The strict definition of HTML 4.01 does not include support for the **align** attribute. Style sheets should be used instead.

<head> (Document Head)

This element indicates the document head that contains descriptive information about the HTML document as well as other supplementary information such as style rules or scripts.

Syntax

```
<head
      dir="ltr | rtl"
      lang="language code"
      profile="url">

</head>
```

XHTML Syntax

Under the XHTML 1.0 specification, the **<head>** element no longer can be implied, but must be used in all documents. The closing tag **</head>** also is mandatory.

Attributes and Events Defined by Internet Explorer 4

```
class="class name(s)"
id="unique alphanumeric identifier"
title="advisory text"
```

Attributes

class   See "Core Attributes Reference," earlier in this chapter.

dir   See "Language Reference," earlier in this chapter.

id   See "Core Attributes Reference," earlier in this chapter.

lang   See "Language Reference," earlier in this chapter.

profile   This attribute specifies a URL for a meta-information dictionary. The specified profile should indicate the format of allowed meta-data and the potential meaning of the data.

title   See "Core Attributes Reference," earlier in this chapter.

Attribute and Event Support

Internet Explorer 4   class, id, lang and title

Internet Explorer 5.5   class, id, and lang

Event Handlers
None

Example

```
<head>
<title>Big Company Home Page</title>
<base href="http://www.bigcompany.com">
<meta name="Keywords"content="BigCompany, SuperWidget">
</head>
```

Compatibility

```
HTML 2, 3.2, 4, 4.01, XHTML 1.0
Internet Explorer 2, 3, 4, 5, and 5.5
Netscape 1, 2, 3, 4–4.7, 6
Opera 4
WebTV
```

Notes

- The **<head>** element must contain a **<title>** element. It also might contain the **<base>**, **<isindex>**, **<link>**, **<meta>**, **<script>**, and **<style>** elements. Internet Explorer 4 supports the inclusion of the **<basefont>** element in the **<head>** element, but **<basefont>** has been deprecated under HTML 4.
- Under XHTML 1.0, the closing **</head>** tag is mandatory.
- Although the HTML 4.01 specification shows support for the **profile** attribute, no browsers appear to support it.
- Internet Explorer 4 defines the **<bgsound>** element as another legal element within **<head>**.
- HTML 2 and 3.2 support no attributes for this element.

<hr> (Horizontal Rule)

This element is used to insert a horizontal rule to visually separate document sections. Rules usually are rendered as a raised or etched line.

Syntax

```
<hr
    align="center | left | right" (transitional)
    class="class name(s)"
    id="unique alphanumeric identifier"
    noshade (transitional)
    size="pixels" (transitional)
    style="style information"
    title="advisory information"
    WIDTH="percentage | pixels" (transitional)
    onclick="script"
    ondblclick="script"
    onkeydown="script"
    onkeypress="script"
    onkeyup="script"
    onmousedown="script"
    onmousemove="script"
    onmouseout="script"
    onmouseover="script"
    onmouseup="script">
```

XHTML Syntax

As an empy element, **<hr>** requires a trailing slash for XHTML compliance:

```
<hr />
```

Attributes and Events Defined by Internet Explorer 4

```
color="color name | #RRGGBB"
lang="language code"
language="javascript | jscript | vbs | vbscript"
src="url"
onbeforeupdate="script"
onblur="script"
ondragstart="script"
onfocus="script"
onhelp="script"
onresize="script"
onrowenter="script"
onrowexit="script"
onselectstart="script"
```

Attributes and Events Defined by Internet Explorer 5.5

```
accesskey="key"
hidefocus="true | false"
tabindex="number"
```

Attributes Defined by WebTV

```
invertborder
```

Attributes

accesskey   This attribute specifies a keyboard navigation accelerator for the element. Pressing ALT or a similar key (depending on the browser and operating system) in association with the specified key selects the anchor element correlated with that key.

align   This attribute controls the horizontal alignment of the rule with respect to the page. The default value is **left**.

class   See "Core Attributes Reference," earlier in this chapter.

color   This attribute sets the rule color using either a named color or a color specified in the hexadecimal *#RRGGBB* format. This attribute currently is supported only by Internet Explorer.

2

hidefocus   This proprietary element, introduced with Internet Explorer 5.5, hides focus on an element's content. Focus must be applied to the element using the **tabindex** attribute.

id   See "Core Attributes Reference," earlier in this chapter.

invertborder   This WebTV-specific attribute creates a horizontal rule that appears raised, as opposed to embossed, on the surface of the page.

lang   See "Language Reference," earlier in this chapter.

language   This attribute specifies the language the current script is written in and invokes the proper scripting engine. The default value is **javascript**. **Javascript** and **jscript** represent that the scripting language is written in JavaScript. **Vbs** and **vbscript** represent that the scripting language is written in VBScript.

noshade   This attribute causes the rule to be rendered as a solid bar without shading.

size   This attribute indicates the height in pixels of the rule.

src   This attribute specifies a URL for an associated file.

style   See "Core Attributes Reference," earlier in this chapter.

tabindex   This attribute uses a number to identify the object's position in the tabbing order for keyboard navigation using the TAB key. Internet Explorer 5.5 applies this attribute to the **hr** element; under IE 5.5, this focus can be disabled with the **hidefocus** attribute.

title   See "Core Attributes Reference," earlier in this chapter.

width   This attribute indicates how wide the rule should be, specified either in pixels or as a percent of screen width, such as 80 percent.

Attribute and Event Support

Netscape 4   **align, noshade, size**, and **width**. (**class, id**, and **style** are implied.)

Internet Explorer 4   All attributes and events defined by W3C and Internet Explorer 4.

Internet Explorer 5.5 All attributes and events defined by W3C and Internet Explorer 4, plus **accesskey**, **hidefocus**, and **tabindex**.

WebTV align, **invertborder**, **noshade**, **size**, and **width**.

Event Handlers

See "Events Reference," earlier in this chapter.

Examples

```
<hr align="left" noshade size="1" width="420">

<hr align="center" width="100%" size="3" color="#000000">
```

XHTML example

```
<hr align="left" noshade size="1" width="350" />
```

Compatibility

HTML 2, 3.2, 4, 4.01, XHTML 1.0
Internet Explorer 2, 3, 4, 5, and 5.5
Netscape 1, 2, 3, 4–4.7, 6
Opera 4
WebTV

Notes

- The HTML 4.01 strict specification removes support for the **align**, **noshade**, **size**, and **width** attributes for horizontal rules. These effects are possible using style sheets.

- XHTML 1.0 requires a trailing slash for this element: **<hr />**.

<html> (HTML Document)

This element identifies a document as containing HTML-tagged content.

Syntax

```
<html
     dir="ltr | rtl"
     lang="language code"
     version="url" (transitional)>

</html>
```

XHTML Syntax

Under the XHTML 1.0 specification, **<html>** can no longer be implied; **<html>** and the closing tag **</html>** both are mandatory for XHTML compliance.

Attributes Defined by Internet Explorer 4

```
class="class name(s)"
id="unique alphanumeric identifier"
```

Attributes and Events Defined by Internet Explorer 5.0

```
dir="ltr | rtl"
xmlns="namespace"
```

Attributes

class   See "Core Attributes Reference," earlier in this chapter.

dir   See "Language Reference," earlier in this chapter.

lang   See "Language Reference," earlier in this chapter.

version   The **version** attribute is used to set the URL of the location of the document type definition (DTD) that the current document conforms to. This attribute is deprecated under HTML 4.0(1), because this information should be defined by the doctype declaration instead.

xmlns   This attribute declares a namespace for XML-based custom tags in the document.

Attribute and Event Support

Internet Explorer 4   class, id

Internet Explorer 5.0   class, dir, id, and **xmlns**

Event Handlers

None

Example

```
<!-- Minimal HTML document -->
<html>
<head><title>Minimal Document</title></head>
<body></body>
</html>
```

Compatibility

HTML 4, 4.01, XHTML 1.0
Internet Explorer 4, 5, 5.5
Netscape 4–4.7, 6
Opera 4
WebTV

Notes

- The **<html>** element is the first element in an **<html>** document. Except for comments, the only tags it directly contains are the **<head>** element followed by either a **<body>** element or a **<frameset>** element.

- The **<html>** element and its closing tag **</html>** both are mandatory under XHTML 1.0.

<i> (Italic)

This element indicates that the enclosed text should be displayed in an italic typeface.

Syntax

```
<i
    class="class name(s)"
    dir="ltr | rtl"
    id="unique alphanumeric identifier"
    lang="language code"
    style="style information"
    title="advisory text"
    onclick="script"
    ondblclick="script"
    onkeydown="script"
    onkeypress="script"
    onkeyup="script"
    onmousedown="script"
    onmousemove="script"
    onmouseout="script"
    onmouseover="script"
    onmouseup="script"

</i>
```

Attributes and Events Defined by Internet Explorer 4

```
language="javascript | jscript | vbs | vbscript"
ondragstart="script"
onhelp="script"
onselectstart="script"
```

Attributes and Events Defined by Internet Explorer 5.5

```
accesskey="key"
contenteditable="false | true | inherit"
hidefocus="true | false"
tabindex="number"
```

Attributes

accesskey   This attribute specifies a keyboard navigation accelerator for the element. Pressing ALT or a similar key (depending on the browser and operating system) in association with the specified key selects the anchor element correlated with that key.

class   See "Core Attributes Reference," earlier in this chapter.

contenteditable   This proprietary Microsoft attribute allows users to edit content rendered in the Internet Explorer 5.5 browser. Values are **false**, **true**, and **inherit**. A value of **false** will prevent content from being edited by users; **true** will allow editing. The default value, **inherit**, applies the value of the affected element's parent element.

dir   See "Language Reference," earlier in this chapter.

hidefocus   This proprietary element, introduced with Internet Explorer 5.5, hides focus on an element's content. Focus must be applied to the element using the **tabindex** attribute.

id   See "Core Attributes Reference," earlier in this chapter.

lang   See "Language Reference," earlier in this chapter.

language   This attribute specifies the language the current script is written in and invokes the proper scripting engine. The default value is **javascript. Javascript** and **jscript** represent that the scripting language is written in JavaScript. **Vbs** and **vbscript** represent that the scripting language is written in VBScript.

style See "Core Attributes Reference," earlier in this chapter.

tabindex This attribute uses a number to identify the object's position in the tabbing order for keyboard navigation using the TAB key. Internet Explorer 5.5 applies this attribute to the **i** element; under IE 5.5, this focus can be disabled with the **hidefocus** attribute.

title See "Core Attributes Reference," earlier in this chapter.

Attribute and Event Support

Netscape 4 **class**, **id**, **lang**, and **style** are implied.

Internet Explorer 4 All attributes and events except **dir**.

Internet Explorer 5.5 All events and attributes, plus **accesskey**, **contenteditable**, **hidefocus**, and **tabindex**.

Event Handlers
See "Events Reference," earlier in this chapter.

Example
```
Here is some <i>italicized</i> text.
```

Compatibility
```
HTML 4, 4.01, XHTML 1.0
Internet Explorer 4, 5, and 5.5
Netscape 4-4.7, 6
Opera 4
WebTV
```

\<iframe\> (Floating Frame)

This element indicates a floating frame, an independently controllable content region that can be embedded in a page.

Syntax (Transitional Only)
```
<iframe
      align="bottom | left | middle | right | top"
      class="class name(s)"
      frameborder="0 | 1"
      height="percentage | pixels"
      id="unique alphanumeric identifier"
```

```
        longdesc="url of description"
        marginheight="pixels"
        marginwidth="pixels"
        name="string"
        scrolling="auto | no | yes"
        src="url of frame contents"
        style="style information"
        title="advisory text"
        width="percentage | pixels">

</iframe>
```

Attributes Defined by Internet Explorer 4

```
        align="absbottom | absmiddle | baseline | texttop"
        border="pixels"
        bordercolor="color name | #RRGGBB"
        datfld="name of column supplying bound data"
        datasrc="id of data source object supplying data"
        frameborder="no | yes | 0 | 1"
        framespacing="pixels"
        hspace="pixels"
        lang="language code"
        language="javascript | jscript | vbs | vbscript"
        noresize="noresize | resize"
        vspace="pixels"
```

Attributes and Events Defined by Internet Explorer 5.5

```
        hidefocus="true | false"
        tabindex="number"
```

Attributes

align   This attribute controls the horizontal alignment of the floating frame with respect to the page. The default is **left**.

border   This attribute specifies the thickness of the border in pixels.

bordercolor   This attribute specifies the color of the border.

class   See "Core Attributes Reference," earlier in this chapter.

datfld   This attribute specifies the column name from the data source object that supplies the bound data.

datasrc   This attribute indicates **id** of the data source object that supplies the data that is bound to this element.

frameborder   This attribute determines whether the frame is surrounded by a border. The HTML 4 specification defines **0** to be off and **1** to be on. The default value is **1**. Internet Explorer also defines the values **no** and **yes**.

framespacing   This attribute creates additional space between the frames.

height   The attribute sets the floating frame's height in pixels.

hidefocus   This proprietary element, introduced with Internet Explorer 5.5, hides focus on an element's content. Focus must be applied to the element using the **tabindex** attribute.

hspace   This attribute specifies margins for the frame.

id   See "Core Attributes Reference," earlier in this chapter.

lang   See "Language Reference," earlier in this chapter.

language   This attribute specifies the language the current script is written in and invokes the proper scripting engine. The default value is **javascript**. **Javascript** and **jscript** represent that the scripting language is written in JavaScript. **Vbs** and **vbscript** represent that the scripting language is written in VBScript.

longdesc   This attribute specifies a URL of a document which contains a long description of the frame's contents. This might be particularly useful as a complement to the **<title>** element.

marginheight   This attribute sets the height in pixels between the floating frame's content and its top and bottom borders.

marginwidth   This attribute sets the width in pixels between the floating frame's content and its left and right borders.

name   This attribute assigns the floating frame a name so that it can be the target destination of hyperlinks.

noresize   When **noresize** is included, the frame cannot be resized by the user.

scrolling   This attribute determines if the frame has scroll bars. A **yes** value forces scroll bars; a **no** value prohibits them.

src   This attribute contains the URL of the content to be displayed in the floating frame. If absent, the frame is blank.

style   See "Core Attributes Reference," earlier in this chapter.

tabindex   This attribute uses a number to identify the object's position in the tabbing order for keyboard navigation using the TAB key. Internet Explorer 5.5 applies this attribute to the **iframe** element; under IE 5.5, this focus can be disabled with the **hidefocus** attribute.

2

title   See "Core Attributes Reference," earlier in this chapter.

vspace   This attribute specifies margins for the frame.

width   This attribute sets the floating frame's width in pixels.

Attribute and Event Support

Internet Explorer 4   All attributes and events except **longdesc**.

Internet Explorer 5.5   Same as IE 4, plus **hidefocus** and **tabindex**.

Event Handlers

See "Events Reference," earlier in this chapter.

Example

```
<iframe src="http://www.democompany.com"
        height="150" width="200"
        name="FloatingFrame1">
Sorry, your browser doesn't support inline frames.
</iframe>
```

Compatibility

HTML 4 (transitional)
Internet Explorer 3, 4, 5, and 5.5
Netscape 6

Notes

- A floating frame does not need to be declared by the **<frameset>** element as part of a frame set.

- WebTV and Netscape 4.x (4.0 through 4.75) do not support floating frames.

- Under HTML 4.01's strict specification, the **<iframe>** element is not defined. Floating frames can be imitated using the **<div>** element and CSS positioning facilities.

<ilayer> (Inflow Layer)

This Netscape-specific element allows the definition of overlapping content layers that can be positioned, hidden or shown, rendered transparent or opaque, reordered front to back, and nested. An *inflow layer* is a layer with a relative position that appears where it would naturally occur in the document, in contrast to a *general layer*, which might be positioned absolutely regardless of its location in a document. The functionality of layers is available using CSS positioning, and page developers are advised not to use this element.

Syntax (Defined by Netscape 4)

```
<ilayer
    above="layer"
    background="url of image"
    below="layer"
    bgcolor="color name | #RRGGBB"
    class="class name(s)"
    clip="x1, y1, x2, y2"
    height="percentage | pixels"
    id="unique alphanumeric identifier"
    left="pixels"
    name="string"
    pagex="pixels"
    pagey="pixels"
    src="url of layer contents"
    style="style information"
    top="pixels"
    visibility="hide | inherit | show"
    width="percentage | pixels"
    z-index="number"
    onblur="script"
    onfocus="script"
    onload="script"
    onmouseout="script"
    onmouseover="script">

</ilayer>
```

Attributes

above This attribute contains the name of the layer to be rendered above the current layer.

background   This attribute contains the URL of a background image for the layer.

below   This attribute contains the name of the layer to be rendered below the current layer.

bgcolor   This attribute specifies a layer's background color. Its value can be either a named color or a color specified in the hexadecimal #*RRGGBB* format.

class   This attribute specifies the class name(s) for access via a style sheet.

clip   This attribute specifies the clipping region or viewable area of the layer. All layer content outside that rectangle will be rendered as transparent. The **clip** rectangle is defined by two x,y pairs: top x, left y, bottom x, and right y. Coordinates are relative to the layer's origin point, **0,0** in its top-left corner.

height   This attribute specifies the height of a layer in pixels or percentage values.

id   See "Core Attributes Reference," earlier in this chapter.

left   This attribute specifies in pixels the horizontal offset of the layer. The offset is relative to its parent layer if it has one or to the left page margin if it does not.

name   This attribute assigns the layer a name that can be referenced by programs in a client-side scripting language. The **id** attribute also can be used.

pagex   This attribute specifies the horizontal position of the layer relative to the browser window.

pagey   This attribute specifies the vertical position of the layer relative to the browser window.

src   This attribute is used to set the URL of a file that contains the content to load into the layer.

style   This attribute specifies an inline style for the layer.

top   This attribute specifies in pixels the top offset of the layer. The offset is relative to its parent layer if it has one or the top page margin if it does not.

visibility   This attribute specifies whether a layer is hidden, shown, or inherits its visibility from the layer that includes it.

width   This attribute specifies a layer's width in pixels.

z-index   This attribute specifies a layer's stacking order relative to other layers. Position is specified with positive integers, with **1** indicating the bottommost layer.

Attribute and Event Support

Netscape 4   All attributes

Event Handlers

None

Example

```
<p>Content comes before.</p>
<ilayer name="background" bgcolor="green">
  <p>Layered information goes here.</p>
</ilayer>
<p>Content comes after.</p>
```

Compatibility

Netscape 4.0–4.7 (Netscape 6 Preview Release 2 did not support this element)

Notes

- This element likely will fall out of fashion because of its lack of cross-browser compatibility. The functionality of **<ilayer>** is possible using the positioning features in CSS. Page developers are discouraged from using this element.

- Applets, plug-ins, and other embedded media forms, generically called *objects,* might be included in a layer; however, they will float to the top of all other layers even if their containing layer is obscured.

<img> (Image)

This element indicates a media object to include in an HTML document. Usually, the object is a graphic image, but some implementations support movies and animations.

Syntax

```
<img
    align="bottom | left | middle | right | top"
        (transitional)
    alt="alternative text"
    border="pixels" (transitional)
    class="class name(s)"
    dir="ltr | rtl"
    height="pixels"
    hspace="pixels" (transitional)
    id="unique alphanumeric identifier"
    ismap
    lang="language code"
    longdesc="url of description file"
    src="url of image"
    style="style information"
    title="advisory text"
    usemap="url of map file"
    vspace="pixels" (transitional)
    width="pixels"
    onclick="script"
    ondblclick="script"
    onkeydown="script"
    onkeypress="script"
    onkeyup="script"
    onmousedown="script"
    onmousemove="script"
    onmouseout="script"
    onmouseover="script"
    onmouseup="script">
```

XHTML Syntax

As an empty element, **<img>** requires a trailing slash for XHTML compliance:

```
<img />
```

Attributes and Events Defined by
Internet Explorer 4

```
    align="absbottom | absmiddle | baseline | texttop"
    datafld="name of column supplying bound data"
    datasrc="id of data source object supplying data"
    dynsrc="url of movie"
    language="javascript | jscript | vbs | vbscript"
    loop="infinite | number"
    lowsrc="url of low-resolution image"
    name="unique alphanumeric identifier"
    onabort="script"
```

```
onafterupdate="script"
onbeforeupdate="script"
onblur="script"
ondragstart="script"
onerror="script"
onfocus="script"
onhelp="script"
onload="script"
onresize="script"
onrowenter="script"
onrowexit="script"
onselectstart="script"
```

Attributes and Events Defined by Internet Explorer 5.5

```
hidefocus="true | false"
tabindex="number"
```

Attributes Defined by Netscape 4

```
align="absbottom | absmiddle | baseline | texttop"
lowsrc="url of low-resolution image"
name="unique alphanumeric identifier"
suppress="true | false"
```

Attributes Defined by WebTV

```
controls
name="unique alphanumeric identifier"
reload="seconds"
selected="x,y pair"
transparency="number (1-100)"
```

Attributes

align   This attribute controls the horizontal alignment of the image with respect to the page. The default value is **left**. Only the Netscape, Internet Explorer 4, and WebTV implementations support the **absbottom**, **absmiddle**, **baseline**, and **texttop** values.

alt   This attribute contains a string to display instead of the image for browsers that cannot display images.

border   This attribute indicates the width in pixels of the border surrounding the image.

class   See "Core Attributes Reference," earlier in this chapter.

controls   Under Internet Explorer 3 and WebTV, it is possible to set the controls to show by placing this attribute in the **<img>** element. This attribute does not appear to be supported under Internet Explorer 4, and users are encouraged to use the **<object>** element to embed video for Internet Explorer.

datafld   This attribute specifies the column name from the data source object that supplies the bound data to set the **src** of the **<img>** element.

datasrc   This attribute indicates the **id** of the data source object that supplies the data that is bound to this **<img>** element.

dir   See "Language Reference," earlier in this chapter.

dynsrc   In the Microsoft and WebTV implementations, this attribute indicates the URL of a movie file and is used instead of the **src** attribute.

height   This attribute indicates the height in pixels of the image.

hidefocus   This proprietary element, introduced with Internet Explorer 5.5, hides focus on an element's content. Focus must be applied to the element using the **tabindex** attribute.

hspace   This attribute indicates the horizontal space in pixels between the image and surrounding text.

id   See "Core Attributes Reference," earlier in this chapter.

ismap   This attribute indicates that the image is a server-side image map. User mouse actions over the image are sent to the server for processing.

lang   See "Language Reference," earlier in this chapter.

language   This attribute specifies the language the current script is written in and invokes the proper scripting engine. The default value is **javascript**. **Javascript** and **jscript** represent that the scripting language is written in JavaScript. **Vbs** and **vbscript** represent that the scripting language is written in VBScript.

longdesc   This attribute specifies a URL of a document which contains a long description of the image. This attribute is used as a complement to the **alt** attribute.

2

loop   In the Microsoft implementation, this attribute is used with the **dynsrc** attribute to cause a movie to loop. Its value is either a numeric loop count or the keyword **infinite**.

lowsrc   In the Netscape implementation, this attribute contains the URL of an image to be initially loaded. Typically, the **lowsrc** image is a low-resolution or black-and-white image that provides a quick preview of the image to follow. Once the primary image is loaded, it replaces the **lowsrc** image.

name   This common attribute is used to bind a name to the image. Older browsers understand the **name** field, and in conjunction with scripting languages it is possible to manipulate images by their defined names to create effects such as "rollover" buttons. The **id** attribute under HTML 4 specifies element identifiers; for backward compatibility, **name** can still be used.

reload   In the WebTV implementation, this attribute indicates in seconds how frequently an image should be reloaded.

selected   In the WebTV implementation, this attribute indicates the initial *x,y* coordinate location on the image. The cursor is placed at that location when the image is loaded. It requires either the **ismap** or the **usemap** attribute.

src   This attribute indicates the URL of an image file to be displayed.

style   See "Core Attributes Reference," earlier in this chapter.

suppress   This Netscape-specific attribute determines if a placeholder icon will appear during image loading. Values are **true** and **false**. **suppress="true"** will suppress display of the placeholder icon as well as display of any **alt** information until the image is loaded. **suppress="false"** will allow the placeholder icon and any tool tips defined by the **alt** information to display while the image is loading. The default value is **false**. If the browser is set to not load images automatically, the **suppress** attribute is ignored.

tabindex   This attribute uses a number to identify the object's position in the tabbing order for keyboard navigation using the TAB key. Internet Explorer 5.5 applies this attribute to the **img** element; under IE 5.5, this focus can be disabled with the **hidefocus** attribute.

title   See "Core Attributes Reference," earlier in this chapter.

transparency   In the WebTV implementation, this attribute allows the background to show through the image. It takes a numeric argument indicating the degree of transparency, from fully opaque (**0**) to fully transparent (**100**).

usemap   This attribute makes the image support client-side image mapping. Its argument is a URL specifying the map file, which associates image regions with hyperlinks.

vspace   This attribute indicates the vertical space in pixels between the image and surrounding text.

width   This attribute indicates the width in pixels of the image.

Attribute and Event Support

Netscape 4   align, alt, border, space, hspace, ismap, lowsrc, name, src, suppress, usemap, vspace, and width.

Internet Explorer 4   All W3C-defined attributes and events except **dir** and **longdesc**, and all attributes and events defined by Internet Explorer 4.

Internet Explorer 5.5   Same as IE 4, plus **dir**, **hidefocus**, and **tabindex**.

WebTV   align, border, height, hspace, id, ismap, name, selected, src, start, transparency, usemap, vspace, width, onabort, onerror, and onload.

Event Handlers
See "Events Reference," earlier in this chapter.

Examples
```
<img src="lakers.jpg" lowsrc="lakersbw.jpg" alt="Los Angeles Lakers"
    height="100" width="300">

<img src="hugeimagemap.gif" usemap="#mainmap" border="0" height="200"
    width="200" alt="Image Map Here">

<a href="home.htm"><IMG SRC="homebutton.gif" width="50" height="20"
    alt="Link to Home Page"></a>
```

XHTML Examples
```
<img src="mikka.jpg" lowsrc="mikkabw.jpg" alt="Grand Prix Driver"
    height="320" width="150" />
```

Compatibility

> HTML 2, 3.2, 4, 4.01, XHTML 1.0
> Internet Explorer 2, 3, 4, 5, and 5.5
> Netscape 1, 2, 3, 4–4.7, 6
> Opera
> WebTV

Notes

- Currently no browser appears to support **longdesc**.

- Typically, when you use the **usemap** attribute, the URL is a fragment, such as #map1, rather than a full URL. Some browsers do not support external client-side map files.

- Under the HTML 4 strict definition, the **<img>** element does not support **align**, **border**, **height**, **hspace**, **vspace**, and **width**. The functionality of these attributes should be possible using style sheet rules.

- Whereas the HTML 4 specification reserves data-binding attributes such as **datafld** or **datasrc**, it is not specified for **<img>**, although Internet Explorer provides support for these attributes.

- XHTML 1.0 requires a trailing slash for this element: **<img />**.

<input> (Input Form Control)

This element specifies an input control for a form. The type of input is set by the **type** attribute and can be a variety of different types, including single-line text field, multiline text field, password style, check box, radio button, or push button.

Syntax

```
<input
     accept="MIME TYPES"
     accesskey="character"
     align="bottom | left | middle | right | top"
           (transitional)
     alt="text"
     checked
     class="class name(s)"
     dir="ltr | rtl"
     disabled
     id="unique alphanumeric identifier"
```

```
lang="language code"
maxlength="maximum field size"
name="field name"
readonly
size="field size"
src="url of image file"
style="style information"
tabindex="number"
title="advisory text"
type="buttom | checkbox | file | hidden | image |
      password | radio | reset | submit | text"
usemap="url of map file"
value="field value"
onblur="script"
onchange="script"
onclick="script"
ondblclick="script"
onfocus="script"
onkeydown="script"
onkeypress="script"
onkeyup="script"
onmousedown="script"
onmousemove="script"
onmouseout="script"
onmouseover="script"
onmouseup="script"
onselect="script">
```

XHTML Syntax

As an empty element, **<input>** requires a trailing slash for XHTML compliance:

```
<input />
```

Attributes and Events Defined by Internet Explorer 4

```
align="center"
language="javascript | jscript | vbs | vbscript"
onafterupdate="script"
onbeforeupdate="script"
ondragstart="script"
onhelp="script"
onselectstart="script"
```

Attributes Defined by Internet Explorer 5.5

```
hidefocus="true | false"
```

Attributes Defined by Netscape 4

```
align="absbottom | absmiddle | baseline | texttop"
```

Attributes Defined by WebTV

```
bgcolor="color name | #RRGGBB"
borderimage="url"
cursor="color name | #RRGGBB"
usestyle
width="pixels"
```

Attributes

accept   This attribute is used to list the MIME types accepted for file uploads when **<input type="file">**.

accesskey   This attribute specifies a keyboard navigation accelerator for the element. Pressing ALT or a similar key in association with the specified character selects the form control correlated with that key sequence. Page designers are forewarned to avoid key sequences already bound to browsers.

align   With image form controls (**type="image"**), this attribute aligns the image with respect to surrounding text. The HTML 4.01 transitional specification defines **bottom**, **left**, **middle**, **right**, and **top** as allowable values. Netscape and Microsoft browsers might also allow the use of attribute values such as **absbottom** or **absmiddle**. Like other presentation-specific aspects of HTML, the **align** attribute is dropped under the strict HTML 4.01 specification.

alt   This attribute is used to display an alternative description of image buttons for text-only browsers. The meaning of **alt** for forms of **<input>** beyond **type="input"** is unclear.

bgcolor   In the WebTV implementation, this attribute specifies the background color of a text form control (**type="text"**). The value of the attribute can be either a named color or a color specified in the hexadecimal *#RRGGBB* format.

borderimage   In the WebTV implementation, this attribute allows specification of a graphical border for **reset**, **submit**, and **text** controls. Its value is the URL of a .bif (Border Image File) graphics file that specifies the border. Border image files tend to reside in WebTV ROM; the common values are **file://ROM/Border/ButtonBorder2.bif** and **file://ROM/Border/ButtonBorder3.bif**, although other values might be present under later versions of WebTV.

2

checked   The **checked** attribute should be used only for check box (**type="checkbox"**) and radio (**type="radio"**) form controls. The presence of this attribute indicates that the control should be displayed in its checked state.

class   See "Core Attributes Reference," earlier in this chapter.

cursor   In the WebTV implementation, this attribute sets the cursor color for a text form control (**type="text"**). The attribute's value is either a named color or a color specified in the hexadecimal *#RRGGBB* format.

dir   See "Language Reference," earlier in this chapter.

disabled   This attribute is used to turn off a form control. Elements will not be submitted, nor will they receive any focus from the keyboard or mouse. Disabled form controls will not be part of the tabbing order. The browser also might gray out the form that is disabled, in order to indicate to the user that the form control is inactive. This attribute requires no value.

hidefocus   This proprietary element, introduced with Internet Explorer 5.5, hides focus on an element's content. Focus must be applied to the element using the **tabindex** attribute.

id   See "Core Attributes Reference," earlier in this chapter.

lang   See "Language Reference," earlier in this chapter.

language   In the Microsoft implementation, this attribute specifies the scripting language to be used with an associated script bound to the element typically through an event handler attribute. Possible values include **javascript**, **jscript**, **vbs** and **vbscript**. Other values that include the version of the language used, such as **JavaScript1.1**, also might be possible.

maxlength   This attribute indicates the maximum content length that can be entered in a text form control (**type="text"**). The maximum number of characters allowed differs from the visible dimension of the form control, which is set with the **size** attribute.

name   This attribute allows a form control to be assigned a name so that it can be referenced by a scripting language. **Name** is supported by older browsers such as Netscape 2 generation browsers, but the W3C encourages the use of the **id** attribute. For compatibility purposes, both might have to be used.

readonly   This attribute prevents the form control's value from being changed. Form controls with this attribute set might receive focus from the user but might not be modified. Because it receives focus, a **readonly** form control will be part of the form's tabbing order. Last, the control's value will be sent on form submission. This attribute can be used only with **<input>** when **type** is set to **text** or **password**. The attribute also is used with the **<textarea>** element.

size   This attribute indicates the visible dimension, in characters, of a text form control (**type="text"**). This differs from the maximum length of content, which can be entered in a form control set by the **maxlength** attribute.

src   This attribute is used with image form controls (**type="image"**) to specify the URL of the image file to load.

style   See "Core Attributes Reference," earlier in this chapter.

tabindex   This attribute takes a numeric value that indicates the position of the form control in the tabbing index for the form. Tabbing proceeds from the lowest positive **tabindex** value to the highest. Negative values for **tabindex** will leave the form control out of the tabbing order. When tabbing is not explicitly set, the browser can tab through items in the order they are encountered. Form controls that are disabled due to the presence of the **disabled** attribute will not be part of the tabbing index, although read-only controls will be.

title   See "Core Attributes Reference," earlier in this chapter.

type   This attribute specifies the type of the form control. A value of **button** indicates a general-purpose button with no well-defined meaning. However, an action can be associated with the button using an event handler attribute, such as **onclick**. A value of **checkbox** indicates a check box control. Check box form controls have a checked and nonchecked set, but even if these controls are grouped together, they allow a user to select multiple check boxes at once. In contrast, a value of **radio** indicates a radio button control. When grouped, radio buttons allow only one of the many choices to be selected at a given time.

A form control type of **hidden** indicates a field that is not visible to the viewer but is used to store information. A hidden form control often is used to preserve state information between pages. A value of **file** for the **type** attribute indicates a control that allows the viewer to upload a file to a server. The filename can be entered in a displayed field, or a user agent might provide a special browse button allowing the user to locate the file. A value of **image** indicates a graphic image form control that a user can click on to invoke an associated action. (Most browsers allow the use of **img**-associated attributes such as **height, width, hspace, vspace** and **alt** when the **type** value is set to **image**.) A value of **password** for the **type** attribute indicates a password entry field. A password field will not display text entered as it is typed; it might instead show a series of dots. Note that password-entered data is not transferred to the server in any secure fashion. A value of **reset** for the **type** attribute is used to insert a button that resets all controls within a form to their default values. A value of **submit** inserts a special submission button that, when pressed, sends the contents of the form to the location indicated by the **action** attribute of the enclosing **<form>** element. Last, a value of **text** (the default) for the **type** attribute indicates a single-line text input field.

usemap   This HTML 4.0 attribute is used to indicate the map file to be associated with an image when the form control is set with **type="image"**. The value of the attribute should be a URL of a map file, but generally will be in the form of a URL fragment referencing a map file within the current file.

usestyle   In the WebTV implementation, the presence of this attribute causes control text to be rendered in the default text style for the page. This attribute requires no value.

value   This attribute has two different uses, depending on the value for the **type** attribute. With data entry controls (**type="text"** and **type="password"**), this attribute is used to set the default value for the control. When used with check box or radio form controls, this attribute specifies the return value for the control when it is turned on, rather than the default Boolean value submitted.

width   This attribute, supported by WebTV and Internet Explorer, is used to set the size of the form control in pixels.

Attribute and Event Support

Netscape 4   name, value, and onclick. (**class, id, lang,** and **style** are implied.)

Internet Explorer 4   All W3C-defined attributes and events except **accept** and **usemap**, and all attributes and events defined by Internet Explorer 4. (Note: Internet Explorer 4 supports only the **center, left,** and **right** values for the **align** attribute.)

Internet Explorer 4   All W3C-defined attributes and events
except **accept**, and **usemap**, and all attributes and events defined
by Internet Explorer 4, and adds **hidefocus**. (Note: Internet
Explorer 4 supports only the **center**, **left**, and **right** values for
the **align** attribute.)

WebTV   align, bgcolor, checked, cursor, id, maxlength, name,
size, type, usestyle, value, width, onblur, onchange, onclick,
onfocus, and onselect.

Event Handlers

See "Events Reference," earlier in this chapter.

Examples

```
<form>
Which is your favorite food?
   <input type="radio" name="favorite" value="Mexican">Mexican
   <input type="radio" name="favorite" value="Russian">Russian
   <input type="radio" name="favorite" value="Japanese">Japanese
   <input type="radio" checked name="favorite" value="Other">Other
<form>

<form>
Enter your name: <input type="text" maxlength="35" size="20"><BR>
Enter your password: <input type="password" maxlength="35"
size="20"><BR>
<br>
   <input type="submit" value="Submit">
   <input type="reset" value="Reset">
</form>
```

XHTML Example

```
<form>
Enter your name: <input type="text" maxlength="35" size="20" /><BR>
Enter your password: <input type="password" maxlength="35"
size="20" /><BR>
<br>
   <input type="submit" value="Submit" />
   <input type="reset" value="Reset" />
</form>
```

Compatibility

HTML 2, 3.2, 4, 4.01, XHTML 1.0
Internet Explorer 2, 3, 4, 5, 5.5
Netscape 1, 2, 3, 4–4.7, 6
Opera 4.0
WebTV

Notes

- The **<input>** element is an empty element and requires no closing tag.

- Some documents suggest the use of **type="textarea"**. Even if this style is supported, it should be avoided in favor of the **<textarea>** element, which is common to all browsers.

- The HTML 2.0 and 3.2 specifications support only the **align, checked, maxlength, name, size, src, type,** and **value** attributes for the **<input>** element.

- The HTML 4.01 specification also reserves the use of the **datafld, dataformatas,** and **datasrc** data-binding attributes.

- Under the strict HTML specification, the **align** attribute is not allowed.

- The XHTML 1.0 specification requires the use of a trailing slash: **<input />**.

<ins> (Inserted Text)

This element is used to indicate that text has been added to the document.

Syntax

```
<ins
    cite="URL"
    class="class name(s)"
    datetime="date"
    id="unique alphanumeric identifier"
    lang="language code"
    style="style information"
    title="advisory text"
    onclick="script"
    ondblclick="script"
    onkeydown="script"
    onkeypress="script"
    onkeyup="script"
    onmousedown="script"
    onmousemove="script"
    onmouseout="script"
    onmouseover="script"
    onmouseup="script">

</ins>
```

Attributes and Events Defined by Internet Explorer 4

```
language="javascript | jscript | vbs | vbscript"
ondragstart="script"
onhelp="script"
```

Attributes and Events Defined by Internet Explorer 5.5

```
accesskey="key"
contenteditable=" false | true | inherit "
dir="ltr | rtl"
hidefocus="true | false"
tabindex="number"
```

Attributes

accesskey This attribute specifies a keyboard navigation accelerator for the element. Pressing ALT or a similar key (depending on the browser and operating system) in association with the specified key selects the anchor element correlated with that key.

cite The value of this attribute is a URL that designates a source document or message for the information inserted. This attribute is intended to point to information explaining why the text was changed.

class See "Core Attributes Reference," earlier in this chapter.

contenteditable This proprietary Microsoft attribute allows users to edit content rendered in the Internet Explorer 5.5 browser. Values are **false**, **true**, and **inherit**. A value of **false** will prevent content from being edited by users; **true** will allow editing. The default value, **inherit**, applies the value of the affected element's parent element.

datetime This attribute is used to indicate the date and time the insertion was made. The value of the attribute is a date in a special format as defined by ISO 8601. The basic date format is

```
yyyy-mm-ddthh:mm:ssTZD
```

where the following is true:

```
yyyy=four-digit year such as 1999
mm=two-digit month (01=January, 02=February, and so on)
```

```
dd=two-digit day of the month (01 through 31)
hh=two-digit hour (00 to 23) (24-hour clock not AM or PM)
mm=two-digit minute (00 to 59)
ss=two-digit second (00 to 59)
tzd=time zone designator
```

2

The time zone designator is either **z**, which indicates UTC (Universal Time Coordinate, or coordinated universal time format), or **+**_hh_**:**_mm_, which indicates that the time is a local time that is _hh_ hours and _mm_ minutes ahead of UTC. Alternatively, the format for the time zone designator could be **-**_hh_**:**_mm_, which indicates that the local time is behind UTC. Note that the letter "T" actually appears in the string, all digits must be used, and **00** values for minutes and seconds might be required. An example value for the **datetime** attribute might be **1999-10-6T09:15:00-05:00**, which corresponds to October 6, 1999, 9:15 A.M., U.S. Eastern Standard Time.

dir   See "Language Reference," earlier in this chapter.

hidefocus   This proprietary element, introduced with Internet Explorer 5.5, hides focus on an element's content. Focus must be applied to the element using the **tabindex** attribute.

id   See "Core Attributes Reference," earlier in this chapter.

lang   See "Language Reference," earlier in this chapter.

language   In the Microsoft implementation, this attribute specifies the scripting language to be used with an associated script bound to the element, typically through an event handler attribute. Possible values might include **javacript**, **jscript**, **vbs**, and **vbscript**. Other values that include the version of the language used, such as **JavaScript1.1**, also might be possible.

style   See "Core Attributes Reference," earlier in this chapter.

tabindex   This attribute uses a number to identify the object's position in the tabbing order for keyboard navigation using the TAB key. Internet Explorer 5.5 applies this attribute to the **ins** element; under IE 5.5, this focus can be disabled with the **hidefocus** attribute.

title   See "Core Attributes Reference," earlier in this chapter.

Attribute and Event Support

Internet Explorer 4   All attributes and events except **cite** and **datetime**.

Event Handlers

See "Events Reference," earlier in this chapter.

Example

```
<ins cite="http://www.bigcompany.com/changes/oct99.htm"
    date="1999-10-06T09:15:00-05:00">
The penalty clause applies to client lateness as well.
</ins>
```

Compatibility

HTML 4, 4.01, XHTML 1.0
Internet Explorer 4, 5, and 5.5
Netscape 6
Opera 4.0

Notes

- Browsers can render inserted (**<ins>**) or deleted (**<del>**) text in a different style to show the changes that have been made to the document. Eventually, a browser could have a way to show a revision history on a document. User agents that do not understand **<del>** or **<ins>** will show the information anyway, so there is no harm in adding information, only in deleting it.

- The **<ins>** element is not supported under the HTML 2 and 3.2 specifications.

<isindex> (Index Prompt)

This element indicates that a document has an associated searchable keyword index. When a browser encounters this element, it inserts a query entry field at that point in the document. The viewer can enter query terms to perform a search. This element is deprecated under the strict HTML 4 specification and should not be used.

Syntax (Transitional Only)

```
<isindex
    class="class name(s)"
```

```
dir="ltr | rtl"
href="url" (nonstandard but common)
id="unique alphanumeric identifier"
lang="language code"
prompt="string"
style="style information"
title="advisory text">
```

2

XHTML Syntax

As an empty element, **<isindex>** requires a trailing slash for
XHTML compliance:

```
<isindex />
```

Attributes Defined by Internet Explorer 4

```
language="javascript | jscript | vbs | vbscript"
```

Attributes and Events Defined by Internet Explorer 5.5

```
accesskey="key"
contenteditable=" false | true | inherit"
hidefocus="true | false"
tabindex="number"
```

Attributes

accesskey   This attribute specifies a keyboard navigation
accelerator for the element. Pressing ALT or a similar key
(depending on the browser and operating system) in association
with the specified key selects the anchor element correlated with
that key.

action   This attribute specifies the URL of the query action to
be executed when the viewer presses the ENTER key. Although
this attribute is not defined under any HTML specification, it is
common to many browsers, particularly Internet Explorer 3, which
defined it.

class   See "Core Attributes Reference," earlier in this chapter.

contenteditable   This proprietary Microsoft attribute allows
users to edit content rendered in the Internet Explorer 5.5 browser.
Values are **false**, **true**, and **inherit**. A value of **false** will prevent
content from being edited by users; **true** will allow editing. The
default value, **inherit**, applies the value of the affected element's
parent element.

dir See "Language Reference," earlier in this chapter.

hidefocus This proprietary element, introduced with Internet Explorer 5.5, hides focus on an element's content. Focus must be applied to the element using the **tabindex** attribute.

href The **href** attribute is used with the **<isindex>** element as a way to indicate what the search document is. Another approach is to use the **<base>** element for the document. The HTML 2 documentation suggests that this is a legal approach and browsers appear to support it; however, it is poorly documented at best.

id See "Core Attributes Reference," earlier in this chapter.

tabindex This attribute uses a number to identify the object's position in the tabbing order for keyboard navigation using the TAB key. Internet Explorer 5.5 applies this attribute to the **dfn** element; under IE 5.5, this focus can be disabled with the **hidefocus** attribute.

lang See "Language Reference," earlier in this chapter.

language In the Microsoft implementation, this attribute specifies the scripting language to be used with an associated script bound to the element, typically through an event handler attribute. Possible values might include **javascript**, **jscript**, **vbs**, and **vbscript**. Other values that include the version of the language used, such as **JavaScript1.1**, also might be possible.

prompt This attribute allows a custom query prompt to be defined. The default prompt is "This is a searchable index. Enter search keywords." WebTV does not implement this attribute.

style See "Core Attributes Reference," earlier in this chapter.

title See "Core Attributes Reference," earlier in this chapter.

Attribute and Event Support

Netscape 4 prompt. (**class**, **id**, **lang**, and **style** are implied.)

Internet Explorer 4 class, **id**, **lang**, **language**, **prompt**, and **style**.

Event Handlers
None

Examples

```
<isindex action="cgi-bin/search" prompt="Enter search terms">

<isindex href="cgi-bin/search" prompt="Keywords:">

<base href="cgi-bin/search">
<isindex prompt="Enter search terms">
```

XHTML Example

```
<isindex action="cgi-bin/search" prompt="Enter search terms" />
```

Compatibility

> HTML 2, 3.2, and 4 (transitional), XHTML 1.0
> Internet Explorer 2, 3, 4, 5, 5.5
> Netscape 1, 2, 3, 4–4.7
> Opera 4.0
> WebTV

Notes

- As an empty element, **<isindex>** requires no closing tag under HTML specifications. The XHTML specification, however, requires a trailing slash: **<isindex />**.

- The HTML 3.2 specification only allows the **prompt** attribute, whereas HTML 2 expected a text description to accompany the search field.

- Netscape 1.1 originated the use of the **prompt** attribute. WebTV does not support this attribute.

- Originally, the W3C intended this element to be used in a document's header. Browser vendors have relaxed this usage to allow the element in a document's body. Early implementations did not support the **action** attribute and used the **<base>** element or an **href** attribute to specify a search function's URL.

- Older versions of Internet Explorer also support the **action** attribute, which specifies the URL to use for the query rather than relying on the URL set in the **<base>** element. Internet Explorer 4 does not support the **action**, **dir**, **href**, or **title** attributes. Microsoft documentation suggests using **<input>** instead of this deprecated element.

<kbd> (Keyboard Input)

This element logically indicates text as keyboard input. A browser generally renders text enclosed by this element in a monospaced font.

Syntax

```
<kbd
      class="class name(s)"
      dir="ltr | rtl"
      id="unique alphanumeric identifier"
      lang="language code"
      style="style information"
      title="advisory text"
      onclick="script"
      ondblclick="script"
      onkeydown="script"
      onkeypress="script"
      onkeyup="script"
      onmousedown="script"
      onmousemove="script"
      onmouseout="script"
      onmouseover="script"
      onmouseup="script">

</kbd>
```

Attributes and Events Defined by Internet Explorer 4

```
      language="javascript | jscript | vbs | vbscript"
      ondragstart="script"
      onhelp="script"
      onselectstart="script"
```

Attributes and Events Defined by Internet Explorer 5.5

```
      accesskey="key"
      contenteditable=" false | true | inherit"
      hidefocus="true | false"
      tabindex="number"
```

Attributes

accesskey   This attribute specifies a keyboard navigation accelerator for the element. Pressing ALT or a similar key (depending on the browser and operating system) in association with the specified key selects the anchor element correlated with that key.

class   See "Core Attributes Reference," earlier in this chapter.

contenteditable   This proprietary Microsoft attribute allows users to edit content rendered in the Internet Explorer 5.5 browser. Values are **false**, **true**, and **inherit**. A value of **false** will prevent content from being edited by users; **true** will allow editing. The default value, **inherit**, applies the value of the affected element's parent element.

dir   See "Language Reference," earlier in this chapter.

hidefocus   This proprietary element, introduced with Internet Explorer 5.5, hides focus on an element's content. Focus must be applied to the element using the **tabindex** attribute.

id   See "Core Attributes Reference," earlier in this chapter.

lang   See "Language Reference," earlier in this chapter.

language   In the Microsoft implementation, this attribute specifies the scripting language to be used with an associated script bound to the element, typically through an event handler attribute. Possible values might include **javascript**, **jscript**, **vbs**, and **vbscript**. Other values that include the version of the language used, such as **JavaScript1.1**, also might be possible.

style   See "Core Attributes Reference," earlier in this chapter.

tabindex   This attribute uses a number to identify the object's position in the tabbing order for keyboard navigation using the TAB key. Internet Explorer 5.5 applies this attribute to the **kbd** element; under IE 5.5, this focus can be disabled with the **hidefocus** attribute.

title   See "Core Attributes Reference," earlier in this chapter.

Attribute and Event Support

Netscape 4   **class**, **id**, **lang**, and **style** are implied.

Internet Explorer 4   All attributes and events except **dir**.

Event Handlers
See "Events Reference," earlier in this chapter.

Example

Enter the change directory command at the prompt as shown below:**
**
**
**
<kbd>CD .. **</kbd>**

Compatibility

> HTML 2, 3.2, 4, and 4.01, XHTML 1.0
> Internet Explorer 2, 3, 4, 5, and 5.5
> Netscape 1, 2, 3, 4–4.7, 6
> Opera 4
> WebTV

Notes

- The HTML 2 and 3.2 specifications support no attributes for this element.

<label> (Form Control Label)

This HTML 4 element is used to relate descriptions to form controls.

Syntax

```
<label
     accesskey="key"
     class="class name(s)"
     dir="ltr | rtl"
     for="id of control"
     id="unique alphanumeric identifier"
     lang="language code"
     style="style information"
     title="advisory text"
     onblur="script"
     onclick="script"
     ondblclick="script"
     onfocus="script"
     onkeydown="script"
     onkeypress="script"
     onkeyup="script"
     onmousedown="script"
     onmousemove="script"
     onmouseout="script"
     onmouseover="script"
     onmouseup="script">

</label>
```

Attributes and Events Defined by Internet Explorer 4

```
datafld="column name"
dataformatas="html | text"
datasrc="data source id"
language="javascript | jscript | vbs | vbscript"
ondragstart="script"
onhelp="script"
onselectstart="script"
```

Attributes and Events Defined by Internet Explorer 5.5

```
contenteditable=" false | true | inherit "
hidefocus="true | false"
tabindex="number"
```

Attributes

accesskey   This attribute specifies a keyboard navigation accelerator for the element. Pressing ALT or a similar key in association with the specified key selects the anchor element correlated with that key.

class   See "Core Attributes Reference," earlier in this chapter.

contenteditable   This proprietary Microsoft attribute allows users to edit content rendered in the Internet Explorer 5.5 browser. Values are **false**, **true**, and **inherit**. A value of **false** will prevent content from being edited by users; **true** will allow editing. The default value, **inherit**, applies the value of the affected element's parent element.

datafld   This attribute is used to indicate the column name in the data source that is bound to the content of the **<label>** element.

dataformatas   This attribute indicates whether the bound data is plain text (**text**) or HTML (**html**). The data bound with **<label>** is used to set the content of the label.

datasrc   The value of this attribute is an identifier indicating the data source to pull data from.

dir   See "Language Reference," earlier in this chapter.

for   This attribute specifies the **id** for the form control element the label references. This is optional when the label encloses the form control it is bound to. In many cases, particularly when a table is used to structure the form, the **<label>** element will not be able to enclose the associated form control, so the **for** attribute should be used. This attribute allows more than one label to be associated with the same control by creating multiple references.

hidefocus   This proprietary element, introduced with Internet Explorer 5.5, hides focus on an element's content. Focus must be applied to the element using the **tabindex** attribute.

id   See "Core Attributes Reference," earlier in this chapter.

lang   See "Language Reference," earlier in this chapter.

language   In the Microsoft implementation, this attribute specifies the scripting language to be used with an associated script bound to the element, typically through an event handler attribute. Possible values might include **javascript**, **jscript**, **vbs**, and **vbscript**. Other values that include the version of the language used, such as **JavaScript1.1**, also might be possible.

style   See "Core Attributes Reference," earlier in this chapter.

tabindex   This attribute uses a number to identify the object's position in the tabbing order for keyboard navigation using the TAB key. Internet Explorer 5.5 applies this attribute to the **label** element; under IE 5.5, this focus can be disabled with the **hidefocus** attribute.

title   See "Core Attributes Reference," earlier in this chapter.

Attribute and Event Support

Internet Explorer 4   All W3C-defined attributes and events except **dir**, **onblur**, and **onfocus**, and all attributes and events defined by Internet Explorer 4.

Event Handlers
See "Events Reference," earlier in this chapter.

Examples
```
<form>
    <label id="usernamelabel">Name
    <input type="text" id="username">
    </label>
</form>
```

Event Handlers

See "Events Reference," earlier in this chapter.

Example

```
<form>
 <fieldset>
   <legend align="top">User Information</legend>
   First Name: <input type="TEXT" id="firstname"
                      size="20"><br>
   Last Name: <input type="text" id="lastname"
                     size="20"><br>
 </fieldset>
</form>
```

2

Compatibility

HTML 4, 4.01, XHTML 1.0
Internet Explorer 4, 5, and 5.5
Netscape 6
Opera 4.0

Notes

- The **<legend>** element should occur only within the **<fieldset>** element. There should be only one **<legend>** per **<fieldset>** element.

- The legend improves accessibility when the **fieldset** is rendered nonvisually.

- The Microsoft implementation can use the **center** option in the **align** attribute. Microsoft also defines the **valign** attribute for legend positioning. However, the **valign** attribute does not appear to work consistently.

- WebTV and Netscape do not yet support this element.

<li> (List Item)

This element is used to indicate a list item as contained in an ordered list (**<ol>**), unordered list (**<ul>**), or older list styles such as **<dir>** and **<menu>**.

Syntax

```
<li
    class="class name(s)"
    dir="ltr | rtl"
    id="unique alphanumeric identifier"
    lang="language code"
    style="style information"
    title="advisory text"
    type="circle | disc | square | a | A | i | I | 1"
        (transitional)
    value="number" (transitional)
    onclick="script"
    ondblclick="script"
    onkeydown="script"
    onkeypress="script"
    onkeyup="script"
    onmousedown="script"
    onmousemove="script"
    onmouseout="script"
    onmouseover="script"
    onmouseup="script">
```

XHTML Syntax

Under the XHTML 1.0 specification, the closing tag **</li>** ceases to be optional and must be used with this element:

```
<li></li>
```

Attributes and Events Defined by Internet Explorer 4

```
    language="javascript | jscript | vbs | vbscript"
    ondragstart="script"
    onhelp="script"
    onselectstart="script"
```

Attributes and Events Defined by Internet Explorer 5.5

```
    accesskey="key"
    contenteditable=" false | true | inherit"
    hidefocus="true | false"
    tabindex="number"
```

Attributes

accesskey   This attribute specifies a keyboard navigation accelerator for the element. Pressing ALT or a similar key

2

(depending on the browser and operating system) in association with the specified key selects the anchor element correlated with that key.

class   See "Core Attributes Reference," earlier in this chapter.

contenteditable   This proprietary Microsoft attribute allows users to edit content rendered in the Internet Explorer 5.5 browser. Values are **false, true,** and **inherit.** A value of **false** will prevent content from being edited by users; **true** will allow editing. The default value, **inherit,** applies the value of the affected element's parent element.

dir   See "Language Reference," earlier in this chapter.

hidefocus   This proprietary element, introduced with Internet Explorer 5.5, hides focus on an element's content. Focus must be applied to the element using the **tabindex** attribute.

id   See "Core Attributes Reference," earlier in this chapter.

lang   See "Language Reference," earlier in this chapter.

language   In the Microsoft implementation, this attribute specifies the scripting language to be used with an associated script bound to the element, typically through an event handler attribute. Possible values might include **javascript, jscript, vbs,** and **vbscript.** Other values that include the version of the language used, such as **JavaScript1.1,** also might be possible.

style   See "Core Attributes Reference," earlier in this chapter.

tabindex   This attribute uses a number to identify the object's position in the tabbing order for keyboard navigation using the TAB key. Internet Explorer 5.5 applies this attribute to the **li** element; under IE 5.5, this focus can be disabled with the **hidefocus** attribute.

title   See "Core Attributes Reference," earlier in this chapter.

type   This attribute indicates the bullet type used in unordered lists or the numbering type used in ordered lists. For ordered lists, a value of **a** indicates lowercase letters, **A** indicates uppercase letters, **i** indicates lowercase Roman numerals, **I** indicates uppercase Roman numerals, and **1** indicates numbers. For unordered lists, values are used to specify bullet types. Although the browser is free to set bullet styles, a value of **disc** generally specifies a filled circle, a value of **circle** specifies an empty circle, and a value of **b** specifies a filled square. Browsers such as WebTV might include other bullet shapes like triangles.

value   This attribute indicates the current number of items in an ordered list as defined by the <ol> element. Regardless of the value of **type** being used to set Roman numerals or letters, the only allowed value for this attribute is a number. List items that follow will continue numbering from the value set. The **value** attribute has no meaning for unordered lists.

Attribute and Event Support

Netscape 4   class, id, style, lang, type, and value.

Internet Explorer 4   All attributes and events except **dir**.

WebTV   type and value.

Event Handlers
See "Events Reference," earlier in this chapter.

Examples
```
<ul>
    <li type="circle">First list item is a circle
    <li type="square">Second list item is a square
    <li type="disc">Third list item is a square
</ul>

<ol>
    <li type="i">Roman Numerals
    <li type="a" value="3">Second list item is letter C
    <li type="a">Continue list in lowercase letters
</ol>
```

XHTML Example
```
<ul>
    <li>First list item </li>
    <li>Second list item </li>
    <li>Third list item</li>
</ul>
```

Compatibility
HTML 2, 3.2, 4, 4.01, XHTML 1.0
Internet Explorer 2, 3, 4, 5, and 5.5

Netscape 1, 2, 3, 4–4.7, 6
Opera 4.0
WebTV

Notes

- Under the strict HTML 4.01 definition, the <li> element loses the **type** and **value** attributes, as these functions can be performed with style sheets.
- Whereas bullet styles can be set explicitly, browsers tend to change styles for bullets when <ul> lists are nested. However, ordered lists generally do not change style automatically, nor do they support outline style number (1.1, 1.1.1, and so on).
- The closing tag </li> is optional under HTML specifications and is not commonly used.
- XHTML 1.0 makes the closing tag </li> mandatory.

<link> (Link to External Files or Set Relationships)

This empty element specifies relationships between the current document and other documents. Possible uses for this element include defining a relational framework for navigation and linking the document to a style sheet.

Syntax

```
<link
    charset="charset list from RFC 2045"
    class="class name(s)"
    dir="ltr | rtl"
    href="URL"
    hreflang="language code"
    id="unique alphanumeric identifier"
    lang="language code"
    media="all | aural | braille | print | projection |
        screen | other"
    rel="relationship value"
    rev="relationship value"
    style="style information"
    target="frame name" (transitional)
    title="advisory information"
    type="content type"
    onclick="script"
    ondblclick="script"
```

```
onkeydown="script"
onkeypress="script"
onkeyup="script"
onmousedown="script"
onmousemove="script"
onmouseout="script"
onmouseover="script"
onmouseup="script">
```

XHTML Syntax

Under the XHTML 1.0 specification, the **<link>** element requires a trailing slash:

```
<link />
```

Attributes Defined by Internet Explorer 4

```
disabled
```

Attributes Defined by Netscape 4

```
src="url"
```

Attributes

charset   This attribute specifies the character set used by the linked document. Allowed values for this attribute are character set names, such as EUC-JP, as defined in RFC 2045.

class   See "Core Attributes Reference," earlier in this chapter.

dir   See "Language Reference," earlier in this chapter.

disabled   This Microsoft-defined attribute is used to disable a link relationship. The presence of the attribute is all that is required to remove a linking relationship. In conjunction with scripting, this attribute could be used to turn on and off various style sheet relationships.

href   This attribute specifies the URL of the linked resource. A URL might be absolute or relative.

hreflang   This attribute is used to indicate the language of the linked resource. See "Language Reference," earlier in this chapter for information on allowed values.

id   See "Core Attributes Reference," earlier in this chapter.

lang   See "Language Reference," earlier in this chapter.

media   This attribute specifies the destination medium for any linked style information, as indicated when the **rel** attribute is set to **stylesheet**. The value of the attribute might be a single media descriptor such as **screen** or a comma-separated list. Possible values for this attribute include **all, aural, braille, print, projection,** and **screen**. Other values also might be defined, depending on the browser. Internet Explorer supports **all, print,** and **screen** as values for this attribute.

rel   This attribute names a relationship between the linked document and the current document. Possible values for this attribute include **alternate, bookmark, chapter, contents, copyright, glossary, help, index, next, prev, section, start, stylesheet,** and **subsection**.

The most common use of this attribute is to specify a link to an external style sheet. The **rel** attribute is set to **stylesheet,** and the **href** attribute is set to the URL of an external style sheet to format the page. WebTV also supports the use of the value **next** for **rel** to preload the next page in a document series.

rev   The value of the **rev** attribute shows the relationship of the current document to the linked document, as defined by the **href** attribute. The attribute thus defines the reverse relationship compared to the value of the **rel** attribute. Values for the **rev** attribute are similar to the possible values for **rel**. They might include **alternate, bookmark, chapter, contents, copyright, glossary, help, index, next, prev, section, start, stylesheet,** and **subsection**.

style   See "Core Attributes Reference," earlier in this chapter.

target   The value of the **target** attribute is used to define the frame or window name that has the defined linking relationship or that will show the rendering of any linked resource.

title   See "Core Attributes Reference," earlier in this chapter.

type   This attribute is used to define the type of the content linked to. The value of the attribute should be a MIME type such as **text/html, text/css,** and so on. The common use of this attribute is to define the type of style sheet linked and the most common current value is **text/css,** which indicates a Cascading Style Sheet format.

Attribute and Event Support

Netscape 4   rel, src, and type. (class, id, lang, and style are implied.)

Internet Explorer 4   disabled, href, id, media (all | print | screen), rel, rev, title, and type.

WebTV   href and rel (value="next").

Event Handlers

See "Event Reference," earlier in this chapter.

Examples

```
<link href="products.htm" rel="parent">

<link href="corpstyle.css" rel="stylesheet" type="text/css" media="all">

<link href="nextpagetoload.htm" rel="next">
```

XHTML Examples

```
<link href="products.htm" rel="parent" />
```

Compatibility

HTML 2, 3.2, 4, 4.01, XHTML 1.0
Netscape 4–4.7, 6
Internet Explorer 3, 4, 5, and 5.5
WebTV

Notes

- As an empty element **<link>** has no closing tag.
- Under XHTML 1.0, empty elements such as **<link>** require a trailing slash: **<link />**.
- The **<link>** element can occur only in the **<head>** element; there could be multiple occurrences of the element.
- HTML 3.2 defines only the **href**, **rel**, **rev**, and **title** attributes for the **<link>** element.
- HTML 2 defines the **href**, **methods**, **rel**, **rev**, **title**, and **urn** attributes for the **<link>** element. The **methods** and **urn** attributes were later removed from specifications.
- The HTML 4.01 specification defines event handlers for the **<link>** element, but it is unclear how they would be used.

<listing> (Code Listing)

This deprecated element from HTML 2 is used to indicate a code listing; it is no longer part of the HTML standard. Text tends to be rendered in a smaller size within this element. Otherwise, the **<pre>** element should be used instead of **<listing>** to indicate preformatted text.

Syntax (HTML 2; Deprecated)

```
<lisitng>
</listing>
```

Attributes and Events Defined by Internet Explorer 4

```
class="class name(s)"
id="unique alphanumeric string"
lang="language code"
language="javascript | jscript | vbs | vbscript"
style="style information"
title="advisory text"
onclick="script"
ondblclick="script"
ondragstart="script"
onhelp="script"
onkeydown="script"
onkeypress="script"
onkeyup="script"
onmousedown="script"
onmousemove="script"
onmouseout="script"
onmouseover="script"
onmouseup="script"
onselectstart="script">
```

Attributes and Events Defined by Internet Explorer 5.5

```
accesskey="key"
contenteditable=" false | true | inherit"
dir="ltr | rtl"
hidefocus="true | false"
tabindex="number"
```

Attributes

accesskey   This attribute specifies a keyboard navigation accelerator for the element. Pressing ALT or a similar key (depending on the browser and operating system) in association with the specified key selects the anchor element correlated with that key.

class　See "Core Attributes Reference," earlier in this chapter.

contenteditable　This proprietary Microsoft attribute allows users to edit content rendered in the Internet Explorer 5.5 browser. Values are **false**, **true**, and **inherit**. A value of **false** will prevent content from being edited by users; **true** will allow editing. The default value, **inherit**, applies the value of the affected element's parent element.

dir　See "Language Reference," earlier in this chapter.

hidefocus　This proprietary element, introduced with Internet Explorer 5.5, hides focus on an element's content. Focus must be applied to the element using the **tabindex** attribute.

id　See "Core Attributes Reference," earlier in this chapter.

lang　See "Language Reference," earlier in this chapter.

language　In the Microsoft implementation, this attribute specifies the scripting language to be used with an associated script bound to the element, typically through an event handler attribute. Possible values might include **javascript**, **jscript**, **vbs**, and **vbscript**. Other values that include the version of the language used, such as **JavaScript1.1**, also might be possible.

style　See "Core Attributes Reference," earlier in this chapter.

tabindex　This attribute uses a number to identify the object's position in the tabbing order for keyboard navigation using the TAB key. Internet Explorer 5.5 applies this attribute to the **listing** element; under IE 5.5, this focus can be disabled with the **hidefocus** attribute.

title　See "Core Attributes Reference," earlier in this chapter.

Attribute and Event Support

Internet Explorer 4　All attributes.

Event Handlers

See "Events Reference," earlier in this chapter.

Example

```
<listing>
This is a code listing. The preformatted text element &lt;PRE&gt;
should be used instead of this deprecated element.
</listing>
```

Compatibility

HTML 2
Internet Explorer 2, 3, 4, 5, and 5.6
Netscape 1, 2, 3, 4–4.7
Opera 6
WebTV

Notes

- As a deprecated element, this element should not be used.
  This element is not supported by HTML 4. It is still
  documented by many browser vendors, however, and does
  creep into some pages. The **<pre>** element should be used
  instead of **<listing>**.

- It appears that Netscape and Internet Explorer browsers also
  make text within **<listing>** one size smaller than normal text,
  probably because the HTML 2 specification suggested that 132
  characters fit to a typical line rather than 80.

- Netscape does not document support for this element,
  although it is still supported. (Netscape 6 Preview Release 2
  did not appear to support this element.)

<map> (Client-Side Image Map)

This element is used to implement client-side image maps. The
element is used to define a map to associate locations on an image
with a destination URL. Each hot region or hyperlink mapping is
defined by an enclosed **<area>** element. A map is bound to a
particular image through the use of the **usemap** attribute in the
<img> element, which is set to the name of the map.

Syntax

```
<map
    class="class name(s)"
    dir="ltr | rtl"
    id="unique alphanumeric identifier"
    lang="language code"
```

```
name="unique alphanumeric identifier"
style="style information"
title="advisory text"
onclick="script"
ondblclick="script"
onkeydown="script"
onkeypress="script"
onkeyup="script"
onmousedown="script"
onmousemove="script"
onmouseout="script"
onmouseover="script"
onmouseup="script">

<area> elements

</map>
```

Events Defined by Internet Explorer 4

```
ondragstart="script"
onhelp="script"
onselectstart="script"
```

Attributes

class   See "Core Attributes Reference," earlier in this chapter.

dir   See "Language Reference," earlier in this chapter.

id   See "Core Attributes Reference," earlier in this chapter.

lang   See "Language Reference," earlier in this chapter.

name   Like **id**, this attribute is used to define a name associated with the element. In the case of the **<map>** element, the **name** attribute is the common way to define the name of the image map to be referenced by the **usemap** attribute within the **<img>** element.

style   See "Core Attributes Reference," earlier in this chapter.

title   See "Core Attributes Reference," earlier in this chapter.

Attribute and Event Support

Netscape 4   name. (class, id, lang, and style are implied.)

Internet Explorer 4   All attributes and events except **dir**.

WebTV   name

Event Handlers

See "Events Reference," earlier in this chapter.

Example

```
<map name="mainmap">
    <area shape="circle" coords="200,250,25"
        href="file1.htm">
    <area shape="rectangle" coords="50,50,100,100"
        href="file2.htm#important">
    <area shape="default" nohref>
</map>
```

Compatibility

> HTML 3.2, 4, 4.01, XHTML 1.0
> Internet Explorer 2, 3, 4, 5, and 5.5
> Netscape 1, 2, 3, 4–4.7, 6
> Opera
> WebTV

Notes

- HTML 3.2 supports only the **name** attribute for the **<map>** element.

- Client-side image maps are not supported under HTML 2. They were first suggested by Spyglass and later incorporated in Netscape and other browsers.

<marquee> (Marquee Display)

This proprietary element specifies a scrolling, sliding, or bouncing text marquee. This is primarily a Microsoft-specific element, although a few other browsers, notably WebTV, support it as well.

Syntax (Defined by Internet Explorer 4)

```
<marquee
    behavior="alternate | scroll | slide"
    bgcolor="color name | #RRGGBB"
    class="class name(s)"
    datafld="column name"
    dataformatas="html | text"
    datasrc="data source id"
    direction="down | left | right | up"
```

```
height="pixels or percentage"
hspace="pixels"
id="unique alphanumeric identifier"
lang="language code"
language="javascript | jscript | vbs | vbscript"
loop="infinite | number"
scrollamount="pixels"
scrolldelay="milliseconds"
style="style information"
title="advisory text"
truespeed
vspace="pixels"
width="pixels or percentage"
onafterupdate="script"
onblur="script"
onbounce="script"
onclick="script"
ondblclick="script"
ondragstart="script"
onfinish="script"
onfocus="script"
onhelp="script"
onkeydown="script"
onkeypress="script"
onkeyup="script"
onmousedown="script"
onmousemove="script"
onmouseout="script"
onmouseover="script"
onmouseup="script"
onresize="script"
onrowenter="script"
onrowexit="script"
onselectstart="script"
onstart="script">

    Marquee text

</marquee>
```

Attributes and Events Defined by Internet Explorer 5.0

```
dir="ltr | rtl"
```

Attributes and Events Defined by Internet Explorer 5.5

```
accesskey="key"
contenteditable=" false | true | inherit"
```

```
hidefocus="true | false"
tabindex="number"
```

Attributes Defined by WebTV

```
align="bottom | center | left | right | top"
transparency="number (0-100)"
```

Attributes

accesskey   This attribute specifies a keyboard navigation accelerator for the element. Pressing ALT or a similar key (depending on the browser and operating system) in association with the specified key selects the anchor element correlated with that key.

align   This WebTV-specific attribute is used to indicate how the marquee should be aligned with surrounding text. The alignment values and rendering are similar to other embedded objects such as images. The default value for this attribute under WebTV is **left**. Microsoft Internet Explorer no longer supports this attribute.

behavior   This attribute controls the movement of marquee text across the marquee. The **alternate** option causes text to completely cross the marquee field in one direction and then cross in the opposite direction. A value of **scroll** for the attribute causes text to wrap around and start over again. This is the default value for a marquee. A value of **slide** for this attribute causes text to cross the marquee field and stop when its leading character reaches the opposite side.

bgcolor   This attribute specifies the marquee's background color. The value for the attribute can either be a color name or a color value defined in the hexadecimal #*RRGGBB* format.

class   See "Core Attributes Reference," earlier in this chapter.

contenteditable   This proprietary Microsoft attribute allows users to edit content rendered in the Internet Explorer 5.5 browser. Values are **false, true,** and **inherit**. A value of **false** will prevent content from being edited by users; **true** will allow editing. The default value, **inherit**, applies the value of the affected element's parent element.

datafld   This attribute is used to indicate the column name in the data source that is bound to the **<marquee>** element.

dataformatas This attribute indicates whether the bound data is plain text (**text**) or HTML (**html**). The data bound with **<marquee>** is used to set the message that is scrolled.

datasrc The value of this attribute is set to an identifier indicating the data source to pull data from. Bound data is used to set the message that is scrolled in the **<marquee>**.

dir See "Language Reference," earlier in this chapter.

direction This attribute specifies the direction in which the marquee should scroll. The default is **left**. Other possible values for **direction** include **down**, **right**, and **up**. WebTV does not support the **down** and **up** values.

height This attribute specifies the height of the marquee in pixels or as a percentage of the window.

hidefocus This proprietary element, introduced with Internet Explorer 5.5, hides focus on an element's content. Focus must be applied to the element using the **tabindex** attribute.

hspace This attribute indicates the horizontal space in pixels between the marquee and surrounding content.

id See "Core Attributes Reference," earlier in this chapter.

lang See "Language Reference," earlier in this chapter.

language In the Microsoft implementation, this attribute specifies the scripting language to be used with an associated script bound to the element, typically through an event handler attribute. Possible values might include **javascript**, **jscript**, **vbs**, and **vbscript**. Other values that include the version of the language used, such as **JavaScript1.1**, also might be possible.

loop This attribute indicates the number of times the marquee content should loop. By default, a marquee loops infinitely unless the **behavior** attribute is set to **slide**. It also is possible to use a value of **infinite** or –1 to set the text to loop indefinitely.

scrollamount This attribute specifies the width in pixels between successive displays of the scrolling text in the marquee.

scrolldelay This attribute specifies the delay in milliseconds between successive displays of the text in the marquee.

style See "Core Attributes Reference," earlier in this chapter.

tabindex   This attribute uses a number to identify the object's position in the tabbing order for keyboard navigation using the TAB key. Internet Explorer 5.5 applies this attribute to the **marquee** element; under IE 5.5, this focus can be disabled with the **hidefocus** attribute.

title   See "Core Attributes Reference," earlier in this chapter.

transparency   In the WebTV implementation, this attribute specifies the marquee's degree of transparency. Values range from **0** (totally opaque) to **100** (totally transparent). A value of **50** is optimized for fast rendering.

truespeed   When this attribute is present, it indicates that the **scrolldelay** value should be honored for its exact value. If the attribute is not present, any values less than 60 are rounded up to 60 milliseconds.

vspace   This attribute indicates the vertical space in pixels between the marquee and surrounding content.

width   This attribute specifies the width of the marquee in pixels or as a percentage of the enclosing window.

Attribute and Event Support

Internet Explorer 4   All Microsoft-defined attributes and events.

WebTV   **align, behavior, bgcolor, direction, height, hspace, loop, scrollamount, scrolldelay, transparency, vspace,** and **width**. (Note: WebTV supports only the **left** and **right** values for the **direction** attribute.)

Event Handlers

The **<marquee>** element has a few unique events. For example, an event is triggered when the text bounces off one side or another on the marquee. This can be caught with the **onbounce** event handler attribute. When the text first starts scrolling, the start event fires, which can be caught with **onstart**; when the marquee is done, a finish event fires, which can be caught with **onfinish**. The other events are common to HTML 4 elements with Microsoft extensions.

Examples

```
<marquee behavior="alternate">
SPECIAL VALUE !!! This week only !!!
</marquee>
```

```
<marquee id="marquee1" bgcolor="red" direction="right"
         height="30" width="80%"
         hspace="10" vspace="10">
The super scroller scrolls again!!
More fun than a barrel of &lt;BLINK&gt; elements.
</marquee>
```

Compatibility

Internet Explorer 3, 4, 5, and 5.5
WebTV

Notes

- The **<marquee>** element is supported only by Microsoft
  and WebTV.

<menu> (Menu List)

This element is used to indicate a short list of items that can occur
in a menu of choices. Like the ordered and unordered lists, the
individual items in the list are indicated by the **<li>** element. Most
browsers render the **<menu>** element exactly the same as the
unordered list, so there is little reason to use it. Under the HTML 4
strict specification, **<menu>** is no longer supported.

Syntax (Transitional Only)

```
<menu
     class="class name(s)"
     compact
     dir="ltr | rtl"
     id="unique alphanumeric string"
     lang="language code"
     style="style information"
     title="advisory text"
     onclick="script"
     ondblclick="script"
     onkeydown="script"
     onkeypress="script"
     onkeyup="script"
     onmousedown="script"
     onmousemove="script"
     onmouseout="script"
     onmouseover="script"
     onmouseup="script">

</menu>
```

Events Defined by Internet Explorer 4

```
ondragstart="script"
onhelp="script"
onselectstart="script"
```

Attributes and Events Defined by Internet Explorer 5.5

```
accesskey="key"
contenteditable=" false | true | inherit"
hidefocus="true | false"
tabindex="number"
```

Attributes

accesskey   This attribute specifies a keyboard navigation accelerator for the element. Pressing ALT or a similar key (depending on the browser and operating system) in association with the specified key selects the anchor element correlated with that key.

class   See "Core Attributes Reference," earlier in this chapter.

compact   This attribute indicates that the list should be rendered in a compact style. Few browsers actually change the rendering of the list regardless of the presence of this attribute. The **compact** attribute requires no value.

contenteditable   This proprietary Microsoft attribute allows users to edit content rendered in the Internet Explorer 5.5 browser. Values are **false**, **true**, and **inherit**. A value of **false** will prevent content from being edited by users; **true** will allow editing. The default value, **inherit**, applies the value of the affected element's parent element.

dir   See "Language Reference," earlier in this chapter.

hidefocus   This proprietary element, introduced with Internet Explorer 5.5, hides focus on an element's content. Focus must be applied to the element using the **tabindex** attribute.

id   See "Core Attributes Reference," earlier in this chapter.

lang   See "Language Reference," earlier in this chapter.

style   See "Core Attributes Reference," earlier in this chapter.

tabindex   This attribute uses a number to identify the object's position in the tabbing order for keyboard navigation using the TAB key. Internet Explorer 5.5 applies this attribute to the **menu** element; under IE 5.5, this focus can be disabled with the **hidefocus** attribute.

title   See "Core Attributes Reference," earlier in this chapter.

Attribute and Event Support

netscape 4   **class**, **id**, **lang**, and **style**.

Internet Explorer 4   All attributes and events except **compact** and **dir**.

Event Handlers

See "Events Reference," earlier in this chapter.

Example

```
<h2>Taco List</h2>
  <menu>
    <li>Fish
    <li>Pork
    <li>Beef
    <li>Chicken
  </menu>
```

Compatibility

HTML 2, 3.2, 4 (transitional), 4.01 (transitional), XHTML 1.0
Internet Explorer 2, 3, 4, 5, and 5.5
Netscape 1, 2, 3, 4–4.7, 6
Opera 4.0
WebTV

Notes

- Under the HTML 4.01 strict specification, this element is not defined. Because most browsers simply render this style of list as an unordered list, using the **<ul>** element instead is preferable.

- Most browsers tend not to support the **compact** attribute.

- The HTML 2.0 and 3.2 specifications support only the **compact** attribute.

<meta> (Meta-Information)

This element specifies general information about a document,
which can be used in document indexing. It also allows a
document to define fields in the HTTP response header
when it is sent from the server. A common use of this element
is for *client-pull* page loading, which allows a document to
automatically load another document after a specified delay.

Syntax

```
<meta
      content="string"
      dir="ltr | rtl"
      http-equiv="http header string"
      lang="language code"
      name="name of meta-information"
      scheme="scheme type">
```

XHTML Syntax

As an empty element, **<meta>** requires a trailing slash for XHTML
1.0 compatibility:

```
<meta />
```

Attributes Defined by WebTV

```
url="url"
```

Attributes

content   This attribute contains the actual meta-information.
The form of the actual meta-information varies greatly, depending
on the value set for **name**.

dir   This attribute defines the text direction (left to right or right
to left) of the content of the **<meta>** element, as defined by the
content attribute.

http-equiv   This attribute binds the meta-information in the
content attribute to an HTTP response header. If this attribute is
present, the **name** attribute should not be used. The **http-equiv**
attribute often is used to create a document that automatically

loads another document after a set time. This is called *client-pull*. An example of a client-pull **<meta>** element is

```
<meta http-equiv="refresh" content="10;URL='nextpage.htm'">
```

Note that the **content** attribute contains two values. The first is the number of seconds to wait, and the second is the identifier URL and the URL to load after the specified time.

lang   This attribute is the language code associated with the language used in the **content** attribute.

name   This attribute associates a name with the meta-information contained in the **content** attribute. If present, the **http-equiv** attribute should not be used.

scheme   The scheme attribute is used to indicate the expected format of the value of the **content** attribute. The particular scheme also can be used in conjunction with the meta-data profile as indicated by the **profile** attribute for the **<head>** element.

Attribute and Event Support

Netscape 4   content, http-equiv, and name.

Internet Explorer 4   All attributes except **dir**.

WebTV   content, http-equiv, and url.

Event Handlers
None

Examples
```
<!-- Use of the meta element to assist document indexing -->
<meta name="keywords" content="html, scripting"
      scheme="Lycos">

<!-- Use of the meta element to implement client-pull to automatically
     load a page -->
<meta http-equiv="refresh"
      content="3;URL='http://www.pint.com/'">

<!-- Use of the META element to add rating information -->
<meta http-equiv="PICS-Label" content="(PICS-1.1
                  'http://www.rsac.org/ratingsv01.html'
                  1 gen true comment 'RSACi North America
                  Server' by 'webmaster@bigcompany.com'
                  for 'http://www.bigcompany.com' on
```

```
'1999.05.26T13:05-0500'
r (n 0 s 0 v 0 1 1))">
```

XHTML Example

```
<meta name="keywords" content="html, scripting" />
```

2

Compatibility

HTML 2, 3.2, 4, 4.01, XHTML 1.0
Internet Explorer 2, 3, 4, 5, and 5.5
Netscape 1.1, 2, 3, 4–4.7, 6
Opera 4.0
WebTV

Notes

- The **<meta>** element can occur only in the **<head>** element. It can be defined multiple times.

- The **<meta>** element is an empty element (as defined in the HTML specifications) and does not have a closing tag nor contain any content.

- Under XHTML 1.0, empty elements such as **<meta>** require a trailing slash: **<meta />**.

- A common use of the **<meta>** element is to set information for indexing tools such as search engines. The common values for the **name** attribute when performing this function include **author**, **description**, and **keywords**; other attributes also might be possible.

- Along the same line as indexing, meta-information is also used for rating pages.

- The HTML 2.0 and 3.2 specifications define only the **content**, **http-equiv**, and **name** attributes.

<multicol> (Multiple Column Text)

This Netscape-specific element renders the enclosed content in multiple columns. This element should not be used in favor of a table, which is a more standard way to render multiple columns of text across browsers. It is likely that style sheets will provide for multicolumn rendering in the future.

Syntax (Defined by Netscape)

```
<multicol
     class="class name(s)"
     cols="number of columns"
     gutter="pixels"
     id="unique alphanumeric identifier"
     style="style information"
     width="pixels">

</multicol>
```

Attributes

class See "Core Attributes Reference," earlier in this chapter.

cols This attribute indicates the number of columns in which to display the text. The browser attempts to fill the columns evenly.

gutter This attribute indicates the width in pixels between the columns. The default value for this attribute is **10** pixels.

id See "Core Attributes Reference," earlier in this chapter.

style See "Core Attributes Reference," earlier in this chapter.

width This attribute indicates the column width for all columns. The width of each column is set in pixels and is equivalent for all columns in the group. If the attribute is not specified, the width of columns will be determined by taking the available window size, subtracting the number of pixels for the gutter between the columns as specified by the **gutter** attribute, and evenly dividing the result by the number of columns in the group as set by the **cols** attribute.

Attribute and Event Support

Netscape 4   All attributes.

Event Handlers

None

Example

```
<multicol cols="3" gutter="20">
Put a long piece of text here....
</multicol>
```

Compatibility

Netscape 3, 4–4.7

Notes

- Do not attempt to use images or other embedded media within a multicolumn layout as defined by **<multicol>**.

- Do not set the number of columns to high or resize the browser window very small, as text will overwrite other lines.

<nobr> (No Breaks)

This proprietary element renders enclosed text without line breaks. Break points for where text may wrap can be inserted using the **<wbr>** element.

Syntax

```
<nobr
    class="class name(s)"
    id="unique alphanumeric identifier"
    style="style information"
    title="advisory text">

</nobr>
```

Attributes and Events Defined by Internet Explorer 5.5

```
    contenteditable=" false | true | inherit "
    dir="ltr | rtl"
```

Attributes

class   See "Core Attributes Reference," earlier in this chapter.

contenteditable   This proprietary Microsoft attribute allows users to edit content rendered in the Internet Explorer 5.5 browser. Values are **false**, **true**, and **inherit**. A value of **false** will prevent content from being edited by users; **true** will allow editing. The default value, **inherit**, applies the value of the affected element's parent element.

dir   See "Language Reference," earlier in this chapter.

id   See "Core Attributes Reference," earlier in this chapter.

style   See "Core Attributes Reference," earlier in this chapter.

title   See "Core Attributes Reference," earlier in this chapter.

Attribute and Event Support

Netscape 4   All attributes.

Internet Explorer 4   id, style, and title.

Event Handlers

None

Examples

`<nobr>`This is really long text ... will not be broken.`</nobr>`

`<nobr>`With this element it is often important to hint where a line may be broken using <wbr>.`<wbr>` This element acts as a soft return.`</nobr>`

Compatibility

Internet Explorer 2, 3, 4, 5, and 5.5
Netscape 1.1, 2, 3, 4–4.7
Opera 4.0
WebTV

Notes

- While many browsers support this attribute, it is not part of any W3C standard.

- Netscape 6 Preview Release 2 did not support this element.

<noembed> (No Embedded Media Support)

This Netscape-specific element is used to indicate alternative content to display on browsers that cannot support an embedded media object. It should occur in conjunction with the **<embed>** element.

Syntax

```
<noembed>

    Alternative content here

</noembed>
```

Attributes

Netscape does not specifically define attributes for this element; however, Netscape documentation suggests that **class**, **id**, **style**, and **title** might be supported for this element.

Event Handlers

None

Example

```
<embed src="trailer.mov" height="150" width="150">
   <noembed>
      <img src="trailer.gif">
      <br>
   Sorry, this browser is not configured to display video.
   </noembed>
</embed>
```

Compatibility

Netscape 2, 3, 4–4.7
WebTV

Notes

- This element will disappear as the **<object>** style of inserting media into a page becomes more common.

<noframes> (No Frame Support Content)

This element is used to indicate alternative content to display on browsers that do not support frames.

Syntax (Transitional Only)

```
<noframes
     class="class name(s)"
     dir="ltr | rtl"
     id="unique alphanumeric identifier"
     lang="language code"
     style="style information"
     title="advisory text"
     onclick="script"
     ondblclick="script"
     onkeydown="script"
     onkeypress="script"
     onkeyup="script"
     onmousedown="script"
     onmousemove="script"
     onmouseout="script"
     onmouseover="script"
     onmouseup="script">

     Alternative content for non-frame-supporting browsers

</noframes>
```

Attributes

class   See "Core Attributes Reference," earlier in this chapter.

dir   See "Language Reference," earlier in this chapter.

id   See "Core Attributes Reference," earlier in this chapter.

lang   See "Language Reference," earlier in this chapter.

style   See "Core Attributes Reference," earlier in this chapter.

title   See "Core Attributes Reference," earlier in this chapter.

Attribute and Event Support

Netscape 4   **class**, **id**, **lang**, and **style** are implied.

Internet Explorer 4   **id**, **style**, and **title**.

Event Handlers

It is interesting to note that whereas the **<noframes>** element does support the common events for nearly all HTML 4 elements, their value seems unclear. The only time that content within a **<noframes>** could be rendered is on a browser that does not support frames; however, browsers that do not support frames are unlikely to support an event model or similar features. With clever scripting it might be possible to access framed and nonframed content, but for now the benefit of the events seems unclear. For more information, see "Events Reference," earlier in this chapter.

Example

```
<frameset rows="100,*">
  <frame src="controls.htm">
  <frame src="content.htm">
    <noframes>
    Sorry, this browser does not support frames.
    </noframes>
</frameset>
```

Compatibility

HTML 4 (transitional), 4.01 (transitional), XHTML 1.0
Internet Explorer 2, 3, 4, 5, and 5.5
Netscape 2, 3, 4–4.7 and 6
Opera 4.0
WebTV

Notes

- This element should be used within the scope of the **<frameset>** element.

- The benefit of events and sophisticated attributes such as **style** is unclear for browsers that would use content within **<noframes>**, given that older browsers that don't support frames probably would not support these features.

<noscript> (No Script Support Content)

This element is used to enclose content that should be rendered on browsers that do not support scripting or that have scripting turned off.

Syntax

```
<noscript
    class="class name(s)"
    dir="ltr | rtl"
    id="unique alphanumeric identifier"
    lang="language code"
    style="style information"
```

```
      title="advisory text"
      onclick="script"
      ondblclick="script"
      onkeydown="script"
      onkeypress="script"
      onkeyup="script"
      onmousedown="script"
      onmousemove="script"
      onmouseout="script"
      onmouseover="script"
      onmouseup="script">

      Alternative content for non-script-supporting browsers

</noscript>
```

Attributes

class   See "Core Attributes Reference," earlier in this chapter.

dir   See "Language Reference," earlier in this chapter.

id   See "Core Attributes Reference," earlier in this chapter.

lang   See "Language Reference," earlier in this chapter.

style   See "Core Attributes Reference," earlier in this chapter.

title   See "Core Attributes Reference," earlier in this chapter.

Attribute and Event Support

Netscape 4   **class**, **id**, **lang**, and **style** are implied.

Internet Explorer 4   **id**

Event Handlers

As defined in the preliminary specification of HTML 4, the benefits of event handlers are not very obvious, considering that content within the **<noscript>** element assumes the browser does not support scripting, whereas the script handlers themselves are for browsers that support scripting. These are standard events for nearly all HTML 4 elements. For definitions, see "Events Reference," earlier in this chapter.

Example

```
Last Updated:
<script language="javascript">
```

```
<!-- document.writeln(document.lastodified); // -->
</script>
<noscript>
1999
</noscript>
```

2

Compatibility

> HTML 4, 4.01, XHTML 1.0
> Internet Explorer 3, 4, 5, and 5.5
> Netscape 2, 3, 4–4.7
> Opera 4.0
> WebTV

Notes

- Improved functionality for the **<noscript>** element might come if it is extended to deal with the lack of support for one scripting language or another. Currently, the element is used only to indicate whether any scripting is supported or not.

- It also is useful to comment out scripting information so non–scripting-aware browsers will not read it.

<object> (Embedded Object)

This element specifies an arbitrary object to be included in an HTML document. Initially, this element was used to insert ActiveX controls, but according to the HTML 4.01 specification, an object can be any media object, document, applet, ActiveX control, or even image.

Syntax

```
<object
     align="bottom | left | middle | right | top"
          (transitional)
     archive="url"
     border="percentage | pixels" (transitional)
     class="class name(s)"
     classid="id"
     codebase="URL"
     codetype="MIME Type"
     data="URL of data"
     declare
     dir="ltr | rtl"
     height="percentage | pixels"
     hspace="percentage | pixels" (transitional)
```

```
    id="unique alphanumeric identifier"
    lang="language code"
    name="unique alphanumeric name"
    standby="standby text string"
    style="style information"
    tabindex="number"
    title="advisory text"
    type="MIME Type"
    usemap="URL"
    vspace="percentage | pixels" (transitional)
    width="percentage | pixels"
    onclick="script"
    ondblclick="script"
    onkeydown="script"
    onkeypress="script"
    onkeyup="script"
    onmousedown="script"
    onmousemove="script"
    onmouseout="script"
    onmouseover="script"
    onmouseup="script">

</object>
```

Attributes and Events Defined by Internet Explorer 4

```
    accesskey="character"
    align="absbottom | absmiddle | baseline | texttop"
    code="url"
    datafld="column name"
    datasrc="id for bound data"
    language="javascript | jscript | vbs | vbscript"
    onafterupdate="script"
    onbeforeupdate="script"
    onblur="script"
    ondragstart="script"
    onfocus="script"
    onhelp="script"
    onreadystatechange="script"
    onresize="script"
    onrowenter="script"
    onrowexit="script"
    onselectstart="script"
```

Attributes and Events Defined by Internet Explorer 5.5

```
    hidefocus="true | false"
```

Attributes

accesskey   This Microsoft attribute specifies a keyboard navigation accelerator for the element. Pressing ALT or a similar key in association with the specified character selects the form control correlated with that key sequence. Page designers are forewarned to avoid key sequences already bound to browsers.

align   This attribute aligns the object with respect to the surrounding text. The default is **left**. The HTML 4.01 specification defines **bottom**, **middle**, **right**, and **top** as well. Browsers might provide an even richer set of alignment values. The behavior of alignment for objects is similar to images. Under the strict HTML 4.01 specification, the **<object>** element does not support this attribute.

archive   This attribute contains a URL for the location of an archive file. An archive file typically is used to contain multiple object files to improve the efficiency of access.

border   This attribute specifies the width of the object's borders in pixels or as a percentage.

class   See "Core Attributes Reference," earlier in this chapter.

classid   This attribute contains a URL for an object's implementation. The URL syntax depends upon the object's type. With ActiveX controls, the value of this attribute does not appear to be a URL but something of the form *CLSID: object-id*; for example, **CLSID: 99B42120-6EC7-11CF-A6C7-00AA00A47DD2**.

code   Under the old Microsoft implementation, this attribute contains the URL referencing a Java applet class file. The way to access a Java applet under the HTML 4.01 specification is to use **<object classid="java: classname.class">**. The pseudo-URL *java:* is used to indicate a Java applet. Microsoft Internet Explorer 4 and beyond support this style, so **code** should not be used.

codebase   This attribute contains a URL to use as a relative base to access the object specified by the **classid** attribute.

codetype   This attribute specifies an object's MIME type. Do not confuse this attribute with **type**, which specifies the MIME type of the data the object may use as defined by the **data** attribute.

data   This attribute contains a URL for data required by an object.

datafld   This attribute is used to indicate the column name in the data source that is bound to the **<object>** element.

datasrc   The value of this attribute is set to an identifier indicating the data source to pull data from.

declare   This attribute declares an object without instantiating it. This is useful when the object will be a parameter to another object.

dir   See "Language Reference," earlier in this chapter.

height   This attribute specifies the height of the object in pixels or as a percentage of the enclosing window.

hidefocus   This proprietary element, introduced with Internet Explorer 5.5, hides focus on an element's content. Focus must be applied to the element using the **tabindex** attribute.

hspace   This attribute indicates the horizontal space in pixels or percentages between the object and surrounding content.

id   See "Core Attributes Reference," earlier in this chapter.

lang   See "Language Reference," earlier in this chapter.

language   In the Microsoft implementation, this attribute specifies the scripting language to be used with an associated script bound to the element, typically through an event handler attribute. Possible values might include **javascript**, **jscript**, **vbs**, and **vbscript**. Other values that include the version of the language used, such as **JavaScript1.1**, also might be possible.

name   This attribute under the Microsoft definition defines the name of the control so scripting can access it. The HTML 4.01 specification suggests that it is a name for form submission, but this meaning is unclear and not supported by browsers.

standby   This attribute contains a text message to be displayed while the object is loading.

style   See "Core Attributes Reference," earlier in this chapter.

tabindex   This attribute takes a numeric value indicating the position of the object in the tabbing index for the document. Tabbing proceeds from the lowest positive **tabindex** value to the highest. Negative values for **tabindex** will leave the object out of the tabbing order. When tabbing is not explicitly set, the browser can tab through items in the order they are encountered.

title   See "Core Attributes Reference," earlier in this chapter.

type   This attribute specifies the MIME type for the object's data. This is different from the **codetype**, which is the MIME type of the object and not the data it uses.

usemap   This attribute contains the URL of the image map to be used with the object. Typically, the URL will be a fragment identifier referencing a **<map>** element somewhere else within the file. The presence of this attribute indicates that the type of object being included is an image.

vspace   This attribute indicates the vertical space in pixels or percentages between the object and surrounding text.

width   This attribute specifies the width of the object in pixels or as a percentage of the enclosing window.

Attribute and Event Support

Netscape 4   **align**, **classid**, **codebase**, **data**, **height**, **type**, and **width**. (**class**, **id**, **lang**, and **style** are implied.)

Internet Explorer 4   **align**, **class**, **classid**, **code**, **codebase**, **codetype**, **data**, **height**, **id**, **lang**, **name**, **style**, **tabindex**, **title**, **type**, **width**, all W3C-defined events, and all attributes and events defined by Internet Explorer 4.

Internet Explorer 5.5   Same as Internet Explorer 4, plus **hidefocus**.

Event Handlers
See "Events Reference," earlier in this chapter.

Examples
```
<object id="IeLabel1" width="325" height="65"
        classid="CLSID:99B42120-6EC7-11CF-A6C7-00AA00A47DD2">
   <param name="_ExtentX" value="6879">
   <param name="_ExtentY" value="1376">
   <param name="Caption" value="Hello World">
   <param name="Alignment" value="4">
   <param name="Mode" value="1">
   <param name="ForeColor" value="#FF0000">
   <param name="FontName" value="Arial">
   <param name="Fontize" value="36">
```

```
<b>Hello World for non-ActiveX users!</b>
</object>

<object classid="java:Blink.class"
        standby="Here it comes"
        height="100" width="300">
   <param name="lbl"
          value="Java is fun, exciting, and new.">
   <param name="speed" value="2">
This will display in non-Java-aware or -enabled
browsers.
</object>

<object data="pullinthisfile.html">
Data not included!
</object>

<object data="bigimage.gif" shapes>
   <a href="page1.htm" shape="rect" coords="10,10,40,40">
   Page 1</a>
   <a href="page2.htm" shape="circle" coords="100,90,20 ">
   Page 2</a>
</object>
```

Compatibility

HTML 4, 4.01, XHTML 1.0
Internet Explorer 3, 4, 5, and 5.5
Netscape 4–4.7, 6

Notes

- Under the strict HTML 4.01 specification the **<object>** element loses most of its presentation attributes, including **align**, **border**, **height**, **hspace**, **vspace**, and **width**. These attributes are replaced by style sheet rules.

- The HTML 4.01 specification reserves the **datafld**, **dataformatas**, and **datasrc** attributes for future use.

- Alternative content should be defined within the **<object>** element after the **<param>** elements.

- The **<object>** element is still mainly used to include binaries in pages. Although the specification defines that it can load in HTML files and create image maps, few, if any, browsers support this.

<ol> (Ordered List)

This element is used to define an ordered or numbered list of items. The numbering style comes in many forms, including letters, Roman numerals, and regular numerals. The individual items within the list are specified by **<li>** elements included with the **<ol>** element.

Syntax

```
<ol
     class="class name(s)"
     compact (transitional)
     dir="ltr | rtl"
     id="unique alphanumeric identifier"
     lang="language code"
     start="number" (transitional)
     style="style information"
     title="advisory text"
     type="a | A | i | I | 1" (transitional)
     onclick="script"
     ondblclick="script"
     onkeydown="script"
     onkeypress="script"
     onkeyup="script"
     onmousedown="script"
     onmousemove="script"
     onmouseout="script"
     onmouseover="script"
     onmouseup="script">

</ol>
```

XHTML Syntax

Because of XHTML 1.0's deprecation of attribute minimization, the **compact** attribute must have a quoted attribute when used:

```
<ol compact="compact"></ol>
```

Attributes and Events Defined by Internet Explorer 4

```
     language="javascript | jscript | vbs | vbscript"
     ondragstart="script"
     onhelp="script"
     onselectstart="script"
```

Attributes and Events Defined by Internet Explorer 5.5

```
accesskey="key"
contenteditable="false | true | inherit"
hidefocus="true | false"
tabindex="number"
```

Attributes

accesskey   This attribute specifies a keyboard navigation accelerator for the element. Pressing ALT or a similar key (depending on the browser and operating system) in association with the specified key selects the anchor element correlated with that key.

class   See "Core Attributes Reference," earlier in this chapter.

compact   This attribute indicates that the list should be rendered in a compact style. Few browsers actually change the rendering of the list regardless of the presence of this attribute. The **compact** attribute requires no value.

contenteditable   This proprietary Microsoft attribute allows users to edit content rendered in the Internet Explorer 5.5 browser. Values are **false**, **true**, and **inherit**. A value of **false** will prevent content from being edited by users; **true** will allow editing. The default value, **inherit**, applies the value of the affected element's parent element.

dir   See "Language Reference," earlier in this chapter.

hidefocus   This proprietary element, introduced with Internet Explorer 5.5, hides focus on an element's content. Focus must be applied to the element using the **tabindex** attribute.

id   See "Core Attributes Reference," earlier in this chapter.

lang   See "Language Reference," earlier in this chapter.

language   In the Microsoft implementation, this attribute specifies the scripting language to be used with an associated script bound to the element, typically through an event handler attribute. Possible values might include **javascript**, **jscript**, **vbs**, and **vbscript**. Other values that include the version of the language used, such as **JavaScript1.1**, might also be possible.

start   This attribute is used to indicate the value to start numbering the individual list items from. Although the ordering type of list elements might be Roman numerals such as **XXXI** or letters, the value of **start** is always represented as number. To start numbering elements from the letter "C," use **<ol type="A" start="3">**.

style   See "Core Attributes Reference," earlier in this chapter.

tabindex   This attribute uses a number to identify the object's position in the tabbing order for keyboard navigation using the TAB key. Internet Explorer 5.5 applies this attribute to the **ol** element; under IE 5.5, this focus can be disabled with the **hidefocus** attribute.

title   See "Core Attributes Reference," earlier in this chapter.

type   This attribute indicates the numbering type: "a" indicates lowercase letters, "A" indicates uppercase letters, "i" indicates lowercase Roman numerals, "I" indicates uppercase Roman numerals, and "1" indicates numbers. Type set in the **<ol>** element is used for the entire list unless a **type** attribute is used within an enclosed **<li>** element.

Attribute and Event Support

Netscape 4   class, id, lang, start, style, and type.

Internet Explorer 4   All attributes and events except **dir**.

Internet Explorer 5.5   All attributes and events.

WebTV   start and type.

Event Handlers
See "Events Reference," earlier in this chapter.

Examples
```
<ol type="1">
   <li>First step
   <li>Second step
   <li>Third step
</ol>

<ol compact type="I" start="30">
   <li>Clause 30
   <li>Clause 31
   <li>Clause 32
</ol>
```

XHTML Example

```
<ol compact="compact" type="I">
    <li>Clause 1</li>
    <li>Clause 2</li>
    <li>Clause 3</li>
</ol>
```

Compatibility

HTML 2, 3.2, 4, 4.01, XHTML 1.0
Internet Explorer 2, 3, 4, 5, and 5.5
Netscape 1, 2, 3, 4–4.7, 6
Opera 4.0
WebTV

Notes

- Under the strict HTML 4.01 specification, the **<ol>** element no longer supports the **compact**, **start**, and **type** attributes. These aspects of lists can be controlled with style sheet rules.

- Under the XHTML 1.0 specification, the **compact** attribute no longer can be minimized, but must have a quoted attribute value: **<ol compact="compact">...</ol>**.

- The HTML 3.2 specification supports only the **compact**, **start**, and **type** attributes. The HTML 2.0 specification supports only the **compact** attribute.

<optgroup> (Option Grouping)

This element specifies a grouping of items in a selection list defined by **<option>** elements so that the menu choices can be presented in a hierarchical menu or similar alternative fashion to improve access through nonvisual browsers.

Syntax

```
<optgroup
    class="class name(s)"
    dir="ltr | rtl"
    disabled
    id="unique alphanumeric identifier"
    label="text description"
```

```
lang="language code"
style="style information"
title="advisory text"
onclick="script"
ondblclick="script"
onkeydown="script"
onkeypress="script"
onkeyup="script"
onmousedown="script"
onmousemove="script"
onmouseout="script"
onmouseover="script"
onmouseup="script">

    <option> elements

</optgroup>
```

Attributes

class   See "Core Attributes Reference," earlier in this chapter.

dir   See "Language Reference," earlier in this chapter.

disabled   Occurrence of this attribute indicates that the enclosed set of options is disabled.

id   See "Core Attributes Reference," earlier in this chapter.

label   This attribute contains a short label that might be more appealing to use when the selection list is rendered as items in a hierarchy.

lang   See "Language Reference," earlier in this chapter.

style   See "Core Attributes Reference," earlier in this chapter.

title   See "Core Attributes Reference," earlier in this chapter.

Attribute and Event Support

Netscape 6   class, disabled, id, label, style, title.

Event Handlers

See "Events Reference," earlier in this chapter.

Example

```
Where would you like to go for your vacation?<br>
<select>
    <option id="ch1" value="China">The Great Wall
  <optgroup label="Mexico">
    <option id="ch2" label="Los Cabos" value="Los Cabos">
    Los Cabos, Mexico
    <option id="ch3" label="Leon" value="Leon">Leon, Mexico
    <option id="ch4" value="MXC">Mexico City
  </optgroup>
    <option id="ch5" value="home" selected>Your backyard
</select>
```

Compatibility

HTML 4, 4.01, XHTML 1.0
Netscape 6

Notes

- This element should occur only within the context of a
  <select> element.

- Netacape 6 Preview Release 2 is the first browser version
  to present this element in a visually meaningful fashion.

<option> (Option in Selection List)

This element specifies an item in a selection list defined by the
<select> element.

Syntax

```
<option
    class="class name(s)"
    dir="ltr | rtl"
    disabled
    id="unique alphanumeric identifier"
    label="text description"
    lang="language code"
    selected
    style="style information"
    title="advisory text"
    value="option value"
    onclick="script"
    ondblclick="script"
    onkeydown="script"
    onkeypress="script"
    onkeyup="script"
```

```
onmousedown="script"
onmousemove="script"
onmouseout="script"
onmouseover="script"
onmouseup="script">
```

```
</option>
```

2

XHTML Syntax

Under the XHTML 1.0 specification, the closing tag **</option>** ceases to be optional and must be used.

Attributes and Events Defined by Internet Explorer 4

```
language="javascript | jscript | vbs | vbscript"
ondragstart="script"
onselectstart="script"
```

Attributes

class   See "Core Attributes Reference," earlier in this chapter.

dir   See "Language Reference," earlier in this chapter.

disabled   Presence of this attribute indicates that the particular item is not selectable.

id   See "Core Attributes Reference," earlier in this chapter.

label   This attribute contains a short label that might be more appealing to use when the selection list is rendered as a hierarchy due to the presence of an **<optgroup>** element.

lang   See "Language Reference," earlier in this chapter.

language   In the Microsoft implementation, this attribute specifies the scripting language to be used with an associated script bound to the element, typically through an event handler attribute. Possible values might include **javascript**, **jscript**, **vbs**, and **vbscript**. Other values that include the version of the language used, such as **JavaScript1.1**, also might be possible.

selected   This attribute indicates that the associated item is the default selection. If not included, the first item in the selection list is the default. If the **<select>** element enclosing the **<option>** elements has the **multiple** attribute, the **selected** attribute might occur in multiple entries. Otherwise, it should occur in only one entry.

style   See "Core Attributes Reference," earlier in this chapter.

title   See "Core Attributes Reference," earlier in this chapter.

value   This attribute indicates the value to include with the form result when the item is selected.

Attribute and Event Support

Netscape 4   **selected** and **value**. (**class**, **id**, **lang**, and **style** are implied.)

Internet Explorer 4   **class**, **id**, **language**, **selected**, **value**, **ondragstart**, and **onselectstart**.

WebTV   **selected** and **value**.

Event Handlers

See "Events Reference," earlier in this chapter.

Example

```
Where would you like to go for your vacation?<br>
<select>
    <option id="choice1" value="China">The Great Wall
    <option id="choice2" value="Mexico">Los Cabos
    <option id="choice3" value="Home" selected>Your backyard
</select>
```

XHTML Example

```
Sorry, you can't go there. How about one of these vacation spots?
<br>
<select>
    <option id="choice1" value="Ohio">Cleveland</option>
    <option id="choice2" value="New Jersey">Paramus</option>
    <option id="choice3" value="almost home" selected="selected">
        Your creepy neighbor's overgrown backyard</option>
</select>
```

Compatibility

HTML 2, 3.2. 4, 4.01, XHTML 1.0
Internet Explorer 2, 3, 4, 5, and 5.5
Netscape 1, 2, 3, 4–4.7, 6
Opera 4.0
WebTV

Notes

- Under HTML specifications, the closing tag for **<option>** is optional.
- For XHTML compatibility, the closing tag **</option>** is required.
- This element should occur only within the context of a **<select>** element.
- The HTML 2.0 and 3.2 specifications define only the **selected** and **value** attributes for this element.

<p> (Paragraph)

This element is used to define a paragraph of text. Browsers typically insert a blank line before and after a paragraph of text.

Syntax

```
<p
    align="center | justify | left | right"
          (transitional)
    class="class name(s)"
    dir="ltr | rtl"
    id="unique alphanumeric identifier"
    lang="language code"
    style="style information"
    title="advisory text"
    onclick="script"
    ondblclick="script"
    onkeydown="script"
    onkeypress="script"
    onkeyup="script"
    onmousedown="script"
    onmousemove="script"
    onmouseout="script"
    onmouseover="script"
    onmouseup="script">

</p>
```

XHTML Syntax

Under XHTML 1.0, the **<p>** element requires the closing tag:

```
<p></p>
```

Attributes and Events Defined by Internet Explorer 4

```
language="javascript | jscript | vbs | vbscript"
ondragstart="script"
onhelp="script"
onselectstart="script"
```

Attributes and Events Defined by Internet Explorer 5.5

```
accesskey="key"
contenteditable="false | true | inherit"
hidefocus="true | false"
tabindex="number"
```

Attributes

accesskey   This attribute specifies a keyboard navigation accelerator for the element. Pressing ALT or a similar key (depending on the browser and operating system) in association with the specified key selects the anchor element correlated with that key.

align   This attribute specifies the alignment of text within a paragraph. The default value is **left**. The transitional specification of HTML 4.01 also defines **center, justify,** and **right**. However, under the strict specification of HTML 4.01, text alignment can be handled through a style sheet rule.

class   See "Core Attributes Reference," earlier in this chapter.

contenteditable   This proprietary Microsoft attribute allows users to edit content rendered in the Internet Explorer 5.5 browser. Values are **false, true,** and **inherit**. A value of **false** will prevent content from being edited by users; **true** will allow editing. The default value, **inherit**, applies the value of the affected element's parent element.

dir   See "Language Reference," earlier in this chapter.

hidefocus   This proprietary element, introduced with Internet Explorer 5.5, hides focus on an element's content. Focus must be applied to the element using the **tabindex** attribute.

id   See "Core Attributes Reference," earlier in this chapter.

lang   See "Language Reference," earlier in this chapter.

language In the Microsoft implementation, this attribute specifies the scripting language to be used with an associated script bound to the element, typically through an event handler attribute. Possible values might include **javascript**, **jscript**, **vbs**, and **vbscript**. Other values that include the version of the language used, such as **JavaScript1.1**, also might be possible.

style See "Core Attributes Reference," earlier in this chapter.

tabindex This attribute uses a number to identify the object's position in the tabbing order for keyboard navigation using the TAB key. Internet Explorer 5.5 applies this attribute to the **p** element; under IE 5.5, this focus can be disabled with the **hidefocus** attribute.

title See "Core Attributes Reference," earlier in this chapter.

Attribute and Event Support

Netscape 4 align. (**class**, **id**, **lang**, and **style** are implied.)

Internet Explorer 4 All attributes and events except **dir**. (Note: The **justify** value for **align** is not supported by Internet Explorer 4.)

Internet Explorer 5.0 All attributes and events.

WebTV align (center | left | right).

Event Handlers

See "Events Reference," earlier in this chapter.

Examples

```
<p align="right">A right-aligned paragraph</p>

<p id="Para1" class="defaultParagraph"
   title="Introduction Paragraph">
This is the introductory paragraph for a very long paper about nothing.
</p>
```

Compatibility

HTML 2, 3.2, 4, and 4.01, XHTML 1.0
Internet Explorer 2, 3, 4, 5, and 5.5
Netscape 1, 2, 3, 4–4.7, 6
Opera 4.0
WebTV

Notes

- Under the strict HTML 4.01 specification the **align** attribute is not supported. Alignment of text can be accomplished using style sheets.

- The closing tag for the **<p>** element is optional under the HTML specification.

- Under the XHTML 1.0 specification, the closing tag **</p>** is required for XHTML compatibility.

- As a logical element, empty paragraphs are ignored by browsers, so do not try to use multiple **<p>** elements in a row, like **<p><p><p><p>**, to add blank lines to a Web page. This will not work; use the **
** element instead.

- The HTML 3.2 specification supports only the **align** attribute with values of **center**, **left**, and **right**.

- The HTML 2.0 specification supports no attributes for the **<p>** element.

<param> (Object Parameter)

This element specifies a parameter to pass to an embedded object using the **<object>** or **<applet>** element. This element should occur only within the scope of one of these elements.

Syntax

```
<param
      id="unique alphanumeric identifier"
      name="parameter name"
      type="mime Type"
      value="parameter value"
      valuetype="data | object | ref">
```

XHTML Syntax

Because **<param>** is an empty element, a closing forward slash is required before the closing bracket of the tag:

```
<param />
```

Attributes Defined by Internet Explorer 4

```
datafld="column name"
dataformatas="html | text"
datasrc="data source id"
```

2

Attributes

datafld   This Internet Explorer–specific attribute is used to indicate the column name in the data source that is bound to the **<param>** element's value.

dataformatas   This Internet Explorer–specific attribute indicates whether the bound data is plain text (**text**) or HTML (**html**).

datasrc   The value of this attribute is set to an identifier indicating the data source to pull data from. Bound data is used to set the value of the parameters passed to the object or applet with which this **<param>** element is associated.

id   See "Core Attributes Reference," earlier in this chapter.

name   This attribute contains the parameter's name. The name of the parameter depends on the particular object being inserted into the page, and it is assumed that the object knows how to handle the passed data. Do not confuse the **name** attribute with the **name** attribute used for form elements. In the latter case, the **name** attribute does not have a similar meaning as **id**, but rather specifies the name of the data to be passed to an enclosing **<object>** element.

type   When the **valuetype** attribute is set to **ref**, the **type** attribute can be used to indicate the type of the information to be retrieved. Legal values for this attribute are in the form of MIME types such as **text/html**.

value   This attribute contains the parameter's value. The actual contents of this attribute depend on the object and the particular parameter being passed in, as determined by the **name** attribute.

valuetype   This HTML 4–specific attribute specifies the type of the **value** attribute being passed in. Possible values for this attribute include **data**, **object**, and **ref**. A value of **data** specifies that the information passed in through the **value** parameter should be treated just as data. A value of **ref** indicates that the information being passed in is a URL that indicates where the data to use is located. The information is not retrieved, but the URL is passed to the object which then can retrieve the information if necessary. The last value of **object** indicates that the value being passed in is the name of an object as set by its **id** attribute. In practice, the **data** attribute is used by default.

Attribute and Event Support

Netscape 4   **name** and **value**. (**id** may be implied.)

Internet Explorer 4   **name, datafld, dataformatas, datasrc,** and **value**.

Event Handlers
None

Examples
```
<applet code="plot.class">
   <param name="min" value="5">
   <param name="max" value="30">
   <param name="ticks" value=".5">
   <param name="line-style" value="dotted">
</applet>

<object classid="clsid:D27CDB6E-AE6D-11cf-96B8-444553540000"
        codebase="swflash.cab#version=2,0,0,0"
        height="100" width="100">
   <param id="param1" name="Movie" value="SplashLogo.swf">
   <param id="param2" name="Play" value="True">
</object>
```

Compatibility

HTML 3.2 and 4
Internet Explorer 3, 4, and 5
Netscape 2, 3, 4, and 4.5

Notes

- The closing tag for this element is forbidden.

- The HTML 3.2 specification supports only the **name** and **value** attributes for this element.

- Under XHTML 1.0, empy elements such as **<param>** require a trailing forward slash: **<param />**.

<plaintext> (Plain Text)

2

This deprecated element from the HTML 2.0 specification renders the enclosed text as plain text and forces the browser to ignore any enclosed HTML. Typically, information affected by the **<plaintext>** element is rendered in monospaced font. This element no longer is part of the HTML standard.

Syntax (HTML 2; Deprecated Under HTML 4)

```
<plaintext>
```

Attributes and Events Defined by Internet Explorer 4

```
class="class name(s)"
dir="ltr | rtl"
id="unique alphanumeric identifier"
lang="language code"
language="javascript | jscript | vbs | vbscript"
style="style information"
title="advisory text"
onclick="script"
ondblclick="script"
ondragstart="script"
onhelp="script"
onkeydown="script"
onkeypress="script"
onkeyup="script"
onmousedown="script"
onmousemove="script"
onmouseout="script"
onmouseover="script"
onmouseup="script"
onselectstart="script"
```

Attributes and Events Defined by Internet Explorer 5.5

```
accesskey="key"
contenteditable="false | true | inherit"
hidefocus="true | false"
tabindex="number"
```

Attributes

accesskey   This attribute specifies a keyboard navigation accelerator for the element. Pressing ALT or a similar key (depending on the browser and operating system) in association with the specified key selects the anchor element correlated with that key.

class   See "Core Attributes Reference," earlier in this chapter.

contenteditable   This proprietary Microsoft attribute allows users to edit content rendered in the Internet Explorer 5.5 browser. Values are **false**, **true**, and **inherit**. A value of **false** will prevent content from being edited by users; **true** will allow editing. The default value, **inherit**, applies the value of the affected element's parent element.

dir   See "Language Reference," earlier in this chapter.

hidefocus   This proprietary element, introduced with Internet Explorer 5.5, hides focus on an element's content. Focus must be applied to the element using the **tabindex** attribute.

id   See "Core Attributes Reference," earlier in this chapter.

lang   See "Language Reference," earlier in this chapter.

language   In the Microsoft implementation, this attribute specifies the scripting language to be used with an associated script bound to the element, typically through an event handler attribute. Possible values might include **javascript**, **jscript**, **vbs**, and **vbscript**. Other values that include the version of the language used, such as **JavaScript1.1**, also might be possible.

style   See "Core Attributes Reference," earlier in this chapter.

tabindex   This attribute uses a number to identify the object's position in the tabbing order for keyboard navigation using the TAB key. Internet Explorer 5.5 applies this attribute to the **plaintext** element; under IE 5.5, this focus can be disabled with the **hidefocus** attribute.

title   See "Core Attributes Reference," earlier in this chapter.

Attribute and Event Support

Netscape 4   **class**, **id**, **lang**, and **style** are implied.

Internet Explorer 4   All attributes and events defined by W3C and Internet Explorer 4.

Internet Explorer 5.5   All attributes and events.

Event Handlers

See "Events Reference," earlier in this chapter.

Example

```
<html>
<head><title>Plaintext Example</title></head>
<body>
    The rest of this file is in plain text.
    <plaintext>
    Even though this is supposed to be <b>bold</b>, the tags still show.
    There is no way to turn plain text off once it is on.  </plaintext>
    does nothing to help. Even </body> and </html> will show up.
```

Compatibility

HTML 2
Internet Explorer 2, 3, 4, 5, and 5.5
Netscape 1, 2, 3, 4–4.7

Notes

- No closing tag for this element is necessary because the browser will ignore all tags after the starting tag.

- This element should not be used. Plain text information can be indicated by a file type, and information can be inserted in a preformatted fashion using the **<pre>** element.

<pre> (Preformatted Text)

This element is used to indicate that the enclosed text is preformatted, meaning that spaces, returns, tabs, and other formatting characters are preserved. Browsers will, however, acknowledge most HTML elements that are found with the **<pre>** element. Preformatted text generally will be rendered by the browsers in a monospaced font.

Syntax

```
<pre
    class="class name(s)"
    dir="ltr | rtl"
```

```
id="unique alphanumeric value"
lang="language code"
style="style information"
title="advisory text"
width="number" (transitional)
onclick="script"
ondblclick="script"
onkeydown="script"
onkeypress="script"
onkeyup="script"
onmousedown="script"
onmousemove="script"
onmouseout="script"
onmouseover="script"
onmouseup="script">
```

</pre>

Attributes and Events Defined by Internet Explorer 4

```
language="javascript | jscript | vbs | vbscript"
ondragstart="script"
onhelp="script"
onselectstart="script"
```

Attributes and Events Defined by Internet Explorer 5.5

```
accesskey="key"
contenteditable="false | true | inherit"
hidefocus="true | false"
tabindex="number"
```

Attributes and Events Defined by Netscape 4

```
col="columns"
wrap
```

Attributes

accesskey   This attribute specifies a keyboard navigation accelerator for the element. Pressing ALT or a similar key (depending on the browser and operating system) in association with the specified key selects the anchor element correlated with that key.

class   See "Core Attributes Reference," earlier in this chapter.

contenteditable   This proprietary Microsoft attribute allows users to edit content rendered in the Internet Explorer 5.5 browser. Values are **false**, **true**, and **inherit**. A value of **false** will prevent content from being edited by users; **true** will allow editing. The default value, **inherit**, applies the value of the affected element's parent element.

dir   See "Language Reference," earlier in this chapter.

hidefocus   This proprietary element, introduced with Internet Explorer 5.5, hides focus on an element's content. Focus must be applied to the element using the **tabindex** attribute.

id   See "Core Attributes Reference," earlier in this chapter.

lang   See "Language Reference," earlier in this chapter.

language   In the Microsoft implementation, this attribute specifies the scripting language to be used with an associated script bound to the element, typically through an event handler attribute. Possible values might include **javascript**, **jscript**, **vbs**, and **vbscript**. Other values that include the version of the language used, such as **JavaScript1.1**, also might be possible.

style   See "Core Attributes Reference," earlier in this chapter.

tabindex   This attribute uses a number to identify the object's position in the tabbing order for keyboard navigation using the TAB key. Internet Explorer 5.5 applies this attribute to the **pre** element; under IE 5.5, this focus can be disabled with the **hidefocus** attribute.

title   See "Core Attributes Reference," earlier in this chapter.

width   This attribute should be set to the **width** of the preformatted region. The value of the attribute should be the number of characters to display. In practice, this attribute is not supported and is dropped under the strict HTML 4.01 specification.

Attribute and Event Support

Netscape 4   class, cols, **id**, **lang**, **style**, and **wrap**.

Internet Explorer 4   All attributes and events defined by W3C and Internet Explorer 4, except **dir** and **width**.

Internet Explorer 5.5   All attributes and events defined by W3C, Internet Explorer 4, and Internet Explorer 5.5, except **width**.

Event Handlers

See "Events Reference," earlier in this chapter.

Example

```
<pre>
   Within PREFORMATTED text      A L L    formatting IS    PRESERVED
   NO  m    a    t    t    e  r how wild it is. Remember that some
   <b>HTML</b> markup is allowed within the &lt;PRE&gt; element.
</pre>
```

Compatibility

HTML 2, 3.2, 4, and 4.01, XHTML 1.0
Internet Explorer 2, 3, 4, 5, and 5.5
Netscape 1, 2, 3, 4–4.7, and 6
Opera 4.0
WebTV

Notes

- The HTML 4.01 transitional specification states that the
  <applet>, **<basefont>**, **<big>**, **<font>**, **<img>**, **<object>**,
  <small>, **<sub>**, and **<sup>** elements should not be used
  within the **<pre>** element. The strict HTML 4 specification
  states that only the **<big>**, **<img>**, **<object>**, **<small>**, **<sub>**,
  and **<sup>** elements should not be used within the **<pre>**
  element. The other excluded elements are missing, as they
  are deprecated from the strict specification. Although these
  attributes should not be used, it appears that the two most
  popular browsers will render them anyway.

- The strict HTML 4.0/4.01 specifications drop support for the
  width attribute, which was not generally supported anyway.

- The HTML 2.0 and 3.2 specifications support only the **width**
  attribute for **<pre>**.

<q> (Quote)

This element indicates that the enclosed text is a short inline
quotation.

Syntax

```
<q
    cite="url of source"
    class="class name(s)"
```

```
dir="ltr | rtl"
id="unique alphanumeric string"
lang="language code"
style="style information"
title="advisory text"
onclick="script"
ondblclick="script"
onkeydown="script"
onkeypress="script"
onkeyup="script"
onmousedown="script"
onmousemove="script"
onmouseout="script"
onmouseover="script"
onmouseup="script">
```

```
</q>
```

Attributes and Events Defined by Internet Explorer 4

```
language="javascript | jscipt | vbs | vbscript"
ondragstart="script"
onhelp="script"
onselectstart="script"
```

Attributes and Events Defined by Internet Explorer 5.5

```
accesskey="key"
contenteditable="false | true | inherit"
hidefocus="true | false"
tabindex="number"
```

Attributes

accesskey   This attribute specifies a keyboard navigation accelerator for the element. Pressing ALT or a similar key (depending on the browser and operating system) in association with the specified key selects the anchor element correlated with that key.

cite   The value of this attribute is a URL that designates a source document or message for the information quoted. This attribute is intended to point to information explaining the context or the reference for the quote.

class   See "Core Attributes Reference," earlier in this chapter.

contenteditable   This proprietary Microsoft attribute allows users to edit content rendered in the Internet Explorer 5.5 browser. Values are **false**, **true**, and **inherit**. A value of **false** will prevent content from being edited by users; **true** will allow editing. The default value, **inherit**, applies the value of the affected element's parent element.

dir   See "Language Reference," earlier in this chapter.

hidefocus   This proprietary element, introduced with Internet Explorer 5.5, hides focus on an element's content. Focus must be applied to the element using the **tabindex** attribute.

id   See "Core Attributes Reference," earlier in this chapter.

lang   See "Language Reference," earlier in this chapter.

language   In the Microsoft implementation, this attribute specifies the scripting language to be used with an associated script bound to the element, typically through an event handler attribute. Possible values might include **javascript**, **jscript**, **vbs**, and **vbscript**. Other values that include the version of the language used, such as **JavaScript1.1**, also might be possible.

style   See "Core Attributes Reference," earlier in this chapter.

tabindex   This attribute uses a number to identify the object's position in the tabbing order for keyboard navigation using the TAB key. Internet Explorer 5.5 applies this attribute to the **q** element; under IE 5.5, this focus can be disabled with the **hidefocus** attribute.

title   See "Core Attributes Reference," earlier in this chapter.

Attribute and Event Support

Internet Explorer 4   All attributes and events defined by the W3C and Internet Explorer 4, except **cite** and **dir**.

Internet Explorer 5.5   All attributes and events, except **cite**.

Event Handlers
See "Events Reference," earlier in this chapter.

Example
```
<q style="color: green">"A few green balls and a rainbow bar will
give you an exciting Web page Christmas Tree!"</q>
```

Compatibility

HTML 4, 4.01, XHTML
Internet Explorer 4, 5, and 5.5
Netscape 6

Notes

- This element is intended for short quotations that don't require paragraph breaks, as compared to text that would be contained within **<blockquote>**. Microsoft documentation continues to indicate this is a block element, when it is not.

- Internet Explorer does not make any sort of style change for quotations, but it is possible to apply a style rule.

- Netscape 6 (Preview Release 2) adds quotes around text enclosed within the **<q>** element.

rt (Ruby Text)

This Microsoft-specific proprietary element is used within the **<ruby>** element to create "ruby text," or annotations or pronunciation guides for words and phrases. The base text should be enclosed in the **<ruby>** element; the annotation, enclosed in the **<rt>** element, will appear as smaller text above the base text. This element was introduced with Internet Explorer 5.0.

Syntax Defined by Internet Explorer 5.0

```
<rt
    accesskey="key"
    class="class name(s)"
    dir="ltr | rtl"
    id="unique alphanumeric identifier"
    lang="language code"
    language="javascript | jscript | vbs | vbscript | xml"
    name="string"
    style="style information"
    tabindex="number"
    title="advisory text"
    onfterupdate="script"
    onbeforecut="script"
    onbeforepaste="script"
    onbeforeupdate="script"
    onblur="script"
    onclick="script"
    oncut="script"
```

```
ondblclick="script"
ondragstart="script"
onerrorupdate="script"
onfilterchange="script"
onfocus="script"
onhelp="script"
onkeydown="script"
onkeypress="script"
onkeyup="script"
onmousedown="script"
onmousemove="script"
onmouseout="script"
onmouseover="script"
onmouseup="script"
onpaste="script"
onreadystatechange="script">
... ruby text ..
```

Syntax Defined by Internet Explorer 5.5

```
contenteditable="false | true | inherit"
hidefocus="true | false"
```

Attributes

accesskey   This attribute specifies a keyboard navigation accelerator for the element. Pressing ALT or a similar key (depending on the browser and operating system) in association with the specified key selects the anchor element correlated with that key.

class   See "Core Attributes Reference," earlier in this chapter.

contenteditable   This proprietary Microsoft attribute allows users to edit content rendered in the Internet Explorer 5.5 browser. Values are **false**, **true**, and **inherit**. A value of **false** will prevent content from being edited by users; **true** will allow editing. The default value, **inherit**, applies the value of the affected element's parent element.

dir   See "Language Reference," earlier in this chapter.

hidefocus   This proprietary element, introduced with Internet Explorer 5.5, hides focus on an element's content. Focus must be applied to the element using the **tabindex** attribute.

id   See "Core Attributes Reference," earlier in this chapter.

lang   See "Language Reference," earlier in this chapter.

language This attribute specifies the language the current script is written in and invokes the proper scripting engine. The default value is **javascript**. **Javascript** and **jscript** represent that the scripting language is written in JavaScript. **Vbs** and **vbscript** represent that the scripting language is written in VBScript.

name Sets a name for the ruby text.

style See "Core Attributes Reference," earlier in this chapter.

tabindex This attribute uses a number to identify the object's position in the tabbing order for keyboard navigation using the TAB key. Internet Explorer 5.5 applies this attribute to the **dfn** element; under IE 5.5, this focus can be disabled with the **hidefocus** attribute.

title See "Core Attributes Reference," earlier in this chapter.

Attribute and Event Support

Internet Explorer 5.0 All attributes and events except **contenteditable** and **hidefocus**.

Internet Explorer 5.5 All attributes and events.

Event Handlers
See "Events Reference," earlier in this chapter.

Example
```
<ruby>Base Text

<rt>Ruby Text

</ruby>
```

Notes

- This element works only in Internet Explorer 5.0 and higher.
- The <rt> element must be used within the <ruby> element.
- Microsoft defines <rt> as an inline element that requires no closing tag; how this might be adapted for XHTML compatibility remains unclear.
- This element should be used only in an Internet Explorer-exclusive environment because other browsers will not interpret it or the <ruby> element.

ruby

This Microsoft-specific proprietary element is used with the **<rt>**
element to create annotations or pronunciation guides for words
and phrases. The base text should be enclosed in the **<ruby>**
element; the annotation, enclosed in the **<rt>** element, will appear
as smaller text above the base text. This element was introduced
with Internet Explorer 5.0.

Syntax Defined by Internet Explorer 5.0

```
ruby
      accesskey="key"
      class="class name(s)"
      dir="ltr | rtl"
      id="unique alphanumeric identifier"
      lang="language code"
      language="javascript | jscript | vbs | vbscript | xml"
      name="string"
      style="style information"
      tabindex="number"
      title="advisory text"
      onfterupdate="script"
      onbeforecut="script"
      onbeforepaste="script"
      onbeforeupdate="script"
      onblur="script"
      onclick="script"
      oncut="script"
      ondblclick="script"
      ondragstart="script"
      onerrorupdate="script"
      onfilterchange="script"
      onfocus="script"
      onhelp="script"
      onkeydown="script"
      onkeypress="script"
      onkeyup="script"
      onmousedown="script"
      onmousemove="script"
      onmouseout="script"
      onmouseover="script"
      onmouseup="script"
      onpaste="script"
      onreadystatechange="script">

      ... base text ...
      <rt>ruby text

</ruby>
```

Syntax Defined by Internet Explorer 5.5

```
contenteditable="false | true | inherit"
hidefocus="true | false"
```

Attributes

accesskey   This attribute specifies a keyboard navigation accelerator for the element. Pressing ALT or a similar key (depending on the browser and operating system) in association with the specified key selects the anchor element correlated with that key.

class   See "Core Attributes Reference," earlier in this chapter.

contenteditable   This proprietary Microsoft attribute allows users to edit content rendered in the Internet Explorer 5.5 browser. Values are **false**, **true**, and **inherit**. A value of **false** will prevent content from being edited by users; **true** will allow editing. The default value, **inherit**, applies the value of the affected element's parent element.

dir   See "Language Reference," earlier in this chapter.

hidefocus   This proprietary element, introduced with Internet Explorer 5.5, hides focus on an element's content. Focus must be applied to the element using the **tabindex** attribute.

id   See "Core Attributes Reference," earlier in this chapter.

lang   See "Language Reference," earlier in this chapter.

language   This attribute specifies the language the current script is written in and invokes the proper scripting engine. The default value is **javascript**. **Javascript** and **jscript** represent that the scripting language is written in JavaScript. **Vbs** and **vbscript** represent that the scripting language is written in VBScript.

name   Sets a name for the ruby base text.

style   See "Core Attributes Reference," earlier in this chapter.

tabindex   This attribute uses a number to identify the object's position in the tabbing order for keyboard navigation using the TAB key. Internet Explorer 5.5 applies this attribute to the **dfn** element; under IE 5.5, this focus can be disabled with the **hidefocus** attribute.

title   See "Core Attributes Reference," earlier in this chapter.

Attribute and Event Support

Internet Explorer 5.0   All attributes and events defined by Internet Explorer 5.0.

Internet Explorer 5.5   All attributes and events defined by Internet Explorer 5.0 and 5.5.

Event Handlers

See "Events Reference," earlier in this chapter.

Example

```
<ruby>This is the base text within the ruby element

<rt>This is the ruby text, which should appear in a smaller font
    above the base text in Internet Explorer 5.0 or higher.

</ruby>
```

Notes

- This element works only in Internet Explorer 5.0 and higher.
- The **<ruby>** element must be used in conjunction with the **<rt>** element; otherwise, it will have no meaning.
- This element should be used only in an Internet Explorer–exclusive environment because other browsers will not interpret it or the **<rt>** element.

<s> (Strikethrough)

This element renders the enclosed text with a line drawn through it.

Syntax (Transitional Only)

```
<s
    class="class name(s)"
    dir="ltr | rtl"
    id="unique alphanumeric identifier"
    lang="language code"
    style="style information"
    title="advisory text"
    onclick="script"
    ondblclick="script"
    onkeydown="script"
    onkeypress="script"
```

```
    onkeyup="script"
    onmousedown="script"
    onmousemove="script"
    onmouseout="script"
    onmouseover="script"
    onmouseup="script">
```

2

`</s>`

Attributes and Events Defined by Internet Explorer 4

```
    language="javascript | jscript | vbs | vbsscript"
    ondragstart="script"
    onhelp="script"
    onselectstart="script"
```

Attributes and Events Defined by Internet Explorer 5.5

```
    accesskey="key"
    contenteditable="false | true | inherit"
    hidefocus="true | false"
    tabindex="number"
```

Attributes

accesskey   This attribute specifies a keyboard navigation accelerator for the element. Pressing ALT or a similar key (depending on the browser and operating system) in association with the specified key selects the anchor element correlated with that key.

class   See "Core Attributes Reference," earlier in this chapter.

contenteditable   This proprietary Microsoft attribute allows users to edit content rendered in the Internet Explorer 5.5 browser. Values are **false**, **true**, and **inherit**. A value of **false** will prevent content from being edited by users; **true** will allow editing. The default value, **inherit**, applies the value of the affected element's parent element.

dir   See "Language Reference," earlier in this chapter.

hidefocus   This proprietary element, introduced with Internet Explorer 5.5, hides focus on an element's content. Focus must be applied to the element using the **tabindex** attribute.

id   See "Core Attributes Reference," earlier in this chapter.

lang   See "Language Reference," earlier in this chapter.

language   In the Microsoft implementation, this attribute specifies the scripting language to be used with an associated script bound to the element, typically through an event handler attribute. Possible values might include **javascript**, **jscript**, **vbs**, and **vbscript**. Other values that include the version of the language used, such as **JavaScript1.1**, might also be possible.

style   See "Core Attributes Reference," earlier in this chapter.

tabindex   This attribute uses a number to identify the object's position in the tabbing order for keyboard navigation using the TAB key. Internet Explorer 5.5 applies this attribute to the **s** element; under IE 5.5, this focus can be disabled with the **hidefocus** attribute.

title   See "Core Attributes Reference," earlier in this chapter.

Attribute and Event Support

Netscape 4   **class**, **id**, **lang**, and **style** are implied.

Internet Explorer 4   All attributes and events defined by the W3C and Internet Explorer 4.0, except **dir**.

Internet Explorer 5.5   All attributes and events.

Event Handlers
See "Events Reference," earlier in this chapter.

Examples
```
This line contains a <s>misstake</s>.
```

```
<s id="strike1"
   onmouseover="this.style.color='red'"
   onmouseout="this.style.color='black'">Fastball</S>
```

Compatibility

> HTML 4 (transitional), 4.01 (transitional), XHTML 1.0
> Internet Explorer 2, 3, 4, 5, and 5.5
> Netscape 3, 4–4.7, 6
> WebTV

Notes

- This element should act the same as the **<strike>** element.

- This HTML 3 element eventually was adopted by Netscape and Microsoft and later was incorporated into the HTML 4 transitional specification.

- This element has been deprecated by the W3C. The strict HTML 4.01 specification does not include the **<s>** element or the **<strike>** element. It is possible to indicate strikethrough text using a style sheet.

<samp> (Sample Text)

This element is used to indicate sample text. Enclosed text generally is rendered in a monospaced font.

Syntax

```
<samp
    class="class name(s)"
    dir="ltr | rtl"
    id="unique alphanumeric string"
    lang="language code"
    style="style information"
    title="advisory text"
    onclick="script"
    ondblclick="script"
    onkeydown="script"
    onkeypress="script"
    onkeyup="script"
    onmousedown="script"
    onmousemove="script"
    onmouseout="script"
    onmouseover="script"
    onmouseup="script">

</samp>
```

Attributes and Events Defined by Internet Explorer 4

```
    language="javascript | jscript | vbs | vbscript"
    ondragstart="script"
    onhelp="script"
    onselectstart="script"
```

Attributes and Events Defined by Internet Explorer 5.5

```
accesskey="key"
contenteditable="false | true | inherit"
hidefocus="true | false"
tabindex="number"
```

Attributes

accesskey   This attribute specifies a keyboard navigation accelerator for the element. Pressing ALT or a similar key (depending on the browser and operating system) in association with the specified key selects the anchor element correlated with that key.

class   See "Core Attributes Reference," earlier in this chapter.

contenteditable   This proprietary Microsoft attribute allows users to edit content rendered in the Internet Explorer 5.5 browser. Values are **false**, **true**, and **inherit**. A value of **false** will prevent content from being edited by users; **true** will allow editing. The default value, **inherit**, applies the value of the affected element's parent element.

dir   See "Language Reference," earlier in this chapter.

hidefocus   This proprietary element, introduced with Internet Explorer 5.5, hides focus on an element's content. Focus must be applied to the element using the **tabindex** attribute.

id   See "Core Attributes Reference," earlier in this chapter.

lang   See "Language Reference," earlier in this chapter.

language   In the Microsoft implementation, this attribute specifies the scripting language to be used with an associated script bound to the element, typically through an event handler attribute. Possible values might include **javascript**, **jscript**, **vbs**, and **vbscript**. Other values that include the version of the language used, such as **JavaScript1.1**, also might be possible.

style   See "Core Attributes Reference," earlier in this chapter.

tabindex   This attribute uses a number to identify the object's position in the tabbing order for keyboard navigation using the TAB key. Internet Explorer 5.5 applies this attribute to the **samp** element; under IE 5.5, this focus can be disabled with the **hidefocus** attribute.

title   See "Core Attributes Reference," earlier in this chapter.

Attribute and Event Support

Internet Explorer 4   All attributes and events defined by the
W3C and Internet Explorer 4.0, except **dir**.

Internet Explorer 5.5   All attributes and events.

Event Handlers
See "Events Reference," earlier in this chapter.

Example
```
Use the following salutation in all e-mail messages to the boss:
<samp>Please excuse the interruption, oh exalted manager.</samp>
```

Compatibility

> HTML 2, 3.2, 4, and 4.01, XHTML 1.0
> Internet Explorer 2, 3, 4, 5, and 5.5
> Netscape 1, 2, 3, 4–4.7, 6
> Opera 4.0
> WebTV

Notes

- As a logical element, **<samp>** is useful to bind style rules to.
- The HTML 2.0 and 3.2 specifications supported no attributes
  for this element.

<script> (Scripting)

This element encloses statements in a scripting language for
client-side processing. Scripting statements can either be included
inline or loaded from an external file and might be commented out
to avoid execution by non–scripting-aware browsers.

Syntax
```
<script
     charset="character set"
     defer
     event="event name" (reserved)
     for="element ID" (reserved)
     language="scripting language name"
```

```
            src="url of script code"
            type="mime type">

</script>
```

Attributes Defined by Internet Explorer 4

```
            class="class name(s)"
            id="unique alphanumeric identifier"
            title="advisory text"
```

Attributes

charset   This attribute defines the character encoding of the script. The value is a space- and/or comma-delimited list of character sets as defined in RFC 2045. The default value is **ISO-8859-1**.

class   This Microsoft-defined attribute does not make much sense given that scripting code would not be bound by style sheet rules. Its meaning as defined in the "Core Attributes Reference" in this chapter is unclear within the context of the **<script>** element.

defer   Presence of this attribute indicates that the browser might defer execution of the script enclosed by the **<script>** element. In practice, deferring code might be more dependent on the position of the **<script>** element or the contents. This attribute was added very late to the HTML 4.01 specification and its support is currently minimal.

event   This Microsoft attribute is used to define a particular event that the script should react to. It must be used in conjunction with the **for** attribute. Event names are the same as event handler attributes; for example, **onclick**, **ondblclick**, and so on.

for   The **for** attribute is used to define the name or ID of the element to which an event defined by the **event** attribute is related. For example, **<script event="onclick" for="button1" language="vbscript">** defines a VBScript that will execute when a click event is issued for an element named button1.

id   See "Core Attributes Reference," earlier in this chapter.

language   This attribute specifies the scripting language being used. The Netscape implementation supports JavaScript. The Microsoft implementation supports JScript (a JavaScript clone) as well as VBScript, which can be indicated by either **vbs** or **vbscript**. Other values that include the version of the language used, such as

JavaScript1.1 and **JavaScript1.2**, also might be possible and are useful to exclude browsers from executing script code that is not supported.

src   This attribute specifies the URL of a file containing scripting code. Typically, files containing JavaScript code will have a .js extension, and a server will attach the appropriate MIME type; if not, the **type** attribute might be used to explicitly set the content type of the external script file. The **language** attribute also might be helpful in determining this.

title   See "Core Attributes Reference," earlier in this chapter.

type   This attribute should be set to the MIME type corresponding to the scripting language used. For JavaScript, for example, this would be **text/javascript**. In practice, the **language** attribute is the more common way to indicate which scripting language is in effect.

Attribute and Event Support

Netscape 4   **language** and **src**.

Internet Explorer 4   All attributes and events except **charset**.

WebTV   **language** and **src**.

Event Handlers

There are no events directly associated with the **<script>** element. However, the Microsoft implementation does allow the **event** attribute to be used to indicate what event a particular script might be associated with.

Examples

```
<script language="JavaScript">
<!-- alert("Hello World !!!"); // -->
</script>

<!-- code in external file -->
<script language="JavaScript1.2" src="superrollover.js">
</script>

<script for ="myButton" event="onclick"
        language="JavaScript">
<!-- alert("I've been clicked!"); // -->
</script>
```

```
<form>
    <input type="BUTTON" name="myButton" value="Click me">
</form>
```

Compatibility

> HTML 4 and 4.01, XHTML 1.0
> Internet Explorer 3, 4, 5, and 5.5
> Netscape 2, 3, 4–4.7, 6
> Opera 4.0

Notes

- It is common practice to comment out statements enclosed by the **<script>** element. Without commenting, scripts are displayed as page content by browsers that do not support scripting. The particular comment style might be dependent on the language being used. For example, in JavaScript use

```
<script language="JavaScript">
<!-- Javacript code here // -->
</script>
```

  and in VBScript use

```
<script language="vbscript">
<!-- VBScript code here -->
</script>
```

- The HTML 3.2 specification defined a placeholder **<script>** element, but otherwise the element is new to HTML 4.

- Refer to the **<noscript>** element reference in this chapter to see how content might be identified for non-scripting-aware browsers.

<select> (Selection List)

This element defines a selection list within a form. Depending on the form of the selection list, the control allows the user to select one or more list options.

Syntax

```
<select
    class="class name(s)"
    dir="ltr | rtl"
```

```
disabled
id="unique alphanumeric identifier"
lang="language code"
multiple
name="unique alphanumeric name"
size="number"
style="style information"
tabindex="number"
title="advisory text"
onblur="script"
onchange="script"
onclick="script"
ondblclick="script"
onfocus="script"
onkeydown="script"
onkeypress="script"
onkeyup="script"
onmousedown="script"
onmousemove="script"
onmouseout="script"
onmouseover="script"
onmouseup="script">
```

```
<option> elements
```

```
</select>
```

Attributes and Events Defined by Internet Explorer 4

```
accesskey="character"
align="absbottom | absmiddle | baseline | bottom |
      left | middle | right | texttop | top"
datafld="column name"
datasrc="data source ID"
language="javascript | jscript | vbs | vbscript"
onafterupdate="script"
onbeforeupdate="script"
ondragstart="script"
onhelp="script"
onresize="script"
onrowenter="script"
onrowexit="script"
onselectstart="script"
```

Attributes and Events Defined by Internet Explorer 5.5

```
hidefocus="true | false"
```

Attributes Defined by WebTV

```
autoactive
bgcolor="color name | #RRGGBB"
exclusive
selcolor="color name | #RRGGBB"
text="color name | #RRGGBB"
usestyle
```

Attributes

accesskey   This Microsoft attribute specifies a keyboard navigation accelerator for the element. Pressing ALT or a similar key in association with the specified character selects the form control correlated with that key sequence. Page designers are forewarned to avoid key sequences already bound to browsers.

align   This Microsoft-specific attribute controls the alignment of the image with respect to the content on the page. The default value is **left**, but other values such as **absbottom**, **absmiddle**, **baseline**, **bottom**, **middle**, **right**, **texttop**, and **top** also might be supported. The meaning of these values should be similar to inserted objects such as images.

auotactive   In the WebTV implementation, this attribute causes the selection list control to immediately activate when the user selects it, allowing the user to quickly use the arrow keys to move up and down. Without this attribute, the process is a two-step procedure to select the control and then move around.

bgcolor   In the WebTV implementation, this attribute specifies the background color of the selection list. The value for this attribute can be either a named color, such as **red**, or a color specified in the hexadecimal *#RRGGBB* format, such as **#FF0000**.

class   See "Core Attributes Reference," earlier in this chapter.

datafld   This attribute is used to indicate the column name in the data source that is bound to the options in the **<select>** element.

datasrc   The value of this attribute is set to an identifier indicating the data source to pull data from.

dir   See "Language Reference," earlier in this chapter.

disabled   This attribute is used to turn off a form control. Elements will not be submitted nor can they receive any focus

from the keyboard or mouse. Disabled form controls will not be part of the tabbing order. The browser also can gray out the form that is disabled in order to indicate to the user that the form control is inactive. This attribute requires no value.

exclusive   In the WebTV implementation, this attribute prevents duplicate entries in the selection list. The attribute requires no value.

hidefocus   This proprietary element, introduced with Internet Explorer 5.5, hides focus on an element's content. Focus must be applied to the element using the **tabindex** attribute.

id   See "Core Attributes Reference," earlier in this chapter.

lang   See "Language Reference," earlier in this chapter.

language   In the Microsoft implementation, this attribute specifies the scripting language to be used with an associated script bound to the element, typically through an event handler attribute. Possible values might include **javascript**, **jscript**, **vbs**, and **vbscript**. Other values that include the version of the language used, such as **JavaScript1.1**, also might be possible.

multiple   This attribute allows the selection of multiple items in the selection list. The default is single-item selection.

name   This attribute allows a form control to be assigned a name so that it can be referenced by a scripting language. **Name** is supported by older browsers such as Netscape 2 generation browsers, but the W3C encourages the use of the **id** attribute. Fo compatibility purposes both might have to be used.

selcolor   In the WebTV implementation, this attribute specifie the background color for selected items. Its value can be either a named color, such as **green**, or a color specified in the hexadeci *#RRGGBB* format, such as **#00FF00**. The default for this attribut WebTV is **#EAEAEA**.

size   This attribute sets the number of visible items in the selection list. When the **multiple** attribute is not present, only one entry should show; however, when **multiple** is present, t attribute is useful to set the size of the scrolling list box.

style   See "Core Attributes Reference," earlier in this chap

tabindex   This attribute takes a numeric value indicating position of the form control in the tabbing index for the form

Tabbing proceeds from the lowest positive **tabindex** value to the highest. Negative values for **tabindex** will leave the form control out of the tabbing order. When tabbing is not explicitly set, the browser might tab through items in the order they are encountered. Form controls that are disabled due to the presence of the **disabled** attribute will not be part of the tabbing index, although read-only controls will be.

text   In the WebTV implementation, this attribute specifies the text color for items in the list. Its value can be either a named color, such as **blue**, or a color specified in the hexadecimal *#RRGGBB* format, such as **#0000FF**.

title   See "Core Attributes Reference," earlier in this chapter.

usestyle   This WebTV-specific attribute causes text to be rendered in the style in effect for the page. The attribute requires no value.

Attribute and Event Support

Netscape 4   multiple, **name**, **size**, **onblur**, **onchange**, and **onfocus**. (**class**, **id**, **lang**, and **style** are implied.)

Internet Explorer 4   All W3C-defined attributes and events except **dir** and **title**, and all attributes and events defined by Internet Explorer 4.

Internet Explorer 5.0   All W3C-defined attributes and events except **title**, and all attributes and events defined by Internet Explorer 4.

Internet Explorer 5.5   Same as Internet Explorer 5.0, plus **hidefocus**.

WebTV   autoactivate, **bgcolor**, **multiple**, **name**, **selcolor**, **size**, **text**, **usestyle**, **onblur**, **onchange**, **onfocus**, and **onclick**.

Event Handlers

See "Events Reference," earlier in this chapter.

Examples

```
Choose your favorite colors
<select multiple size="2">
   <option>Red
   <option>Blue
```

```
    <option>Green
    <option>Yellow
</select>

Taco Choices
<select name="tacomenu">
    <option value="SuperChicken">Chicken
    <option value="Baja">Fish
    <option value="RX-Needed">Carnitas
</select>
```

Compatibility

HTML 2, 3.2, 4, and 4.01, XHTML 1.0
Internet Explorer 2, 3, 4, 5, and 5.5
Netscape 1, 2, 3, 4–4.7, 6
Opera 4
WebTV

Notes

- The HTML 4.01 specification reserves the attributes **datafld** and **datasrc** for future use.

- The HTML 2.0 and 3.2 specifications define only **multiple**, **name**, and **size** attributes.

<small> (Small Text)

This element renders the enclosed text one font size smaller than a document's base font size unless it is already set to the smallest size.

Syntax

```
<small
    class="class name(s)"
    dir="ltr | rtl"
    id="unique alphanumeric string"
    lang="language code"
    style="style information"
    title="advisory text"
    onclick="script"
    ondblclick="script"
    onkeydown="script"
    onkeypress="script"
    onkeyup="script"
    onmousedown="script"
    onmousemove="script"
```

```
onmouseout="script"
onmouseover="script"
onmouseup="script">
```

```
</small>
```

Attributes and Events Defined by Internet Explorer 4

```
language="javascript | jscript | vbs | vbscript"
ondragstart="script"
onhelp="script"
onselectstart="script"
```

Attributes and Events Defined by Internet Explorer 5.5

```
accesskey="key"
contenteditable="false | true | inherit"
hidefocus="true | false"
tabindex="number"
```

Attributes

accesskey   This attribute specifies a keyboard navigation accelerator for the element. Pressing ALT or a similar key (depending on the browser and operating system) in association with the specified key selects the anchor element correlated with that key.

class   See "Core Attributes Reference," earlier in this chapter.

contenteditable   This proprietary Microsoft attribute allows users to edit content rendered in the Internet Explorer 5.5 browser. Values are **false**, **true**, and **inherit**. A value of **false** will prevent content from being edited by users; **true** will allow editing. The default value, **inherit**, applies the value of the affected element's parent element.

dir   See "Language Reference," earlier in this chapter.

hidefocus   This proprietary element, introduced with Internet Explorer 5.5, hides focus on an element's content. Focus must be applied to the element using the **tabindex** attribute.

id   See "Core Attributes Reference," earlier in this chapter.

lang   See "Language Reference," earlier in this chapter.

language   In the Microsoft implementation, this attribute specifies the scripting language to be used with an associated script bound to the element, typically through an event handler attribute. Possible values might include **javascript**, **jscript**, **vbs**, and **vbscript**. Other values that include the version of the language used, such as **JavaScript1.1**, also might be possible.

2

style   See "Core Attributes Reference," earlier in this chapter.

tabindex   This attribute uses a number to identify the object's position in the tabbing order for keyboard navigation using the TAB key. Internet Explorer 5.5 applies this attribute to the **small** element; under IE 5.5, this focus can be disabled with the **hidefocus** attribute.

title   See "Core Attributes Reference," earlier in this chapter.

Attribute and Event Support

Netscape 4   **class**, **id**, **lang**, and **style** are implied.

Internet Explorer 4   All attributes and events defined by the W3C and Internet Explorer 4, except **dir**.

Internet Explorer 5.5   All attributes and events.

Event Handlers
See "Events Reference," earlier in this chapter.

Examples
Here is some **<small>**small text**</small>**.

This element can be applied **<small><small><small>**multiple times**</small></small></small>**to make things even smaller.

Compatibility

HTML 3.2, 4, and 4, XHTML 1.0
Internet Explorer 2, 3, 4, 5, and 5.5
Netscape 2, 3, 4–4.7, 6
WebTV

Notes

- The <small> element can be used multiple times to decrease the size of text to a greater degree. Using more than six

<small> elements together doesn't make sense because browsers currently only support relative font sizes from 1 to 7. As style sheets become more common, this element might fall out of favor.

• The default base font size for a document typically is 3, although it can be changed with the **<basefont>** element.

<spacer> (Extra Space)

This proprietary element specifies an invisible region for pushing content around a page.

Syntax (Defined by Netscape 3)

```
<spacer
      align="absmiddle | absbottom | baseline | bottom |
            left | middle | right | texttop | top"
      height="pixels"
      size="pixels"
      type="block | horizontal | vertical"
      width="pixels">
```

Attributes

align   This attribute specifies the alignment of the spacer with respect to surrounding text. It is used only with spacers with **type="block"**. The default value for the **align** attribute is **bottom**. The meanings of the **align** values are similar to those used with the **<img>** element.

height   This attribute specifies the height of the invisible region in pixels. It is used only with spacers with **type="block"**.

size   Used with **type="block"** and **type="horizontal"** spacers, this attribute sets the spacer's width in pixels. Used with a **type="vertical"** spacer, this attribute is used to set the spacer's height.

type   This attribute indicates the type of invisible region. A **horizontal** spacer adds horizontal space between words and objects. A **vertical** spacer is used to add space between lines. A **block** spacer defines a general-purpose positioning rectangle like an invisible image that text can flow around.

width   This attribute is used only with the **type="block"** spacer and is used to set the width of the region in pixels.

Attribute and Event Support

Netscape 4   All attributes

WebTV   All attributes

Examples

A line of text with two **<spacer type="horizontal" size="20">**words separated by 20 pixels. Here is a line of text.**
**
<spacer type="vertical" size="50">

Here is another line of text with a large space between the two lines.**<spacer align="left" type="block" height="100" width="100">** This is a bunch of text that flows around an invisible block region. You could have easily performed this layout with a table.

Compatibility

> Netscape 3, 4–4.7, 6
> WebTV

Notes

- This element should not be used. If the effect of this element is required and style sheets cannot be used, an invisible pixel trick might be a more appropriate choice. The invisible pixel trick requires a transparent image, which then is resized with the **height** and **width** attributes of the **<img>** element:

  ```
  <img src="pixel.gif" height="100" width="100">
  ```

- This is an empty element; no closing tag is allowed.

<span> (Text Span)

This element typically is used to group inline text so scripting or style rules can be applied to the content. As it has no preset or rendering meaning, this is the most useful inline element for associating style and script with content.

Syntax

```
<span
    class="class name(s)"
    datafld="column name" (reserved)
    dataformatas="html | text" (reserved)
    datasrc="data source id" (reserved)
```

```
dir="ltr | rtl"
id="unique alphanumeric string"
lang="language code"
style="style information"
title="advisory text"
onclick="script"
ondblclick="script"
onkeydown="script"
onkeypress="script"
onkeyup="script"
onmousedown="script"
onmousemove="script"
onmouseout="script"
onmouseover="script"
onmouseup="script">
```

```
</span>
```

Attributes and Events Defined by Internet Explorer 4

```
language="javascript | jscript | vbs | vbscript"
ondragstart="script"
onhelp="script"
onselectstart="script"
```

Attributes and Events Defined by Internet Explorer 5.5

```
accesskey="key"
contenteditable="false | true | inherit"
hidefocus="true | false"
tabindex="number"
```

Attributes

accesskey   This attribute specifies a keyboard navigation accelerator for the element. Pressing ALT or a similar key (depending on the browser and operating system) in association with the specified key selects the anchor element correlated with that key.

class   See "Core Attributes Reference," earlier in this chapter.

contenteditable   This proprietary Microsoft attribute allows users to edit content rendered in the Internet Explorer 5.5 browser. Values are **false**, **true**, and **inherit**. A value of **false** will prevent content from being edited by users; **true** will allow editing. The default value, **inherit**, applies the value of the affected element's parent element.

datafld   This attribute is used to indicate the column name in the data source that is bound to the contents of the **\<span\>** element.

dataformatas   This attribute indicates whether the bound data is plain text (**text**) or HTML (**html**). The data bound with **\<span\>** should be used to set the content of the element and might include HTML markup.

2

datasrc   The value of this attribute is set to an identifier indicating the data source to pull data from.

dir   See "Language Reference," earlier in this chapter.

hidefocus   This proprietary element, introduced with Internet Explorer 5.5, hides focus on an element's content. Focus must be applied to the element using the **tabindex** attribute.

id   See "Core Attributes Reference," earlier in this chapter.

lang   See "Language Reference," earlier in this chapter.

language   In the Microsoft implementation, this attribute specifies the scripting language to be used with an associated script bound to the element, typically through an event handler attribute. Possible values might include **javascript**, **jscript**, **vbs**, and **vbscript**. Other values that include the version of the language used, such as **JavaScript1.1**, also might be possible.

style   See "Core Attributes Reference," earlier in this chapter.

tabindex   This attribute uses a number to identify the object's position in the tabbing order for keyboard navigation using the TAB key. Internet Explorer 5.5 applies this attribute to the **span** element; under IE 5.5, this focus can be disabled with the **hidefocus** attribute.

title   See "Core Attributes Reference," earlier in this chapter.

Attribute and Event Support

Netscape 4   class, **id**, **lang**, and **style**.

Internet Explorer 4   All attributes and events defined by the W3C and Internet Explorer 4, except **dir**.

Internet Explorer 5.5   All attributes and events.

Event Handlers

See "Events Reference," earlier in this chapter.

Examples

```
Here is some <span style="font-size: 14pt; color: purple">very
strange</span> text.
```

```
<span id="toggletext"
      onclick="this.style.color='red'"
      ondblclick="this.style.color='black'">
Click and Double Click Me
</span>
```

Compatibility

> HTML 4, 4.01, XHTML 1.0
> Internet Explorer 3, 4, 5, and 5.5
> Netscape 4–4.7, 6

Notes

- The HTML 4.01 specification reserves the **datafld**, **dataformatas**, and **datasrc** attributes for future use. Internet Explorer 4 supports them.

- Unlike the block level element **<div>**, as an inline element **<span>** does not cause any line breaks.

<strike> (Strikeout Text)

This element is used to indicate strikethrough text, namely text with a line drawn through it. The **<s>** element provides shorthand notation for this element.

Syntax (Transitional Only)

```
<strike
    class="class name(s)"
    dir="ltr | rtl"
    id="unique alphanumeric string"
    lang="language code"
    style="style information"
    title="advisory text"
    onclick="script"
    ondblclick="script"
    onkeydown="script"
    onkeypress="script"
```

```
        onkeyup="script"
        onmousedown="script"
        onmousemove="script"
        onmouseout="script"
        onmouseover="script"
        onmouseup="script">
```

```
</strike>
```

Attributes and Events Defined by
Internet Explorer 4

```
        language="javascript | jscript | vbs | vbscript"
        ondragstart="script"
        onhelp="script"
        onselectstart="script"
```

Attributes and Events Defined by
Internet Explorer 5.5

```
        accesskey="key"
        contenteditable="false | true | inherit"
        hidefocus="true | false"
        tabindex="number"
```

Attributes

accesskey   This attribute specifies a keyboard navigation accelerator for the element. Pressing ALT or a similar key (depending on the browser and operating system) in association with the specified key selects the anchor element correlated with that key.

class   See "Core Attributes Reference," earlier in this chapter.

contenteditable   This proprietary Microsoft attribute allows users to edit content rendered in the Internet Explorer 5.5 browser. Values are **false**, **true**, and **inherit**. A value of **false** will prevent content from being edited by users; **true** will allow editing. The default value, **inherit**, applies the value of the affected element's parent element.

dir   See "Language Reference," earlier in this chapter.

hidefocus   This proprietary element, introduced with Internet Explorer 5.5, hides focus on an element's content. Focus must be applied to the element using the **tabindex** attribute.

id   See "Core Attributes Reference," earlier in this chapter.

lang   See "Language Reference," earlier in this chapter.

language   In the Microsoft implementation, this attribute specifies the scripting language to be used with an associated script bound to the element, typically through an event handler attribute. Possible values might include **javascript**, **jscript**, **vbs**, and **vbscript**. Other values that include the version of the language used, such as **JavaScript1.1**, also might be possible.

style   See "Core Attributes Reference," earlier in this chapter.

tabindex   This attribute uses a number to identify the object's position in the tabbing order for keyboard navigation using the TAB key. Internet Explorer 5.5 applies this attribute to the **strike** element; under IE 5.5, this focus can be disabled with the **hidefocus** attribute.

title   See "Core Attributes Reference," earlier in this chapter.

Attribute and Event Support

Netscape 4   **class**, **id**, **lang**, and **style** are implied.

Internet Explorer 4   All attributes and events defined by the W3C and Internet Explorer 4, except **dir**.

Internet Explorer 5.5   All attributes and events.

Event Handlers
See "Events Reference," earlier in this chapter.

Example
```
This line contains a spelling <strike>misstake</strike> mistake.
```

Compatibility

> HTML 3.2, 4 (transitional), and 4.01 (transitional), XHTML 1.0
> Internet Explorer 2, 3, 4, 5, and 5.5
> Netscape 3, 4–4.7, 6
> Opera 4.0
> WebTV

Notes

- This element should act the same as the **<s>** element.
- This element has been deprecated by the W3C. The strict HTML 4.01 specification does not include the **<strike>** element nor the **<s>** element. It is possible to indicate strikethrough text using a style sheet.

<strong> (Strong Emphasis)

This element indicates strongly emphasized text. It usually is rendered in a bold typeface, but is a logical element rather than a physical one.

Syntax

```
<strong
     class="class name(s)"
     dir="ltr | rtl"
     id="unique alphanumeric string"
     lang="language code"
     style="style information"
     title="advisory text"
     onclick="script"
     ondblclick="script"
     onkeydown="script"
     onkeypress="script"
     onkeyup="script"
     onmousedown="script"
     onmousemove="script"
     onmouseout="script"
     onmouseover="script"
     onmouseup="script">

</strong>
```

Attributes and Events Defined by Internet Explorer 4

```
     language="javascript | jscript | vbs | vbscript"
     ondragstart="script"
     onhelp="script"
     onselectstart="script"
```

Attributes and Events Defined by Internet Explorer 5.5

```
accesskey="key"
contenteditable="false | true | inherit"
hidefocus="true | false"
tabindex="number"
```

Attributes

accesskey   This attribute specifies a keyboard navigation accelerator for the element. Pressing ALT or a similar key (depending on the browser and operating system) in association with the specified key selects the anchor element correlated with that key.

class   See "Core Attributes Reference," earlier in this chapter.

contenteditable   This proprietary Microsoft attribute allows users to edit content rendered in the Internet Explorer 5.5 browser. Values are **false**, **true**, and **inherit**. A value of **false** will prevent content from being edited by users; **true** will allow editing. The default value, **inherit**, applies the value of the affected element's parent element.

dir   See "Language Reference," earlier in this chapter.

hidefocus   This proprietary element, introduced with Internet Explorer 5.5, hides focus on an element's content. Focus must be applied to the element using the **tabindex** attribute.

id   See "Core Attributes Reference," earlier in this chapter.

lang   See "Language Reference," earlier in this chapter.

language   In the Microsoft implementation, this attribute specifies the scripting language to be used with an associated script bound to the element, typically through an event handler attribute. Possible values might include **javascript**, **jscript**, **vbs**, and **vbscript**. Other values that include the version of the language used, such as **JavaScript1.1**, also might be possible.

style   See "Core Attributes Reference," earlier in this chapter.

tabindex   This attribute uses a number to identify the object's position in the tabbing order for keyboard navigation using the TAB

2

key. Internet Explorer 5.5 applies this attribute to the **strong** element; under IE 5.5, this focus can be disabled with the **hidefocus** attribute.

title   See "Core Attributes Reference," earlier in this chapter.

Attribute and Event Support

Netscape 4   **class**, **id**, **lang**, and **style** are implied.

Internet Explorer 4   All attributes and events defined by the W3C and Internet Explorer 4, except **dir**.

Internet Explorer 5.5   All attributes and events.

Event Handlers

See "Events Reference," earlier in this chapter.

Examples

```
It is really <strong>important</STRONG> to pay attention.

<strong style="font-family: impact; font-size: 28pt">
Important Info
</strong>
```

Compatibility

> HTML 2, 3.2, 4, and 4.01, XHTML 1.0
> Internet Explorer 2, 3, 4, 5, and 5.5
> Netscape 1, 2, 3, 4–4.7, 6
> Opera 4.0
> WebTV

Notes

- This element generally renders as bold text. As a logical element, however, **<strong>** is useful to bind style rules to.

- As compared to **<b>**, this element does have meaning and voice browsers can state **<strong>** enclosed text in a different voice than text that is enclosed by **<b>**.

<style> (Style Information)

This element is used to surround style sheet rules for a document. This element should be found only in the **<head>** of a document. Style rules within a document's **<body>** element should be set with the style attribute for a particular element.

Syntax

```
<style
    dir="ltr | rtl"
    lang="language code"
    media="all | print | screen | others"
    title="advisory text"
    type="MIME Type">

</style>
```

Attributes Defined by Internet Explorer 4

```
disabled
```

Attributes

dir   This attribute is used to set the text direction of the title for the style sheet, either left to right (**ltr**) or right to left (**rtl**).

disabled   This Microsoft-defined attribute is used to disable a style sheet. The presence of the attribute is all that is required to disable the style sheet. In conjunction with scripting, this attribute could be used to turn on and off various style sheets in a document.

lang   The value of this attribute is a language code like all other **lang** attributes; however, this attribute defines the language of the **title** attribute rather than the content of the element.

media   This attribute specifies the destination medium for the style information. The value of the attribute can be a single media descriptor like **screen** or a comma-separated list. Possible values for this attribute include **all**, **aural**, **braille**, **print**, **projection**, **screen**, and **tv**. Other values also might be defined, depending on the browser. Internet Explorer supports **all**, **print**, and **screen** as values for this attribute.

title   This attribute associates an informational title with the style sheet.

type   This attribute is used to define the type of style sheet. The value of the attribute should be the MIME type of the style sheet language used. The most common current value for this attribute is **text/css**, which indicates a Cascading Style Sheet format.

Attribute and Event Support

Netscape 4   type

Internet Explorer 4   disabled, media (all | print | screen), title, and **type**.

Event Handlers

None

Example

```
<html>
<head>
<title>Style Sheet Example</title>
<style type="text/css">
<!--
   body {background: black; color: white;
   font: 12pt Helvetica}
   h1 {color: red; font: 14pt Impact}
-->
</style>
</head>

<body>
<h1>A 14-point red Impact heading on a black
background</h1>
Regular body text, which is 12 point white Helvetica
</body>
</html>
```

Compatibility

> HTML 4, 4.01, XHTML 1.0
> Netscape 4–4.7, 6
> Internet Explorer 3, 4, 5, and 5.5
> Opera 4.0

Notes

- Style information also can be specified in external style sheets as defined by the **<link>** element.

- Style information can also be associated with a particular element using the **style** attribute.
- Style rules generally are commented out within the **<style>** element to avoid interpretation by nonconforming browsers.

<sub> (Subscript)

This element renders its content as subscripted text.

Syntax

```
<sub
     class="class name(s)"
     dir="ltr | rtl"
     id="unique alphanumeric string"
     lang="language code"
     style="style information"
     title="advisory text"
     onclick="script"
     ondblclick="script"
     onkeydown="script"
     onkeypress="script"
     onkeyup="script"
     onmousedown="script"
     onmousemove="script"
     onmouseout="script"
     onmouseover="script"
     onmouseup="script">

</sub>
```

Attributes and Events Defined by Internet Explorer 4

```
     language="javascript | jscript | vbs | vbscript"
     ondragstart="script"
     onhelp="script"
     onselectstart="script"
```

Attributes and Events Defined by Internet Explorer 5.5

```
     accesskey="key"
     contenteditable="false | true | inherit"
     hidefocus="true | false"
     tabindex="number"
```

Attributes

accesskey   This attribute specifies a keyboard navigation accelerator for the element. Pressing ALT or a similar key (depending on the browser and operating system) in association with the specified key selects the anchor element correlated with that key.

class   See "Core Attributes Reference," earlier in this chapter.

contenteditable   This proprietary Microsoft attribute allows users to edit content rendered in the Internet Explorer 5.5 browser. Values are **false**, **true**, and **inherit**. A value of **false** will prevent content from being edited by users; **true** will allow editing. The default value, **inherit**, applies the value of the affected element's parent element.

dir   See "Language Reference," earlier in this chapter.

hidefocus   This proprietary element, introduced with Internet Explorer 5.5, hides focus on an element's content. Focus must be applied to the element using the **tabindex** attribute.

id   See "Core Attributes Reference," earlier in this chapter.

lang   See "Language Reference," earlier in this chapter.

language   In the Microsoft implementation, this attribute specifies the scripting language to be used with an associated script bound to the element, typically through an event handler attribute. Possible values might include **javascript**, **jscript**, **vbs**, and **vbscript**. Other values that include the version of the language used, such as **JavaScript1.1**, also might be possible.

style   See "Core Attributes Reference," earlier in this chapter.

tabindex   This attribute uses a number to identify the object's position in the tabbing order for keyboard navigation using the TAB key. Internet Explorer 5.5 applies this attribute to the **sub** element; under IE 5.5, this focus can be disabled with the **hidefocus** attribute.

title   See "Core Attributes Reference," earlier in this chapter.

Attribute and Event Support

Netscape 4   class, **id**, **lang**, and **style** are implied.

Internet Explorer 4   All attributes and events defined by the
W3C and Internet Explorer 4, except **dir**.

Internet Explorer 5.5   All attributes and events.

Event Handlers
See "Events Reference," earlier in this chapter.

Example
```
Here is some <sub>subscripted</sub> text.
```

Compatibility

> HTML 3.2, 4, and 4.01, XHTML 1.0
> Internet Explorer 2, 3, 4, 5, and 5.5
> Netscape 2, 3, 4–4.7, 6
> Opera 4.0
> WebTV

Notes

- The HTML 3.2 specification supports no attributes for the
  <sub> element.

<sup> (Superscript)

This element renders its content as superscripted text.

Syntax
```
<sup
    class="class name(s)"
    dir="ltr | rtl"
    id="unique alphanumeric string"
    lang="language code"
    style="style information"
    title="advisory text"
    onclick="script"
    ondblclick="script"
    onkeydown="script"
    onkeypress="script"
    onkeyup="script"
    onmousedown="script"
    onmousemove="script"
    onmouseout="script"
    onmouseover="script"
```

```
        onmouseup="script">

</sup>
```

Attributes and Events Defined by Internet Explorer 4

```
        language="javascript | jscript | vbs | vbscript"
        ondragstart="script"
        onhelp="script"
        onselectstart="script"
```

Attributes and Events Defined by Internet Explorer 5.5

```
        accesskey="key"
        contenteditable="false | true | inherit"
        hidefocus="true | false"
        tabindex="number"
```

Attributes

accesskey   This attribute specifies a keyboard navigation accelerator for the element. Pressing ALT or a similar key (depending on the browser and operating system) in association with the specified key selects the anchor element correlated with that key.

class   See "Core Attributes Reference," earlier in this chapter.

contenteditable   This proprietary Microsoft attribute allows users to edit content rendered in the Internet Explorer 5.5 browser. Values are **false**, **true**, and **inherit**. A value of **false** will prevent content from being edited by users; **true** will allow editing. The default value, **inherit**, applies the value of the affected element's parent element.

dir   See "Language Reference," earlier in this chapter.

hidefocus   This proprietary element, introduced with Internet Explorer 5.5, hides focus on an element's content. Focus must be applied to the element using the **tabindex** attribute.

id   See "Core Attributes Reference," earlier in this chapter.

lang   See "Language Reference," earlier in this chapter.

language   In the Microsoft implementation, this attribute specifies the scripting language to be used with an associated script bound to the element, typically through an event handler attribute. Possible values might include **javascript**, **jscript**, **vbs**, and **vbscript**. Other values that include the version of the language used, such as **JavaScript1.1**, also might be possible.

style   See "Core Attributes Reference," earlier in this chapter.

tabindex   This attribute uses a number to identify the object's position in the tabbing order for keyboard navigation using the TAB key. Internet Explorer 5.5 applies this attribute to the **sup** element; under IE 5.5, this focus can be disabled with the **hidefocus** attribute.

title   See "Core Attributes Reference," earlier in this chapter.

Attribute and Event Support

Netscape 4   **class**, **id**, **lang**, and **style** are implied.

Internet Explorer 4   All attributes and events defined by the W3C and Internet Explorer 4, except **dir**.

Internet Explorer 5.5   All attributes and events.

Event Handlers
See "Events Reference," earlier in this chapter.

Example
```
Here is some <sup>superscripted</sup> text.
```

Compatibility

> HTML 3.2, 4, and 4.01, XHTML 1.0
> Internet Explorer 2, 3, 4, 5, and 5.5
> Netscape 2, 3, 4–4.7, 6
> Opera 4.0
> WebTV

Notes

- The HTML 3.2 specification defines no attributes for this element.

\<table\> (Table)

This element is used to define a table. Tables are used to organize data as well as to provide structure for laying out pages.

Syntax

```
<table
    align="center | left | right" (transitional)
    bgcolor="color name | #RRGGBB" (transitional)
    border="pixels"
    cellpadding="pixels"
    cellspacing="pixels"
    class="class name(s)"
    datapagesize="number of records to display"
    dir="ltr | rtl"
    frame="above | below | border | box | hsides |
           lhs | rhs | void | vsides"
    id="unique alphanumeric identifier"
    lang="language code"
    rules="all | cols | groups | none | rows"
    style="style information"
    summary="summary information"
    title="advisory text"
    width="percentage | pixels"
    onclick="script"
    ondblclick="script"
    onkeydown="script"
    onkeypress="script"
    onkeyup="script"
    onmousedown="script"
    onmousemove="script"
    onmouseout="script"
    onmouseover="script"
    onmouseup="script">

</table>
```

Attributes and Events Defined by Internet Explorer 4

```
    background="url"
    bordercolor="color name | #RRGGBB"
    bordercolordark="color name | #RRGGBB"
    bordercolorlight="color name | #RRGGBB"
    cols="number"
    datasrc="data source id"
    height="percentage | pixels"
    language="javascript | jscript | vbs | vbscript"
    onafterupdate="script"
    onbeforeupdate="script"
    onblur="script"
    ondragstart="script"
    onfocus="script"
    onhelp="script"
    onresize="script"
```

```
onrowenter="script"
onrowexit="script"
onselectstart="script"
```

Attributes and Events Defined by Internet Explorer 5.5

```
accesskey="key"
hidefocus="true | false"
tabindex="number"
```

Attributes Defined by Netscape 4

```
background="url of image" file
bordercolor="color name | #RRGGBB"
cols="number of columns"
height="pixels"
hspace="pixels"
vspace="pixels"
```

Attributes Defined by WebTV

```
align="bleedleft | bleedright | justify"
background="url of image file"
cellborder="pixels"
gradangle="gradient angle"
gradcolor="color value"
href="url"
hspace="pixels"
name="string"
nowrap
transparency="number (0-100)"
vspace="pixels"
```

Attributes

accesskey   This attribute specifies a keyboard navigation accelerator for the element. Pressing ALT or a similar key (depending on the browser and operating system) in association with the specified key selects the anchor element correlated with that key.

align   This attribute specifies the alignment of the table with respect to surrounding text. The HTML 4.01 specification defines **center**, **left**, and **right**. WebTV also defines **bleedleft** and **bleedright**, which cause the table to bleed over the right and left margins of the page, and **justify**, which is used to justify the table within the browser window. Some browsers also might support alignment values, such as **absmiddle**, that are common to block objects.

background   This nonstandard attribute, which is supported by Internet Explorer, Netscape, and WebTV, specifies the URL of a background image for the table. The image is tiled if it is smaller than the table dimensions. Netscape displays the background image in each table cell, rather than behind the complete table like in Internet Explorer.

bgcolor   This attribute specifies a background color for a table. Its value can be either a named color, such as **red**, or a color specified in the hexadecimal *#RRGGBB* format, such as **#FF0000**.

border   This attribute specifies in pixels the width of a table's borders. A value of **0** makes a borderless table, which is useful for graphic layout.

bordercolor   This attribute, supported by Internet Explorer 4 and Netscape 4, is used to set the border color for a table. The attribute should be used only with a positive value for the **border** attribute. The value of the attribute can be either a named color, such as **green**, or a color specified in the hexadecimal *#RRGGBB* format, such as **#00FF00**. Internet Explorer colors the entire table border, including cell borders; Netscape colors only the outer border of the table.

bordercolordark   This Internet Explorer–specific attribute specifies the darker of two border colors used to create a three-dimensional effect for cell borders. It must be used with the **border** attribute set to a positive value. The attribute value can be either a named color, such as **blue**, or a color specified in the hexadecimal *#RRGGBB* format, such as **#00FF00**.

bordercolorlight   This Internet Explorer–specific attribute specifies the lighter of two border colors used to create a three-dimensional effect for cell borders. It must be used with the **border** attribute set to a positive value. The attribute value can be either a named color, such as **red**, or a color specified in the hexadecimal *#RRGGBB* format, such as **#FF0000**.

cellborder   In the WebTV implementation, this attribute sets the width in pixels of the border between table cells. If this value is not present, the default border as specified by the **border** attribute is used.

cellpadding   This attribute sets the width in pixels between the edge of a cell and its content.

cellspacing This attribute sets the width in pixels between individual cells.

class See "Core Attributes Reference," earlier in this chapter.

cols This attribute specifies the number of columns in the table and is used to help quickly calculate the size of the table. This attribute was part of the preliminary specification of HTML 4.0, but was later dropped. A few browsers, notably Netscape 4 and higher, already support it.

datapagesize The value of this Microsoft-specific attribute is the number of records that can be displayed in the table when data binding is used.

datasrc The value of this Microsoft-specific attribute is an identifier indicating the data source to pull data from.

dir See "Language Reference," earlier in this chapter.

frame This attribute specifies which edges of a table are to display a border frame. A value of **above** indicates only the top edge; **below** indicates only the bottom edge; and **border** and **box** indicate all edges, which is the default when the **border** attribute is a positive integer. A value of **hsides** indicates only the top and bottom edges should be displayed; **lhs** indicates the left-hand edge should be displayed; **rhs** indicates the right-hand edge should be displayed; **vsides** indicates the left and right edges both should be displayed; and **void** indicates no border should be displayed.

gradangle This WebTV-specific attribute defines the gradient angle for a table, ranging from 90 to –90 degrees. **gradangle="0"** yields a left-to-right gradient, whereas **gradangle="90"** yields a top-to-bottom gradient. The beginning color of the gradient is defined by the **bgcolor** attribute, and the ending color is defined by the **gradcolor** attribute.

gradcolor This WebTV-specific attribute defines the end color of a table's background gradient, in conjunction with the gradient angle defined by the **gradangle** attribute and the starting color defined by the **bgcolor** attribute.

height For Netscape 4, this attribute allows the author to specify the height of the table in pixels. Internet Explorer 4 allows both pixels and percentages.

hidefocus   This proprietary element, introduced with Internet Explorer 5.5, hides focus on an element's content. Focus must be applied to the element using the **tabindex** attribute.

href   This WebTV-specific attribute is used to make the entire table function as a hyperlink anchor to the specified URL.

2

hspace   This Netscape-specific attribute indicates the horizontal space in pixels between the table and surrounding content. This attribute also is supported by WebTV but, oddly, not by Internet Explorer.

id   See "Core Attributes Reference," earlier in this chapter.

lang   See "Language Reference," earlier in this chapter.

language   In the Microsoft implementation, this attribute specifies the scripting language to be used with an associated script bound to the element, typically through an event handler attribute. Possible values might include **javascript**, **jscript**, **vbs**, and **vbscript**. Other values that include the version of the language used, such as **JavaScript1.1**, also might be possible.

name   This WebTV attribute is used to assign the table a unique name. It is synonymous with the **id** attribute.

nowrap   This WebTV-specific attribute keeps table rows from wrapping if they extend beyond the right margin. The attribute requires no value.

rules   This attribute controls the display of dividing rules within a table. A value of **all** specifies dividing rules for rows and columns. A value of **cols** specifies dividing rules for columns only. A value of **groups** specifies horizontal dividing rules between groups of table cells defined by the **<thead>**, **<tbody>**, **<tfoot>**, or **<colgroup>** elements. A value of **rows** specifies dividing rules for rows only. A value of **NONE** indicates no dividing rules and is the default.

style   See "Core Attributes Reference," earlier in this chapter.

summary   This attribute is used to provide a text summary of the table's purpose and structure. This element is used for accessibility, and its presence is important for nonvisual user agents.

tabindex   This attribute uses a number to identify the object's position in the tabbing order for keyboard navigation using the TAB key. Internet Explorer 5.5 applies this attribute to the **table**

element; under IE 5.5, this focus can be disabled with the
hidefocus attribute.

title   See "Core Attributes Reference," earlier in this chapter.

transparency   This WebTV-specific attribute specifies the
degree of transparency of the table. Values range from **0** (totally
opaque) to **100** (totally transparent). A value of **50** is optimized for
fast rendering.

vspace   This Netscape attribute indicates the vertical space in
pixels between the table and surrounding content. This attribute
also is supported by WebTV but, oddly, not by Internet Explorer.

width   This attribute specifies the width of the table either in
pixels or as a percentage value of the enclosing window.

Attribute and Event Support

Netscape 4   **align (left | right)**, **bgcolor**, **border**, **cellpadding**,
cellspacing, **cols**, **height**, **hpace**, **vspace**, and **width**. (**class**, **id**,
lang, and **style** are implied.)

Internet Explorer 4   All W3C-defined attributes and events
except **dir** and **summary**, and all attributes and events defined
by Internet Explorer 4.

Internet Explorer 5.5   All attributes and events defined by
the W3C, Internet Explorer 4, and Internet Explorer 5.5.

WebTV   **align (bleedleft | bleedright | center | left | right)**,
background, **bgcolor**, **border**, **cellpadding**, **cellspacing**, **gradangle**,
gradcolor, **hspace**, **id**, **nowrap**, **transparency**, and **width**.

Event Handlers
See "Events Reference," earlier in this chapter.

Examples

```
<table bgcolor="white" border="2">
    <tr>
        <td>Cell 1</td>
        <td>Cell 2</td>
        <td>Cell 3</td>
        <td>Cell 4</td>
    </tr>
```

2

```
      <tr>
         <td>Cell 5</td>
         <td>Cell 6</td>
      </tr>
   </table>

<table rules="all" bgcolor="yellow">
<caption>Widgets by Area</caption>
<thead align="center" bgcolor="green" valign="middle">
   <td>This is a Header</td>
</thead>

<tfoot align="right" bgcolor="red" valign="bottom">
   <td>This is part of the footer.</td>
   <td>This is also part of the footer.</td>
</tfoot>

<tbody>
   <tr>
      <td> </td>
      <th>Regular Widget</th>
      <th>Super Widget</th>
   </tr>

   <tr>
      <th>West Coast</th>
      <td>10</td>
      <td>12</td>
   </tr>

   <tr>
      <th>East Coast</th>
      <td>1</td>
      <td>20</td>
   </tr>
</tbody>
</table>
```

Compatibility

HTML 3.2, 4, and 4.01, XHTML 1.0
Internet Explorer 2, 3, 4, 5, and 5.5
Netscape 1.1, 2, 3, 4–4.7, 6
Opera 4.0
WebTV

Notes

- In addition to displaying tabular data, tables are used to support graphic layout and design.
- The HTML 4.01 specification reserves the future use of the **datafld**, **dataformatas**, and **datasrc** attributes for the **<table>** element.
- The HTML 3.2 specification defines only the **align**, **border**, **cellpadding**, **cellspacing**, and **width** attributes for the **<table>** element.
- The **cols** attribute might provide an undesirable result under Netscape, which assumes the size of each column in the table is exactly the same.

<tbody> (Table Body)

This element is used to group the rows within the body of a table so that common alignment and style defaults can easily be set for numerous cells.

Syntax

```
<tbody
        align="center | char | justify | left | right"
        char="character"
        charoff="offset"
        class="class name(s)"
        dir="ltr | rtl"
        id="unique alphanumeric identifier"
        lang="language code"
        style="style information"
        title="advisory text"
        valign="baseline | bottom | middle | top"
        onclick="script"
        ondblclick="script"
        onkeydown="script"
        onkeypress="script"
        onkeyup="script"
        onmousedown="script"
        onmousemove="script"
        onmouseout="script"
        onmouseover="script"
        onmouseup="script">

</tbody>
```

Syntax

Under the XHTML 1.0 specification, the closing tag **</tbody>** no longer can be considered optional.

Attributes and Events Defined by Internet Explorer 4

```
bgcolor="color name | #RRGGBB"
language="javascript | jscript | vbs | vbscript"
valign="center"
ondragstart="script"
onhelp="script"
onselectstart="script"
```

Attributes and Events Defined by Internet Explorer 5.5

```
accesskey="key"
hidefocus="true | false"
tabindex="number"
```

Attributes

accesskey   This attribute specifies a keyboard navigation accelerator for the element. Pressing ALT or a similar key (depending on the browser and operating system) in association with the specified key selects the anchor element correlated with that key.

align   This attribute is used to align the contents of the cells within the **<tbody>** element. Common values are **center**, **justify**, **left**, and **right**. The HTML 4.01 specification also defines a value of **char**. When **align** is set to **char**, the attribute **char** must be present and set to the character to which cells should be aligned. A common use of this approach would be to set cells to align on a decimal point.

bgcolor   This attribute specifies a background color for the cells within the **<tbody>** element. Its value can be either a named color, such as **red**, or a color specified in the hexadecimal *#RRGGBB* format, such as **#FF0000**.

char   This attribute is used to define the character to which element contents are aligned when the **align** attribute is set to the **char** value.

charoff   This attribute contains an offset as a positive or negative integer to align characters as related to the **char** value. A value of **2**, for example, would align characters in a cell two characters to the right of the character defined by the **char** attribute.

class   See "Core Attributes Reference," earlier in this chapter.

dir   See "Language Reference," earlier in this chapter.

hidefocus   This proprietary element, introduced with Internet Explorer 5.5, hides focus on an element's content. Focus must be applied to the element using the **tabindex** attribute.

id   See "Core Attributes Reference," earlier in this chapter.

lang   See "Language Reference," earlier in this chapter.

language   In the Microsoft implementation, this attribute specifies the scripting language to be used with an associated script bound to the element, typically through an event handler attribute. Possible values might include **javascript**, **jscript**, **vbs**, and **vbscript**. Other values that include the version of the language used, such as **JavaScript1.1**, also might be possible.

style   See "Core Attributes Reference," earlier in this chapter.

tabindex   This attribute uses a number to identify the object's position in the tabbing order for keyboard navigation using the TAB key. Internet Explorer 5.5 applies this attribute to the **tbody** element; under IE 5.5, this focus can be disabled with the **hidefocus** attribute.

title   See "Core Attributes Reference," earlier in this chapter.

valign   This attribute is used to set the vertical alignment for the table cells with the <tbody> element. HTML 4.01 defines **baseline**, **bottom**, **middle**, and **top**. Internet Explorer replaces **middle** with **center**; the effect should be the same.

Attribute and Event Support

Internet Explorer 4   All W3C-defined attributes and events except **char**, **charoff**, and **dir**. (Note: Internet Explorer 4 does not support the **char** and **justify** values for **align**, nor the **middle** value for **valign**.)

Internet Explorer 5.5   All W3C-defined attributes and events except **char** and **charoff**, and all attributes and events defined by Internet Explorer 4 and 5.5.

Event Handlers

See "Events Reference," earlier in this chapter.

Example

```
<table rule="all" bgcolor="yellow">

<tbody align="center" bgcolor="red" style="bodystyle"
      valign="baseline">
   <tr>
      <td> </td>
      <th>Regular Widget</th>
      <th>Super Widget</th>
   </tr>

   <tr>
      <th>West Coast</th>
      <td>10</td>
      <td>12</td>
   </tr>

   <tr>
      <th>East Coast</th>
      <td>1</td>
      <td>20</td>
   </tr>
</tbody>
</table>
```

Compatibility

> HTML 4, 4.01, XHTML 1.0
> Internet Explorer 4, 5, and 5.5
> Netscape 6

Notes

- This element is contained by the **<table>** element and contains one or more table rows as indicated by the **<tr>** element.
- For XHTML compatibility, the closing **</tbody>** tag must be used with this element.

<td> (Table Data)

This element specifies a data cell in a table. The element should occur within a table row as defined by the **<tr>** element.

Syntax

```
<td
     abbr="abbreviation"
     align="center | justify | left | right"
     axis="group name"
     bgcolor="color name | #RRGGBB" (transitional)
     char="character"
     charoff="offset"
     class="class name"
     colspan="number"
     dir="ltr | rtl"
     headers="space-separated list of associated header
              cells' id values"
     height="pixels" (transitional)
     id="unique alphanumeric identifier"
     lang="language code"
     nowrap (transitional)
     rowspan="number"
     scope="col | colgroup | row | rowgroup"
     style="style information"
     title="advisory text"
     valign="baseline | bottom | middle | top"
     width="pixels" (transitional)
     onclick="script"
     ondblclick="script"
     onkeydown="script"
     onkeypress="script"
     onkeyup="script"
     onmousedown="script"
     onmousemove="script"
     onmouseout="script"
     onmouseover="script"
     onmouseup="script">

</td>
```

XHTML Syntax

Under the XHTML 1.0 specification, the closing **</td>** tag is mandatory.

Attributes and Events Defined by Internet Explorer 4

```
background="url of image file"
bordercolor="color name | #RRGGBB"
bordercolordark="color name | #RRGGBB"
bordercolorlight="color name | #RRGGBB"
language="javascript | jscript | vbs | vbscript"
valign="center"
onafterupdate="script"
onbeforeupdate="script"
onblur="script"
ondragstart="script"
onfocus="script"
onhelp="script"
onresize="script"
onrowenter="script"
onrowexit="script"
onscroll="script"
onselectstart="script"
```

Attributes and Events Defined by Internet Explorer 5.5

```
accesskey="key"
hidefocus="true | false"
tabindex="number"
```

Attributes Defined by Netscape 4

```
background="url of image file"
bordercolor="color name | #RRGGBB"
```

Attributes Defined by WebTV

```
absheight="pixels"
abswidth="pixels"
background="url of image file"
gradangle="gradient angle"
gradcolor="color"
maxlines="number"
transparency="number (0-100)"
```

Attributes

abbr   The value of this attribute is an abbreviated name for a header cell. This might be useful when attempting to display large tables on small screens.

absheight This WebTV-specific attribute sets the absolute height of a cell in pixels. Content that does not fit within this height is clipped.

abswidth This WebTV-specific attribute sets the absolute width of a cell in pixels. Content that does not fit within this width is clipped.

accesskey This attribute specifies a keyboard navigation accelerator for the element. Pressing ALT or a similar key (depending on the browser and operating system) in association with the specified key selects the anchor element correlated with that key.

align This attribute is used to align the contents of the cells within the <**tbody**> element. Common values are **center**, **justify**, **left**, and **right**.

axis This attribute is used to provide a name for a group of related headers.

background This nonstandard attribute, which is supported by Internet Explorer, Netscape, and WebTV, specifies the URL of a background image for the table cell. The image is tiled if it is smaller than the cell's dimensions.

bgcolor This attribute specifies a background color for a table cell. Its value can be either a named color, such as **red**, or a color specified in the hexadecimal *#RRGGBB* format, such as **#FF0000**. (Netscape Navigator often fails to render a cell with a colored background unless a nonbreaking space, at least, is inserted in the cell.)

bordercolor This attribute, supported by Internet Explorer and Netscape, is used to set the border color for a table cell. The attribute should be used only with a positive value for the **border** attribute. The value of the attribute can be either a named color, such as **green**, or a color specified in the hexadecimal *#RRGGBB* format, such as **#00FF00**.

bordercolordark This Internet Explorer–specific attribute specifies the darker of two border colors used to create a three-dimensional effect for a cell's borders. It must be used with the **border** attribute set to a positive value. The attribute value can be either a named color, such as **blue**, or a color specified in the hexadecimal *#RRGGBB* format, such as **#00FF00**.

bordercolorlight   This Internet Explorer–specific attribute specifies the lighter of two border colors used to create a three-dimensional effect for a cell's borders. It must be used with the **border** attribute set to a positive value. The attribute value can be either a named color, such as **red**, or a color specified in the hexadecimal *#RRGGBB* format, such as **#FF0000**.

char   This attribute is used to define the character to which element contents are aligned when the **align** attribute is set to the **char** value.

charoff   This attribute contains an offset as a positive or negative integer to align characters as related to the **char** value. A value of **2**, for example, would align characters in a cell two characters to the right of the character defined by the **char** attribute.

class   See "Core Attributes Reference," earlier in this chapter.

colspan   This attribute takes a numeric value that indicates how many columns wide a cell should be. This is useful to create tables with cells of different widths.

dir   See "Language Reference," earlier in this chapter.

gradangle   This WebTV-specific attribute defines the gradient angle for a table cell, ranging from 90 to –90 degrees. **gradangle="0"** yields a left-to-right gradient, while **gradangle="90"** yields a top-to-bottom gradient. The beginning color of the gradient is defined by the **bgcolor** attribute, and the ending color is defined by the **gradcolor** attribute.

gradcolor   This WebTV-specific attribute defines the end color of a table cell's background gradient, in conjunction with the gradient angle defined by the **gradangle** attribute and the starting color defined by the **bgcolor** attribute.

headers   This attribute takes a space-separated list of **id** values that correspond to the header cells related to this cell.

height   This attribute indicates the height of the cell in pixels.

hidefocus   This proprietary element, introduced with Internet Explorer 5.5, hides focus on an element's content. Focus must be applied to the element using the **tabindex** attribute.

id   See "Core Attributes Reference," earlier in this chapter.

lang See "Language Reference," earlier in this chapter.

language In the Microsoft implementation, this attribute specifies the scripting language to be used with an associated script bound to the element, typically through an event handler attribute. Possible values might include **javascript**, **jscript**, **vbs**, and **vbscript**. Other values that include the version of the language used, such as **JavaScript1.1**, also might be possible.

maxlines This WebTV-specific attribute takes a numeric argument indicating the maximum number of content lines to display. Content beyond these lines is clipped.

nowrap This attribute keeps the content within a table cell from automatically wrapping.

rowspan This attribute takes a numeric value that indicates how many rows high a table cell should span. This attribute is useful in defining tables with cells of different heights.

scope This attribute specifies the table cells that the current cell provides header information for. A value of **col** indicates that the cell is a header for the the rest of the column below it. A value of **colgroup** indicates that the cell is a header for its current column group. A value of **row** indicates that that the cell contains header information for the rest of the row it is in. A value of **rowgroup** indicates that the cell is a header for its row group. This attribute might be used in place of the **header** attribute and is useful for rendering assistance by nonvisual browsers. This attribute was added very late to the HTML 4 specification so support for this attribute is minimal.

style See "Core Attributes Reference," earlier in this chapter.

tabindex This attribute uses a number to identify the object's position in the tabbing order for keyboard navigation using the TAB key. Internet Explorer 5.5 applies this attribute to the **td** element; under IE 5.5, this focus can be disabled with the **hidefocus** attribute.

title See "Core Attributes Reference," earlier in this chapter.

transparency This WebTV-specific attribute specifies the degree of transparency of the table cell. Values range from **0** (totally opaque) to **100** (totally transparent). A value of **50** is optimized for fast rendering.

valign This attribute is used to set the vertical alignment for the table cell. HTML 4 defines **baseline, bottom, middle,** and **top.** Internet Explorer replaces **middle** with **center**; the effect should be the same.

width This attribute specifies the width of a cell in pixels.

Attribute and Event Support

Netscape 4 align, background, bgcolor, bordercolor, colspan, height, nowrap, rowspan, valign, and width. (class, id, lang, and style are implied.)

Internet Explorer 4 All W3C-defined attributes and events except **abbr, axis, char, charoff, dir, headers,** and **height,** and all attributes and events defined by Internet Explorer 4. (Note: Internet Explorer 4 does not support the **justify** value for **align,** nor the **middle** value for **valign.**)

Internet Explorer 5.5 All W3C-defined attributes and events except **abbr, axis, char, charoff,** and **headers,** and all attributes and events defined by Internet Explorer 4 and 5.5.

WebTV align (center | left | right), background, bgcolor, colspan, gradangle, gradcolor, height, rowspan, transparency, valign (baseline | bottom | middle | top), and width.

Event Handlers

See "Events Reference," earlier in this chapter.

Examples

```
<table>
<tr>
<td align="left" valign="top">
 Put me in the top left corner.
</td>
<td align="right" bgcolor="red" valign="bottom">
 Put me in the bottom right corner.
</td>
</tr>
</table>


<table border="1" width="80%">
  <tr>
    <td colspan="3">
    A pretty wide cell
    </td>
```

```
<tr>
    <td>Item 2</td>
    <td>Item 3</td>
    <td>Item 4</td>
</tr>
</table>
```

Compatibility

HTML 3.2, 4, and 4.0, XHTML 1.0
Internet Explorer 2, 3, 4, 5, and 5.5
Netscape 1.1, 2, 3, 4–4.7, 6
Opera 4.0
WebTV

Notes

- Under the XHTML 1.0 specification, the closing **</td>** tag ceases to be optional.

- The HTML 3.2 specification defines only **align**, **colspan**, **height**, **nowrap**, **rowspan**, **valign**, and **width** attributes.

- This element should always be within the **<tr>** element.

<textarea> (Multiline Text Input)

This element specifies a multiline text input field contained within a form.

Syntax

```
<textarea
    accesskey="character"
    class="class name"
    cols="number"
    dir="ltr | rtl"
    disabled
    id="unique alphanumeric identifier"
    lang="language code"
    name="unique alphanumeric identifier"
    readonly
    rows="number"
    style="style information"
    tabindex="number"
    title="advisory text"
    onblur="script"
    onchange="script"
    onclick="script"
```

```
ondblclick="script"
onfocus="script"
onkeydown="script"
onkeypress="script"
onkeyup="script"
onmousedown="script"
onmousemove="script"
onmouseout="script"
onmouseover="script"
onmouseup="script"
onselect="script">
```

```
</textarea>
```

Attributes and Events Defined by Internet Explorer 4

```
align="absbottom | absmiddle | baseline | bottom |
      left | middle | right | texttop | tcp"
datafld="column name"
datasrc="data source ID"
language="javascript | jscript | vbs | vbscript"
wrap="off | physical | virtual"
onafterupdate="script"
onbeforeupdate="script"
ondragstart="script"
onhelp="script"
onresize="script"
onrowenter="script"
onrowexit="script"
onscroll="script"
onselectstart="script"
onstart="script"
```

Attributes and Events Defined by Internet Explorer 5.5

```
contenteditable="false | true | inherit"
hidefocus="true | false"
```

Attributes Defined by Netscape 4

```
wrap="hard | off | soft"
```

Attributes Defined by WebTV

```
allcaps
autoactivate
autocaps
bgcolor="color name | #RRGGBB"
cursor="color name | #RRGGBB"
```

```
growable
nohardbreaks
nosoftbreaks
numbers
showkeyboard
usestyle
```

Attributes

accesskey   This Microsoft-specific attribute specifies a keyboard navigation accelerator for the element. Pressing ALT or a similar key in association with the specified character selects the form control correlated with that key sequence. Page designers are forewarned to avoid key sequences already bound to browsers.

align   Microsoft defines alignment values for this element. The values for this attribute should behave similarly to any included object or image.

allcaps   This WebTV-specific attribute renders all viewer-entered text in capital letters. This attribute requires no value.

autoactivate   This WebTV-specific attribute causes the text input control to immediately activate. This attribute requires no value.

autocaps   This WebTV-specific attribute renders the first letter of all viewer-entered words in a capital letter. This attribute requires no value.

bgcolor   This WebTV-specific attribute specifies the background color for the text input area. Its value can be either a named color, such as **red**, or a color specified in the hexadecimal *#RRGGBB* format, such as **#FF0000**. The default color for the **<textarea>** element under WebTV is **#EAEAEA**.

class   See "Core Attributes Reference," earlier in this chapter.

cols   This attribute sets the width in characters of the text area. The typical default values for the size of a **<textarea>** element when this attribute is not set is **20** characters.

contenteditable   This proprietary Microsoft attribute allows users to edit content rendered in the Internet Explorer 5.5 browser. Values are **false**, **true**, and **inherit**. A value of **false** will prevent content from being edited by users; **true** will allow editing. The default value, **inherit**, applies the value of the affected element's parent element.

2

cursor   This WebTV-specific attribute is used to indicate the cursor color for the text input area. Its value can be either a named color, such as **red**, or a color specified in the hexadecimal *#RRGGBB* format, such as **#FF0000**. The default value for the cursor color in the WebTV browser is **darkblue (#3333AA)**.

datafld   This attribute is used to indicate the column name in the data source that is bound to the content enclosed by the **<textarea>** element.

datasrc   The value of this attribute is an identifier indicating the data source to pull data from.

dir   See "Language Reference," earlier in this chapter.

disabled   This attribute is used to turn off a form control. Elements will not be submitted nor can they receive any focus from the keyboard or mouse. Disabled form controls will not be part of the tabbing order. The browser also can gray out the form that is disabled in order to indicate to the user that the form control is inactive. This attribute requires no value.

growable   This WebTV-specific attribute allows the text input area to expand vertically to accommodate extra text entered by the user. This attribute requires no value.

hidefocus   This proprietary element, introduced with Internet Explorer 5.5, hides focus on an element's content. Focus must be applied to the element using the **tabindex** attribute.

id   See "Core Attributes Reference," earlier in this chapter.

lang   See "Language Reference," earlier in this chapter.

language   In the Microsoft implementation, this attribute specifies the scripting language to be used with an associated script bound to the element, typically through an event handler attribute. Possible values might include **javascript**, **jscript**, **vbs**, and **vbscript**. Other values that include the version of the language used, such as **JavaScript1.1**, also might be possible.

name   This attribute allows a form control to be assigned a name so that it can be referenced by a scripting language. **Name** is supported by older browsers, such as Netscape 2 generation browsers, but the W3C encourages the use of the **id** attribute. For compatibility purposes, both attributes might have to be used.

nohardbreaks This WebTV-specific attribute causes a press of the ENTER key to select the next form element rather than causing a line break in the text input area. The attribute requires no value.

nosoftbreaks This attribute removes breaks automatically inserted into the text by line wrapping when the form is submitted. The attribute requires no value.

numbers This WebTV-specific attribute causes the number "1" to be selected in the onscreen keyboard in anticipation of the viewer entering a numeric value.

readonly This attribute prevents the form control's value from being changed. Form controls with this attribute set might receive focus from the user but might not be modified. Because they receive focus, a **readonly** form control will be part of the form's tabbing order. Finally the control's value will be sent on form submission. The attribute can be used with **<input>** only when **type** is set to **text** or **password**. The attribute also is used with the **<textarea>** element.

rows This attribute sets the number of rows in the text area. The value of the attribute should be a positive integer.

showkeyboard In the WebTV implementation, this attribute causes the onscreen keyboard to be displayed when the **<textarea>** element is selected.

style See "Core Attributes Reference," earlier in this chapter.

tabindex This attribute takes a numeric value indicating the position of the form control in the tabbing index for the form. Tabbing proceeds from the lowest positive **tabindex** value to the highest. Negative values for **tabindex** will leave the form control out of the tabbing order. When tabbing is not explicitly set, the browser can tab through items in the order they are encountered. Form controls that are disabled due to the presence of the **disabled** attribute will not be part of the tabbing index, although read-only controls will be.

title See "Core Attributes Reference," earlier in this chapter.

usestyle This WebTV-specific attribute causes text to be rendered in the style in effect for the page. The attribute requires no value.

wrap In Netscape and Microsoft browsers, this attribute controls word wrap behavior. A value of **off** for the attribute forces the

<textarea> not to wrap text, so the viewer must manually enter line breaks. A value of **hard** causes word wrap and includes line breaks in text submitted to the server. A value of **soft** causes word wrap but removes line breaks from text submitted to the server. Internet Explorer supports a value of **physical**, which is equivalent to Netcape's **hard** value, and a value of **virtual**, which is equivalent to Netscape's **soft** value. If the **wrap** attribute is not included, text will still wrap under Internet Explorer, but under Netscape it will scroll horizontally in the text box. It is always a good idea to include the **wrap** attribute.

Attribute and Event Support

Netscape 4   cols, name, rows, wrap (hard I off I soft), onblur, onchange, onfocus, and onselect. (class, id, lang, and style are implied.)

Internet Explorer 4   All W3C-defined events and attributes except **dir**, and all attributes and events defined by Internet Explorer 4.

Internet Explorer 4   All events and attributes defined by the W3C, Internet Explorer 4, and Internet Explorer 5.5.

WebTV   bgcolor, cols, cursor, name, rows, usestyle, onblur, onchange, and onfocus.

Event Handlers

See "Events Reference," earlier in this chapter.

Examples

```
<textarea name="CommentBox" cols="40" rows="8">
Default text in field
</textarea>

<textarea name="comment" rows="10" cols="40" wrap="virtual"
          align="center">
</textarea>
```

Compatibility

HTML 2, 3.2, 4, and 4.01, XHTML 1.0
Internet Explorer 2, 3, 4, 5, and 5.5
Netscape 1, 2, 3, 4–4.7, 6
Opera 4.0
WebTV

Notes

- Any text between the **<textarea>** and **</textarea>** tags is rendered as the default entry for the form control.
- The HTML 2.0 and 3.2 specifications define only the **cols**, **name**, and **rows** attribute for this element.
- The HTML 4.01 specification reserves the **datafld** and **datasrc** attributes for future use with the **<textarea>** element.

<tfoot> (Table Footer)

This element is used to group the rows within the footer of a table so that common alignment and style defaults can easily be set for numerous cells. This element might be particularly useful when setting a common footer for tables that are dynamically generated.

Syntax

```
<tfoot
     align="center | char | justify | left | right"
     bgcolor="color name | #RRGGBB" (transitional)
     char="character"
     charoff="offset"
     class="class name(s)"
     dir="ltr | rtl"
     id="unique alphanumeric identifier"
     lang="language code"
     style="style information"
     title="advisory text"
     valign="baseline | bottom | middle | top"
     onclick="script"
     ondblclick="script"
     onkeydown="script"
     onkeypress="script"
     onkeyup="script"
     onmousedown="script"
     onmousemove="script"
     onmouseout="script"
     onmouseover="script"
     onmouseup="script">

</tfoot>
```

XHTML Syntax

Under the XHTML 1.0 specification, the closing **</tfoot>** tag is mandatory.

Attributes and Events Defined by Internet Explorer 4

```
language="javascript | jscript | vbs | vbscript"
valign="center"
ondragstart="script"
onhelp="script"
onselectstart="script"
```

2

Attributes and Events Defined by Internet Explorer 5.5

```
accesskey="key"
hidefocus="true | false"
tabindex="number"
```

Attributes

accesskey   This attribute specifies a keyboard navigation accelerator for the element. Pressing ALT or a similar key (depending on the browser and operating system) in association with the specified key selects the anchor element correlated with that key.

align   This attribute is used to align the contents of the cells within the <tfoot> element. Common values are **center**, **justify**, **left**, and **right**. The HTML 4 specification also defines a value of **char**. When **align** is set to **char**, the attribute **char** must be present and set to the character to which cells should be aligned. A common use of this approach would be to set cells to align on a decimal point.

bgcolor   This attribute specifies a background color for the cells within the <tfoot> element. Its value can be either a named color, such as **red**, or a color specified in the hexadecimal #*RRGGBB* format, such as **#FF0000**.

char   This attribute is used to define the character to which element contents are aligned when the **align** attribute is set to the **char** value.

charoff   This attribute contains an offset as a positive or negative integer to align characters as related to the **char** value. A value of **2**, for example, would align characters in a cell two characters to the right of the character defined by the **char** attribute.

class   See "Core Attributes Reference," earlier in this chapter.

dir   See "Language Reference," earlier in this chapter.

hidefocus   This proprietary element, introduced with Internet Explorer 5.5, hides focus on an element's content. Focus must be applied to the element using the **tabindex** attribute.

id   See "Core Attributes Reference," earlier in this chapter.

lang   See "Language Reference," earlier in this chapter.

language   In the Microsoft implementation, this attribute specifies the scripting language to be used with an associated script bound to the element, typically through an event handler attribute. Possible values might include **javascript**, **jscript**, **vbs**, and **vbscript**. Other values that include the version of the language used, such as **JavaScript1.1**, also might be possible.

style   See "Core Attributes Reference," earlier in this chapter.

tabindex   This attribute uses a number to identify the object's position in the tabbing order for keyboard navigation using the TAB key. Internet Explorer 5.5 applies this attribute to the **tfoot** element; under IE 5.5, this focus can be disabled with the **hidefocus** attribute.

title   See "Core Attributes Reference," earlier in this chapter.

valign   This attribute is used to set the vertical alignment for the table cells with the **<tfoot>** element. HTML 4 defines **baseline**, **bottom**, **middle**, and **top**. Internet Explorer replaces **middle** with **center**; the effect should be the same.

Attribute and Event Support

Internet Explorer 4   All events and attributes except **char**, **charoff**, and **dir**. (Note: Internet Explorer 4 does not support the **justify** value for the **align** attribute.)

Internet Explorer 5.5   All W3C-defined attributes and events except **char** and **charoff**, and all attributes and events defined by Internet Explorer 4 and 5.5.

Event Handlers
None

Example

```
<table border="1" bgcolor="yellow" width="80%">
<tbody class="tablebody">
   <tr>
      <td>The contents of the table!</td>
   </tr>
</tbody>

<tfoot align="center" bgcolor="red" class="footer"
      valign="bottom">
   <td>This is part of the footer.</td>
   <td>This is also part of the footer.</td>
</tfoot>
</table>
```

Compatibility

> HTML 4, 4.01, XHTML 1.0
> Internet Explorer 4, 5, and 5.5
> Netscape 6

Notes

- This element is contained only by the **<table>** element and contains table rows as delimited by **<tr>** elements.

- Under the XHTML 1.0 specification, the closing **</tfoot>** tag ceases to be optional.

<th> (Table Header)

This element specifies a header cell in a table. The element should occur within a table row as defined by a **<tr>** element. The main difference between this element and **<td>** is that browsers might render table headers slightly differently.

Syntax

```
<th
    abbr="abbreviation"
    align="center | justify | left | right"
    axis="group name"
    bgcolor="color name | #RRGGBB" (transitional)
    char="character"
    charoff="offset"
    class="class name"
    colspan="number"
    dir="ltr | rtl"
```

```
headers="space-separated list of associated header
        cells' id values"
height="pixels" (transitional)
id="unique alphanumeric identifier"
lang="language code"
nowrap (transitional)
rowspan="number"
scope="col | colgroup | row | rowgroup"
style="style information"
title="advisory text"
valign="baseline | bottom | middle | top"
width="pixels" (transitional)
onclick="script"
ondblclick="script"
onkeydown="script"
onkeypress="script"
onkeyup="script"
onmousedown="script"
onmousemove="script"
onmouseout="script"
onmouseover="script"
onmouseup="script">
```

```
</th>
```

XHTML Syntax

Under the XHTML 1.0 specification, the closing **</th>** tag is mandatory.

Attributes and Events Defined by Internet Explorer 4

```
background="url of image" file
bordercolor="color name | #RRGGBB"
bordercolordark="color name | #RRGGBB"
bordercolorlight="color name | #RRGGBB"
language="javascript | jscript | vbs | vbscript"
valign="center"
ondragstart="script"
onhelp="script"
onscroll="script"
onselectstart="script"
```

Attributes and Events Defined by Internet Explorer 5.5

```
accesskey="key"
hidefocus="true | false"
tabindex="number"
```

Attributes Defined by Netscape 4

```
background="url of image file"
bordercolor="color name | #RRGGBB"
```

Attributes Defined by WebTV

```
absheight="pixels"
abswidth="pixels"
background="url of image" file
gradangle
gradcolor
maxlines="number"
transparency="number (0-100)"
```

Attributes

abbr   The value of this attribute is an abbreviated name for a header cell. This might be useful when attempting to display large tables on small screens.

absheight   This WebTV-specific attribute sets the absolute height of a cell in pixels. Content that does not fit within this height is clipped.

abswidth   This WebTV-specific attribute sets the absolute width of a cell in pixels. Content that does not fit within this width is clipped.

accesskey   This attribute specifies a keyboard navigation accelerator for the element. Pressing ALT or a similar key (depending on the browser and operating system) in association with the specified key selects the anchor element correlated with that key.

align   This attribute is used to align the contents of the cells within the **<tbody>** element. Common values are **center**, **justify**, **left**, and **right**.

axis   This attribute is used to provide a name for a group of related headers.

background   This nonstandard attribute, which is supported by Internet Explorer, Netscape, and WebTV, specifies the URL of a background image for the table cell. The image is tiled if it is smaller than the cell's dimensions.

bgcolor   This attribute specifies a background color for a table cell. Its value can be either a named color, such as red, or a color specified in the hexadecimal *#RRGGBB* format, such as **#FF0000**.

bordercolor   This attribute, supported by Internet Explorer and Netscape, is used to set the border color for a table cell. The attribute should be used only with a positive value for the **border** attribute. The value of the attribute can be either a named color, such as **green**, or a color specified in the hexadecimal *#RRGGBB* format, such as **#00FF00**.

bordercolordark   This Internet Explorer–specific attribute specifies the darker of two border colors used to create a three-dimensional effect for a cell's borders. It must be used with the **border** attribute set to a positive value. The attribute value can be either a named color, such as **blue**, or a color specified in the hexadecimal *#RRGGBB* format, such as **#00FF00**.

bordercolorlight   This Internet Explorer–specific attribute specifies the lighter of two border colors used to create a three-dimensional effect for a cell's borders. It must be used with the **border** attribute set to a positive value. The attribute value can be either a named color, such as **red**, or a color specified in the hexadecimal *#RRGGBB* format, such as **#FF0000**.

char   This attribute is used to define the character to which element contents are aligned when the **align** attribute is set to the **char** value.

charoff   This attribute contains an offset as a positive or negative integer to align characters as related to the **char** value. A value of **2**, for example, would align characters in a cell two characters to the right of the character defined by the **char** attribute.

class   See "Core Attributes Reference," earlier in this chapter.

colspan   This attribute takes a numeric value that indicates how many columns wide a cell should be. This is useful to create tables with cells of different widths.

dir   See "Language Reference," earlier in this chapter.

gradangle   This WebTV-specific attribute defines the gradient angle for a table header, ranging from 90 to –90 degrees. **gradangle="0"** yields a left-to-right gradient, whereas **gradangle="90"** yields a top-to-bottom gradient. The beginning color of the gradient is defined by the **bgcolor** attribute, and the ending color is defined by the **gradcolor** attribute.

2

gradcolor   This WebTV-specific attribute defines the end color of a table header's background gradient, in conjunction with the gradient angle defined by the **gradangle** attribute and the starting color defined by the **bgcolor** attribute.

headers   This attribute takes a space-separated list of **id** values that correspond to the header cells related to this cell.

height   This attribute indicates the height in pixels of the header cell.

hidefocus   This proprietary element, introduced with Internet Explorer 5.5, hides focus on an element's content. Focus must be applied to the element using the **tabindex** attribute.

id   See "Core Attributes Reference," earlier in this chapter.

lang   See "Language Reference," earlier in this chapter.

language   In the Microsoft implementation, this attribute specifies the scripting language to be used with an associated script bound to the element, typically through an event handler attribute. Possible values might include **javascript**, **jscript**, **vbs**, and **vbscript**. Other values that include the version of the language used, such as **JavaScript1.1**, also might be possible.

maxlines   This WebTV-specific attribute takes a numeric argument indicating the maximum number of content lines to display. Content beyond these lines is clipped.

nowrap   This attribute keeps the content within a table header cell from automatically wrapping.

rowspan   This attribute takes a numeric value that indicates how many rows high a table cell should span. This attribute is useful in defining tables with cells of different heights.

scope   This attribute specifies the table cells for which the current cell provides header information. A value of **col** indicates that the cell is a header for the the rest of the column below it. A value of **colgroup** indicates that the cell is a header for its current column group. A value of **row** indicates that that the cell contains header information for the rest of the row it is in. A value of **rowgroup** indicates that the cell is a header for its row group. This attribute can be used in place of the **header** attribute and is useful for rendering assistance by nonvisual browsers. This attribute was added very late to the HTML 4.0 specification so support for this attribute is minimal.

style   See "Core Attributes Reference," earlier in this chapter.

tabindex   This attribute uses a number to identify the object's position in the tabbing order for keyboard navigation using the TAB key. Internet Explorer 5.5 applies this attribute to the **th** element; under IE 5.5, this focus can be disabled with the **hidefocus** attribute.

title   See "Core Attributes Reference," earlier in this chapter.

transparency   This WebTV-specific attribute specifies the degree of transparency of the table header. Values range from **0** (totally opaque) to **100** (totally transparent). A value of **50** is optimized for fast rendering.

valign   This attribute is used to set the vertical alignment for the table cell. HTML 4 defines **baseline**, **bottom**, **middle**, and **top**. Internet Explorer further defines **center**, which should act just like **middle**.

width   This attribute specifies the width of a header cell in pixels.

Attribute and Event Support

Netscape 4   align, background, bgcolor, bordercolor, colspan, height, nowrap, rowspan, valign, and width. (class, id, lang, and style are implied.)

Internet Explorer 4   align (center | left | right), bgcolor, class, colspan, id, lang, nowrap, rowspan, style, title, and valign (baseline | bottom | top), all W3C-defined events, and all attributes and events defined by Internet Explorer 4.

Internet Explorer 5.5   All W3C-defined attributes and events except abbr, axis, char, and charoff, and all attributes and events defined by Internet Explorer 4 and 5.5.

WebTV   align (center | left | right), bgcolor, colspan, gradangle, gradcolor, nowrap, rowspan, transparency, valign (baseline | bottom | middle | top), and width.

Event Handlers

See "Events Reference," earlier in this chapter.

Examples

```
<table border="1">
   <tr>
      <th>Names</th>
      <th>Apples</th>
      <th>Oranges</th>
   </tr>

   <tr>
      <td>Bobby</td>
      <td>10</td>
      <td>5</td>
   </tr>

   <tr>
      <td>Ruby Sue</td>
      <td>20</td>
      <td>3</td>
   </tr>
</table>
```

Compatibility

HTML 3.2, 4, and 4.01, XHTML 1.0
Internet Explorer 2, 3, 4, 5, and 5.5
Netscape 1.1, 2, 3, 4–4.7, 6
Opera 4.0
WebTV

Notes

- The HTML 3.2 specification defines only **align**, **colspan**, **height**, **nowrap**, **rowspan**, **valign**, and **width** attributes.
- This element should always be within the **<tr>** element.
- Under the XHTML 1.0 specification, the closing **</th>** tag ceases to be optional.

<thead> (Table Header)

This element is used to group the rows within the header of a table so that common alignment and style defaults can easily be set for numerous cells. This element might be particularly useful when setting a common head for tables that are dynamically generated.

Syntax

```
<thead
    align="center | char | justify | left | right"
    char="character"
    charoff="offset"
    class="class name(s)"
    dir="ltr | rtl"
    id="unique alphanumeric identifier"
    lang="language code"
    style="style information"
    title="advisory text"
    valign="baseline | bottom | middle | top"
    onclick="script"
    ondblclick="script"
    onkeydown="script"
    onkeypress="script"
    onkeyup="script"
    onmousedown="script"
    onmousemove="script"
    onmouseout="script"
    onmouseover="script"
    onmouseup="script">

</thead>
```

XHTML Syntax

Under the XHTML 1.0 specification, the closing **</thead>** tag is mandatory.

Attributes and Events Defined by Internet Explorer 4

```
    bgcolor="color name | #RRGGBB"
    language="javascript | jscript | vbs | vbscript"
    valign="center"
    ondragstart="script"
    onhelp="script"
    onselectstart="script"
```

Attributes and Events Defined by Internet Explorer 5.5

```
    accesskey="key"
    hidefocus="true | false"
    tabindex="number"
```

2

Attributes

accesskey   This attribute specifies a keyboard navigation accelerator for the element. Pressing ALT or a similar key (depending on the browser and operating system) in association with the specified key selects the anchor element correlated with that key.

align   This attribute is used to align the contents of the cells within the **<thead>** element. Common values are **center**, **justify**, **left**, and **right**. The HTML 4 specification also defines a value of **char**. When **align** is set to **char**, the attribute **char** must be present and set to the character to which cells should be aligned. A common use of this approach would be to set cells to align on a decimal point.

bgcolor   This attribute specifies a background color for the cells within the **<thead>** element. Its value can be either a named color, such as **red**, or a color specified in the hexadecimal *#RRGGBB* format, such as **#FF0000**.

char   This attribute is used to define the character to which element contents are aligned when the **align** attribute is set to the **char** value.

charoff   This attribute contains an offset as a positive or negative integer to align characters as related to the **char** value. A value of **2**, for example, would align characters in a cell two characters to the right of the character defined by the **char** attribute.

class   See "Core Attributes Reference," earlier in this chapter.

dir   See "Language Reference," earlier in this chapter.

hidefocus   This proprietary element, introduced with Internet Explorer 5.5, hides focus on an element's content. Focus must be applied to the element using the **tabindex** attribute.

id   See "Core Attributes Reference," earlier in this chapter.

lang   See "Language Reference," earlier in this chapter.

language   In the Microsoft implementation, this attribute specifies the scripting language to be used with an associated script bound to the element, typically through an event handler attribute. Possible values might include **javascript**, **jscript**, **vbs**, and **vbscript**. Other values that include the version of the language used, such as **JavaScript1.1**, also might be possible.

style   See "Core Attributes Reference," earlier in this chapter.

tabindex   This attribute uses a number to identify the object's position in the tabbing order for keyboard navigation using the TAB key. Internet Explorer 5.5 applies this attribute to the **thead** element; under IE 5.5, this focus can be disabled with the **hidefocus** attribute.

title   See "Core Attributes Reference," earlier in this chapter.

valign   This attribute is used to set the vertical alignment for the table cells with the **<thead>** element. HTML 4.01 defines **baseline**, **bottom**, **middle**, and **top**. Internet Explorer replaces **middle** with **center**; the effect should be the same.

Attribute and Event Support

Internet Explorer 4   All attributes and events except **char**, **charoff**, and **dir**. (Note: Internet Explorer 4 does not support the **justify** value for the **align** attribute.)

Internet Explorer 5.5   All W3C-defined attributes and events except **char** and **charoff**, and all attributes and events defined by Internet Explorer 4 and 5.5.

Event Handlers

See "Events Reference," earlier in this chapter.

Example

```
<table border="1" bgcolor="yellow" width="80%">
<thead align="center" bgcolor="red" class="footer"
      valign="bottom">
   <td>This is the Important Table Headline</td>
</thead>

<tbody class="tablebody">
   <tr>
      <td>The contents of the table!</td>
   </tr>
</tbody>
</table>
```

Compatibility

HTML 4, 4.01, XHTML 1.0
Internet Explorer 3, 4, 5, and 5.5
Netscape 6

Notes

- This element is contained only by the **<table>** element and contains table rows as delimited by **<tr>** elements.

- Under the XHTML 1.0 specification, the closing **</thead>** tag ceases to be optional.

2

<title> (Document Title)

This element encloses the title of an HTML document. It must occur within a document's **<head>** element and must be present in all valid documents. Meaningful titles are very important because they are used for bookmarking a page and might be used by search engines attempting to index the document.

Syntax

```
<title
    dir="ltr | rtl"
    lang="language code">

</title>
```

Attributes Defined by Internet Explorer 4

```
    id="unique alphanumeric identifier"
    title="advisory text"
```

Attributes

dir   See "Language Reference," earlier in this chapter.

id   See "Core Attributes Reference," earlier in this chapter.

lang   See "Language Reference," earlier in this chapter.

title   See "Core Attributes Reference," earlier in this chapter.

Attribute and Event Support

Internet Explorer 4   **id** and **title**

Event Handlers

None

Example

`<head><title>`Big Company: Products: Super Widget`</title></head>`

Compatibility

> HTML 2, 3.2, 4, and 4.01
> Internet Explorer 2, 3, 4, 5, and 5.5
> Netscape 1, 2, 3, 4–4.7, 6
> Opera 4.0
> WebTV

Notes

- Meaningful names should provide information about the document. A poor title would be something like "My Home Page," whereas a better title would be "Joe Smith Home."

- Older versions of Netscape allowed for multiple occurrences of the `<title>` element. When multiple `<title>` elements were encountered, they could be used to simulate an animated title bar. This was a bug with the Netscape browser, however, and the effect of multiple `<title>` elements no longer works.

- Browsers can be extremely sensitive with the `<title>` element. If the title element is malformed or not closed, the page might not even render in the browser.

- The HTML 2.0 and 3.2 specifications define no attributes for the `<title>` element.

`<tr>` (Table Row)

This element specifies a row in a table. The individual cells of the row are defined by the `<th>` and `<td>` elements.

Syntax

```
<tr
    align="center | justify | left | right"
    bgcolor="color name | #RRGGBB" (transitional)
    char="character"
    charoff="offset"
    class="class name(s)"
    dir="ltr | rtl"
    id="unique alphanumeric identifier"
    lang="language code"
    style="style information"
    title="advisory text"
```

```
valign="baseline | bottom | middle | top"
onclick="script"
ondblclick="script"
onkeydown="script"
onkeypress="script"
onkeyup="script"
onmousedown="script"
onmousemove="script"
onmouseout="script"
onmouseover="script"
onmouseup="script">
```

2

```
</tr>
```

XHTML Syntax

Under the XHTML 1.0 specification, the closing **</tr>** tag is
mandatory.

Attributes and Events Defined by
Internet Explorer 4

```
bordercolor="color name | #RRGGBB"
bordercolordark="color name | #RRGGBB"
bordercolorlight="color name | #RRGGBB"
language="javascript | javascript | vbs | vbscript"
valign="center"
onafterupdate="script"
onbeforeupdate="script"
onblur="script"
ondragstart="script"
onfocus="script"
onhelp="script"
onresize="script"
onrowenter="script"
onrowexit="script"
onselectstart="script
```

Attributes and Events Defined by
Internet Explorer 5.5

```
accesskey="key"
hidefocus="true | false"
tabindex="number"
```

Attributes Defined by WebTV

```
nowrap
transparency="number (0-100)"
```

Attributes

accesskey This attribute specifies a keyboard navigation accelerator for the element. Pressing ALT or a similar key (depending on the browser and operating system) in association with the specified key selects the anchor element correlated with that key.

align This attribute is used to align the contents of the cells within the **<thead>** element. Common values are **center, justify, left,** and **right.**

bgcolor This attribute specifies a background color for all the cells in a row. Its value can be either a named color, such as **red,** or a color specified in the hexadecimal *#RRGGBB* format, such as **#FF0000.**

bordercolor This attribute, supported by Internet Explorer and Netscape, is used to set the border color for table cells in the row. The attribute should be used only with a positive value for the **border** attribute. The value of the attribute can be either a named color, such as **green,** or a color specified in the hexadecimal *#RRGGBB* format, such as **#00FF00.**

bordercolordark This Internet Explorer–specific attribute specifies the darker of two border colors used to create a three-dimensional effect for the cell's borders. It must be used with the **border** attribute set to a positive value. The attribute value can be either a named color, such as **blue,** or a color specified in the hexadecimal *#RRGGBB* format, such as **#00FF00.**

bordercolorlight This Internet Explorer–specific attribute specifies the lighter of two border colors used to create a three-dimensional effect for a cell's borders. It must be used with the **border** attribute set to a positive value. The attribute value can be either a named color, such as **red,** or a color specified in the hexadecimal *#RRGGBB* format, such as **#FF0000.**

char This attribute is used to define the character to which element contents are aligned when the **align** attribute is set to the **char** value.

charoff This attribute contains an offset as a positive or negative integer to align characters as related to the **char** value. A value of **2,** for example, would align characters in a cell two characters to the right of the character defined by the **char** attribute.

class   See "Core Attributes Reference," earlier in this chapter.

dir   See "Language Reference," earlier in this chapter.

hidefocus   This proprietary element, introduced with Internet Explorer 5.5, hides focus on an element's content. Focus must be applied to the element using the **tabindex** attribute.

id   See "Core Attributes Reference," earlier in this chapter.

lang   See "Language Reference," earlier in this chapter.

language   In the Microsoft implementation, this attribute specifies the scripting language to be used with an associated script bound to the element, typically through an event handler attribute. Possible values might include **javascript**, **jscript**, **vbs**, and **vbscript**. Other values that include the version of the language used, such as **JavaScript1.1**, also might be possible.

nowrap   This WebTV-specific attribute keeps table rows from wrapping if they extend beyond the right margin.

style   See "Core Attributes Reference," earlier in this chapter.

tabindex   This attribute uses a number to identify the object's position in the tabbing order for keyboard navigation using the TAB key. Internet Explorer 5.5 applies this attribute to the **tr** element; under IE 5.5, this focus can be disabled with the **hidefocus** attribute.

title   See "Core Attributes Reference," earlier in this chapter.

transparency   This WebTV-specific attribute specifies the degree of transparency of the table. Values range from **0** (totally opaque) to **100** (totally transparent). A value of **50** is optimized for fast rendering.

valign   This attribute is used to set the vertical alignment for the table cells with the <**tr**> element. HTML 4.01 defines **baseline**, **bottom**, **middle**, and **top**. Internet Explorer replaces **middle** with **center**; the effect should be the same.

Attribute and Event Support

Netscape 4   **align**, **bgcolor**, and **valign**. (**class**, **id**, **lang**, and **style** are implied.)

Internet Explorer 4 align (center | left | right), bgcolor, id, lang, style, title, and valign (baseline | bottom | top), all W3C-defined events, and all attributes and events defined by Internet Explorer 4.

Internet Explorer 5.5 align (center | left | right | justify), bgcolor, id, lang, style, title, and valign (baseline | bottom | top | middle), all W3C-defined events, and all attributes and events defined by Internet Explorer 4 and 5.5.

WebTV align (center | left | right), bgcolor, nowrap, transparency, and valign (baseline | bottom | middle | top).

Event Handlers

See "Events Reference," earlier in this chapter.

Example

```
<table width="300" border="1">
    <tr bgcolor="red" align="center" valign="middle">
        <td>3</td>
        <td>5.6</td>
        <td>7.9</td>
    </tr>
</table>
```

Compatibility

HTML 3.2, 4, and 4.01, XHTML 1.0
Internet Explorer 2, 3, 4, 5, and 5.5
Netscape 1.1, 2, 3, 4–4.7, 6
Opera 4.0
WebTV

Notes

- This element is contained by the **<table>**, **<thead>**, **<tbody>**, and **<tfoot>** elements. It contains the **<th>** and **<td>** elements.

- The HTML 3.2 specification defines only the **align** and **valign** attributes for this element.

- Under the XHTML 1.0 specification, the closing **</tr>** tag ceases to be optional.

<tt> (Teletype Text)

This element is used to indicate that text should be rendered in a monospaced font similar to teletype text.

2

Syntax

```
<tt
     class="class name(s)"
     dir="ltr | rtl"
     id="unique alphanumeric identifier"
     lang="language code"
     style="style information"
     title="advisory text"
     onclick="script"
     ondblclick="script"
     onkeydown="script"
     onkeypress="script"
     onkeyup="script"
     onmousedown="script"
     onmousemove="script"
     onmouseout="script"
     onmouseover="script"
     onmouseup="script">

</tt>
```

Attributes and Events Defined by Internet Explorer 4

```
     language="javascript | jscript | vbs | vbscript"
     ondragstart="script"
     onhelp="script"
     onselectstart="script"
```

Attributes and Events Defined by Internet Explorer 5.5

```
     accesskey="key"
     contenteditable="false | true | inherit"
     hidefocus="true | false"
     tabindex="number"
```

Attributes

accesskey   This attribute specifies a keyboard navigation accelerator for the element. Pressing ALT or a similar key (depending on the browser and operating system) in association with the specified key selects the anchor element correlated with that key.

class   See "Core Attributes Reference," earlier in this chapter.

contenteditable   This proprietary Microsoft attribute allows users to edit content rendered in the Internet Explorer 5.5 browser. Values are **false**, **true**, and **inherit**. A value of **false** will prevent content from being edited by users; **true** will allow editing. The default value, **inherit**, applies the value of the affected element's parent element.

dir   See "Language Reference," earlier in this chapter.

hidefocus   This proprietary element, introduced with Internet Explorer 5.5, hides focus on an element's content. Focus must be applied to the element using the **tabindex** attribute.

id   See "Core Attributes Reference," earlier in this chapter.

lang   See "Language Reference," earlier in this chapter.

language   In the Microsoft implementation, this attribute specifies the scripting language to be used with an associated script bound to the element, typically through an event handler attribute. Possible values might include **javascript**, **jscript**, **vbs**, and **vbscript**. Other values that include the version of the language used, such as **JavaScript1.1**, also might be possible.

style   See "Core Attributes Reference," earlier in this chapter.

tabindex   This attribute uses a number to identify the object's position in the tabbing order for keyboard navigation using the TAB key. Internet Explorer 5.5 applies this attribute to the **tt** element; under IE 5.5, this focus can be disabled with the **hidefocus** attribute.

title   See "Core Attributes Reference," earlier in this chapter.

Attribute and Event Support

Netscape 4   **class**, **id**, **lang**, and **style** are implied.

Internet Explorer 4   All attributes and events defined by the W3C and Internet Explorer 4, except **dir**.

Internet Explorer 5.5   All attributes and events.

2

Event Handlers
See "Events Reference," earlier in this chapter.

Example
```
Here is some <tt>monospaced text</tt>.
```

Compatibility

HTML 2, 3.2, 4, and 4.01, XHTML 1.0
Internet Explorer 2, 3, 4, 5, and 5.5
Netscape 1, 2, 3, 4–4.7, 6
Opera 4.0
WebTV

<u> (Underline)

This element is used to indicate that the enclosed text should be displayed underlined.

Syntax (Transitional Only)
```
<u
      class="class name(s)"
      dir="ltr | rtl"
      id="unique alphanumeric string"
      lang="language code"
      style="style information"
      title="advisory text"
      onclick="script"
      ondblclick="script"
      onkeydown="script"
      onkeypress="script"
      onkeyup="script"
      onmousedown="script"
      onmousemove="script"
      onmouseout="script"
      onmouseover="script"
      onmouseup="script">

</u>
```

Attributes and Events Defined by Internet Explorer 4

```
language="javascript | jscript | vbs | vbscript"
ondragstart="script"
onhelp="script"
onselectstart="script"
```

Attributes and Events Defined by Internet Explorer 5.5

```
accesskey="key"
contenteditable="false | true | inherit"
hidefocus="true | false"
tabindex="number"
```

Attributes

accesskey   This attribute specifies a keyboard navigation accelerator for the element. Pressing ALT or a similar key (depending on the browser and operating system) in association with the specified key selects the anchor element correlated with that key.

class   See "Core Attributes Reference," earlier in this chapter.

contenteditable   This proprietary Microsoft attribute allows users to edit content rendered in the Internet Explorer 5.5 browser. Values are **false**, **true**, and **inherit**. A value of **false** will prevent content from being edited by users; **true** will allow editing. The default value, **inherit**, applies the value of the affected element's parent element.

dir   See "Language Reference," earlier in this chapter.

hidefocus   This proprietary element, introduced with Internet Explorer 5.5, hides focus on an element's content. Focus must be applied to the element using the **tabindex** attribute.

id   See "Core Attributes Reference," earlier in this chapter.

lang   See "Language Reference," earlier in this chapter.

language   In the Microsoft implementation, this attribute specifies the scripting language to be used with an associated script bound to the element, typically through an event handler attribute. Possible values might include **javascript**, **jscript**, **vbs**, and **vbscript**. Other values that include the version of the language used, such as **JavaScript1.1**, also might be possible.

style   See "Core Attributes Reference," earlier in this chapter.

2

tabindex   This attribute uses a number to identify the object's position in the tabbing order for keyboard navigation using the TAB key. Internet Explorer 5.5 applies this attribute to the **u** element; under IE 5.5, this focus can be disabled with the **hidefocus** attribute.

title   See "Core Attributes Reference," earlier in this chapter.

Attribute and Event Support

Netscape 4   **class**, **id**, **lang**, and **style** are implied.

Internet Explorer 4   All attributes and events defined by the W3C and Internet Explorer 4, except **dir**.

Internet Explorer 4   All attributes and events.

Event Handlers
See "Events Reference," earlier in this chapter.

Examples
```
Here is some <u>underlined text</u>.

Be careful with <u>underlined</u> text; it looks like
<a href="http://www.yahoo.com/">links</a>.
```

Compatibility

HTML 3.2, 4 (transitional), 4.01 (transitional), XHTML 1.0
Internet Explorer 2, 3, 4, 5, and 5.5
Netscape 3, 4–4.7, 6
Opera 4.0
WebTV

Notes

- This element has been deprecated by the W3C. Under the strict HTML 4.01 specification, the <u> element is not defined. The capabilities of this element are possible using style sheets.

- Underlining text can be problematic because it looks similar to a link, especially in a black-and-white environment.

<ul> (Unordered List)

This element is used to indicate an unordered list, namely a collection of items that do not have a numerical ordering. The individual items in the list are defined by the **<li>** element, which is the only allowed element within **<ul>**.

Syntax

```
<ul
    class="class name(s)"
    compact (transitional)
    dir="ltr | rtl"
    id="unique alphanumeric identifier"
    lang="language code"
    style="style information"
    title="advisory text"
    type="circle | disc | square" (transitional)
    onclick="script"
    ondblclick="script"
    onkeydown="script"
    onkeypress="script"
    onkeyup="script"
    onmousedown="script"
    onmousemove="script"
    onmouseout="script"
    onmouseover="script"
    onmouseup="script">

    List items specified by <li> elements

</ul>
```

XHTML Syntax

Due to XHTML 1.0's deprecation of attribute minimization, the **compact** attribute must have a quoted attribute when used:

```
<ul compact="compact"></ul>
```

Attributes and Events Defined by Internet Explorer 4

```
    language="javascript | jscript | vbs | vbscript"
    ondragstart="script"
    onhelp="script"
    onselectstart="script"
```

Attributes and Events Defined by Internet Explorer 5.5

```
accesskey="key"
contenteditable="false | true | inherit"
hidefocus="true | false"
tabindex="number"
```

Attributes

accesskey   This attribute specifies a keyboard navigation accelerator for the element. Pressing ALT or a similar key (depending on the browser and operating system) in association with the specified key selects the anchor element correlated with that key.

class   See "Core Attributes Reference," earlier in this chapter.

compact   This attribute indicates that the list should be rendered in a compact style. Few browsers actually change the rendering of the list regardless of the presence of this attribute. The **compact** attribute requires no value.

contenteditable   This proprietary Microsoft attribute allows users to edit content rendered in the Internet Explorer 5.5 browser. Values are **false**, **true**, and **inherit**. A value of **false** will prevent content from being edited by users; **true** will allow editing. The default value, **inherit**, applies the value of the affected element's parent element.

dir   See "Language Reference," earlier in this chapter.

hidefocus   This proprietary element, introduced with Internet Explorer 5.5, hides focus on an element's content. Focus must be applied to the element using the **tabindex** attribute.

id   See "Core Attributes Reference," earlier in this chapter.

lang   See "Language Reference," earlier in this chapter.

language   In the Microsoft implementation, this attribute specifies the scripting language to be used with an associated script bound to the element, typically through an event handler attribute. Possible values might include **javascript**, **jscript**, **vbs**, and **vbscript**. Other values that include the version of the language used, such as **JavaScript1.1**, also might be possible.

style   See "Core Attributes Reference," earlier in this chapter.

tabindex   This attribute uses a number to identify the object's position in the tabbing order for keyboard navigation using the TAB key. Internet Explorer 5.5 applies this attribute to the **ul** element; under IE 5.5, this focus can be disabled with the **hidefocus** attribute.

title   See "Core Attributes Reference," earlier in this chapter.

type   The **type** attribute is used to set the bullet style for the list. The values defined under HTML 3.2 and the transitional version of HTML 4.0/4.01 are **circle**, **disc**, and **square**. A user agent might decide to use a different bullet depending on the nesting level of the list unless the **type** attribute is used. The WebTV interface also supports a triangle bullet. The **type** attribute is dropped under the strict version of HTML 4.0 because style sheets can provide richer bullet control.

Attribute and Event Support

Netscape 4   **class**, **id**, **lang**, **style**, and **type**.

Internet Explorer 4   All attributes and events defined by the W3C and Internet Explorer 4 except **compact** and **dir**.

Internet Explorer 4   All attributes and events.

WebTV   **type**.

Event Handlers

See "Events Reference," earlier in this chapter.

Examples

```
<ul compact title="Sushi Short List" type="circle">
    <li>Maguro
    <li>Ebi
    <li>Hamachi
</ul>

<!-- Common but bad example -->
<ul>Indenting using lists should not be used, though it is common.
Many Web editors generate code laden with nonbreaking spaces and
unordered lists.</ul>
```

Compatibility

> HTML 2, 3.2, 4, and 4.01, XHTML 1.0
> Internet Explorer 2, 3, 4, 5, and 5.5
> Netscape 1, 2, 3, 4–4.7, 6
> Opera 4.0
> WebTV

Notes

- HTML 2.0 supports only the **compact** attribute.

- The HTML 3.2 specification supports **compact** and **type**.

- Under the strict HTML 4.01 specification, the **<ul>** element does not support the **compact** attribute or the **type** attribute. Both of these attributes can be safely replaced with style rules.

- Many Web page designers and page development tools use the **<ul>** element to indent text. Be aware that the only element that should occur within a **<ul>** element is **<li>**, according to HTML standards, so such HTML markup does not conform to standards. However, this common practice is likely to continue.

<var> (Variable)

This element is used to indicate a variable. Variables are identifiers that occur in a programming language or a mathematical expression. The element is logical, although enclosed text often is rendered in italics.

Syntax

```
<var
    class="class name(s)"
    dir="ltr | rtl"
    id="unique alphanumeric value"
    lang="language code"
    style="style information"
    title="advisory text"
    onclick="script"
    ondblclick="script"
    onkeydown="script"
    onkeypress="script"
```

```
onkeyup="script"
onmousedown="script"
onmousemove="script"
onmouseout="script"
onmouseover="script"
onmouseup="script">
```

```
</var>
```

Attributes and Events Defined by Internet Explorer 4

```
language="javascript | jscript | vbs | vbscript"
ondragstart="script"
onhelp="script"
onselectstart="script"
```

Attributes and Events Defined by Internet Explorer 5.5

```
accesskey="key"
contenteditable="false | true | inherit"
hidefocus="true | false"
tabindex="number"
```

Attributes

accesskey   This attribute specifies a keyboard navigation accelerator for the element. Pressing ALT or a similar key (depending on the browser and operating system) in association with the specified key selects the anchor element correlated with that key.

class   See "Core Attributes Reference," earlier in this chapter.

contenteditable   This proprietary Microsoft attribute allows users to edit content rendered in the Internet Explorer 5.5 browser. Values are **false**, **true**, and **inherit**. A value of **false** will prevent content from being edited by users; **true** will allow editing. The default value, **inherit**, applies the value of the affected element's parent element.

dir   See "Language Reference," earlier in this chapter.

hidefocus   This proprietary element, introduced with Internet Explorer 5.5, hides focus on an element's content. Focus must be applied to the element using the **tabindex** attribute.

id   See "Core Attributes Reference," earlier in this chapter.

lang   See "Language Reference," earlier in this chapter.

language   In the Microsoft implementation, this attribute specifies the scripting language to be used with an associated script bound to the element, typically through an event handler attribute. Possible values might include **javascript**, **jscript**, **vbs**, and **vbscript**. Other values that include the version of the language used, such as **JavaScript1.1**, also might be possible.

style   See "Core Attributes Reference," earlier in this chapter.

tabindex   This attribute uses a number to identify the object's position in the tabbing order for keyboard navigation using the TAB key. Internet Explorer 5.5 applies this attribute to the **var** element; under IE 5.5, this focus can be disabled with the **hidefocus** attribute.

title   See "Core Attributes Reference," earlier in this chapter.

Attribute and Event Support

Netscape 4   **class**, **id**, **lang**, and **style** are implied.

Internet Explorer 4   All attributes and events defined by the W3C and Internet Explorer 4, except **dir**.

Internet Explorer 5.5   All attributes and events.

Event Handlers

See "Events Reference," earlier in this chapter.

Example

```
Assign the value 5 to the variable <var>x</var>.
```

Compatibility

HTML 2, 3.2, 4, and 4.01, XHTML 1.0
Internet Explorer 2, 3, 4, 5, and 5.5
Netscape 1, 2, 3, 4–4.7, 6
Opera 4.0
WebTV

Notes

- As a logical element, **<var>** is a perfect candidate for style sheet binding.

- The HTML 2.0 and 3.2 specifications support no attributes for this element.

<wbr> (Word Break)

This nonstandard element is used to indicate a place where a line break can occur if necessary. This element is used in conjunction with the **<nobr>** element, which is used to keep text from wrapping. When used this way, **<wbr>** can be thought of as a soft line break in comparison to the **
** element. This element is common to both Netscape and Microsoft implementations, though it is not part of any HTML standard.

Syntax

```
<wbr
    class="class name(s)"
    id="unique alphanumeric value"
    language="javascript | jscript | vbs | vbscript"
    style="style information"
    title="advisory text">
```

Attributes

class   See "Core Attributes Reference," earlier in this chapter.

id   See "Core Attributes Reference," earlier in this chapter.

language   In the Microsoft implementation, this attribute specifies the scripting language to be used with an associated script bound to the element, typically through an event handler attribute. Possible values might include **javascript**, **jscript**, **vbs**, and **vbscript**. Other values that include the version of the language used, such as **JavaScript1.1**, also might be possible.

style   See "Core Attributes Reference," earlier in this chapter.

title   See "Core Attributes Reference," earlier in this chapter.

Attribute and Event Support

Netscape 4   **class**, **id**, **style**, and **title** are implied.

Internet Explorer 4   All attributes.

Event Handlers

See "Events Reference," earlier in this chapter.

Example

```
<nobr>A line break can occur here<wbr>but not
elsewhere, even if the line is really long.</nobr>
```

2

Compatibility

Internet Explorer 2, 3, 4, 5, and 5.5
Netscape 1.1, 2, 3, 4–4.7

Notes

- This element was introduced in Netscape 1.1.
- This is an empty element, so no closing tag is required.

xml (XML Data Island)

This proprietary element introduced by Microsoft can be used to embed islands of xml (Extensible Markup Language) data into HTML documents; this will work only under Internet Explorer 5.0 or later. The **<xml>** element can be used to reference outside data sources using the **src** attribute, or surround XML data in the HTML document itself.

Syntax (Defined by Internet Explorer 5.0)

```
<xml
    id="unique alphanumeric value"
    ns="url of xml namespace"
    prefix="xml prefix"
    src="url of xml data file"
    ondataavailable="script"
    ondatasetchanged="script"
    ondatasetcomplete="script"
    onreadystatechange="script"
    onrowenter="script"
    onrowexit="script">

. . . embedded xml code . . .

</xml>
```

Attributes

id   See "Core Attributes Reference," earlier in this chapter.

ns This attribute, still largely theoretical at the time of this writing, references the URL of an xml namespace.

prefix This attribute references the URL of an XML namespace prefix in conjunction with the **ns** attribute.

src This attribute references an external xml data file.

Event Handlers

ondataavailable See "Extended Events," earlier in this chapter.

ondatasetchanged See "Extended Events," earlier in this chapter.

ondatasetcomplete See "Extended Events," earlier in this chapter.

onreadystatechange See "Extended Events," earlier in this chapter.

onrowenter See "Extended Events," earlier in this chapter.

onrowexit See "Extended Events," earlier in this chapter.

Attribute and Event Support

Internet Explorer 5 id, src, ondataavailable, ondatasetchanged, ondatasetcomplete, onreadystatechange, onrowenter, onrowexit

Examples

```
<!-- This code embeds xml data directly into a document.
     All code between the xml tags is not HTML, but a
     hypothetical example of xml. -->

<xml id="tasty">
   <combomeal>
      <burger>
       <name>Tasty Burger</name>
         <bun bread="white">
            <meat />
            <cheese />
            <meat />
         </bun>
      </burger>
      <fries size="large" />
```

```
    <drink size="large" flavor="Cola" />
  </combomeal>
</xml>

<!-- This code fragment uses the src attribute to reference an
external file containing xml data. -->

<xml src="combomeal.xml"></xml>
```

Compatibility

Internet Explorer 5

Notes

- Support of the **<xml>** element currently is exclusive to Internet Explorer 5.0 and later.

<xmp> (Example)

This deprecated element indicates that the enclosed text is an example. Example text generally is rendered in a monospaced font, and the spaces, tabs, and returns are preserved, as with the **<pre>** element. As the **<xmp>** element is no longer standard, the **<pre>** or **<samp>** elements should be used instead.

Syntax (Defined by HTML 2; Deprecated Under HTML 4)

```
<xmp>
</xmp>
```

Attributes and Events Defined by Internet Explorer 4

```
class="class name(s)"
id="unique alphanumeric value"
lang="language code"
language="javascript | jscript | vbs | vbscript"
style="style information"
title="advisory text"
onclick="script"
ondblclick="script"
ondragstart="script"
onhelp="script"
```

```
onkeydown="script"
onkeypress="script"
onkeyup="script"
onmousedown="script"
onmousemove="script"
onmouseout="script"
onmouseover="script"
onmouseup="script"
onselectstart="script"
```

Attributes and Events Defined by Internet Explorer 5.5

```
accesskey="key"
contenteditable="false | true | inherit"
hidefocus="true | false"
tabindex="number"
```

Attributes

accesskey   This attribute specifies a keyboard navigation accelerator for the element. Pressing ALT or a similar key (depending on the browser and operating system) in association with the specified key selects the anchor element correlated with that key.

class   See "Core Attributes Reference," earlier in this chapter.

contenteditable   This proprietary Microsoft attribute allows users to edit content rendered in the Internet Explorer 5.5 browser. Values are **false**, **true**, and **inherit**. A value of **false** will prevent content from being edited by users; **true** will allow editing. The default value, **inherit**, applies the value of the affected element's parent element.

hidefocus   This proprietary element, introduced with Internet Explorer 5.5, hides focus on an element's content. Focus must be applied to the element using the **tabindex** attribute.

id   See "Core Attributes Reference," earlier in this chapter.

lang   See "Language Reference," earlier in this chapter.

language   In the Microsoft implementation, this attribute specifies the scripting language to be used with an associated script bound to the element, typically through an event handler attribute. Possible values might include **javascript**, **jscript**, **vbs**, and **vbscript**. Other values that include the version of the language used, such as **JavaScript1.1**, also might be possible.

style   See "Core Attributes Reference," earlier in this chapter.

tabindex   This attribute uses a number to identify the object's position in the tabbing order for keyboard navigation using the TAB key. Internet Explorer 5.5 applies this attribute to the **xmp** element; under IE 5.5, this focus can be disabled with the **hidefocus** attribute.

title   See "Core Attributes Reference," earlier in this chapter.

Attribute and Event Support

Netscape 4   **class**, **id**, **style**, and **title**.

Internet Explorer 4   All attributes defined by the W3C and Internet Explorer 4.

Internet Explorer 5.5   All attributes.

Event Handlers

See "Events Reference," earlier in this chapter.

Example

`<xmp>`This is a large block of text used as an example. Note that returns as well as   S P A C E S are preserved.`</xmp>`

Compatibility

> HTML 2
> Internet Explorer 2, 3, 4, and 5
> Netscape 1, 2, 3, 4–4.7
> Opera 4.0
> WebTV

Note

- This element is very old, although it continues to be documented. It was first deprecated under HTML 3.2 and continues to be unsupported under HTML 4.0.

- Page designers should not use this element. Internet Explorer documentation supports this element but recommends use of **<pre>** or **<samp>** instead.

Chapter 3
Special Characters

This chapter lists the special characters available in standard HTML and HTML 4.0x. Note that browser support of elements in this chapter is based on testing in the following browser versions: Netscape 1.22, Netscape 2.02, Netscape 3.01, Netscape Communicator 4.0, Netscape Communicator 4.5, Netscape Communicator 4.73, Internet Explorer 3.02, Internet Explorer 4.0, Internet Explorer 5.0, Internet Explorer 5.5, Opera 4.02, and WebTV's browser simulator. Testing also was performed in preview releases of Netscape 6. In the tables in this chapter, the following abbreviations are used for the different Netscape and Internet Explorer versions:

N1 = Netscape 1.22	N6 = Netscape Communicator 6*
N2 = Netscape 2.02	IE3 = Internet Explorer 3.02
N3 = Netscape 3.01	IE4 = Internet Explorer 4.0
N4 = Netscape Communicator 4.0	IE5 = Internet Explorer 5.0
N4.5 = Netscape Communicator 4.5	IE5.5 = Internet Explorer 5.5
N4.7 = Netscape Communicator 4.73	O4 = Opera 4.02

* Netscape 6 support based upon Preview Release 2

"Standard" HTML Character Entities

As discussed throughout the book, Web browsers do not render certain characters if they appear in an HTML document. Some keyboard characters such as < and > have special meanings to HTML because they are part of HTML tags. Other characters such as certain foreign language accent characters and special symbols can be difficult to insert as well. HTML uses a set of character entity codes in order to display these special characters. These codes consist of numbered entities and some, but not all, of these numbered entities have corresponding named entities. For example, the numbered entity Ë produces the character Ë. The named entity Ë produces the same character. Note that the named entity suggests the intended rendering of the character, which provides a handy mnemonic device for dedicated HTML coders.

While Ë is widely supported, not all character entities work in all browsers. Theoretically, a browser vendor could even create arbitrary interpretations of these codes. For instance, WebTV has assigned its own unique renderings for the entities numbered 128 and 129. Under the HTML specifications, 128 and 129 are not assigned a character. The codes numbered 32 through 255 (with some gaps) were assigned standard keyboard characters. Some of these codes duplicate characters that Web browsers can already interpret. The entity 5 represents the numeral five, while A represents "A." Character entities become more practical when it is necessary to employ characters used in foreign languages, such as "Œ" or "Å," or special characters such as "¶ ." The following chart lists these "standard" entities and their intended renderings, and identifies which browsers support each.

Named Entity	Browser Support	Numbered Entity	Browser Support	Intended Rendering	Description
		&#32;	N: 1, 2, 3, 4, 4.5, 4.7, 6 IE: 3, 4, 5, 5.5, Opera 4.02, WebTV		Space
		&#33;	N: 1, 2, 3, 4, 4.5, 4.7, 6 IE: 3, 4, 5, 5.5, Opera 4.02, WebTV	!	Exclamation point
&quot;	N: 1, 2, 3, 4, 4.5, 4.7, 6 IE: 3, 4, 5, 5.5, Opera 4.02, WebTV	&#34;	N: 1, 2, 3, 4, 4.5, 4.7, 6 IE: 3, 4, 5, 5.5, Opera 4.02, WebTV	"	Double quotes
		&#35;	N: 1, 2, 3, 4, 4.5, 4.7, 6 IE: 3, 4, 5, 5.5, Opera 4.02, WebTV	#	Number symbol
		&#36;	N: 1, 2, 3, 4, 4.5, 4.7, 6 IE: 3, 4, 5, 5.5, Opera 4.02, WebTV	$	Dollar symbol

Named Entity	Browser Support	Numbered Entity	Browser Support	Intended Rendering	Description
		&#37;	N: 1, 2, 3, 4, 4.5, 4.7, 6 IE: 3, 4, 5, 5.5, Opera 4.02, WebTV	%	Percent symbol
&amp;	N: 1, 2, 3, 4, 4.5, 4.7, 6 IE: 3, 4, 5, 5.5, Opera 4.02, WebTV	&#38;	N: 1, 2, 3, 4, 4.5, 4.7, 6 IE: 3, 4, 5, 5.5, Opera 4.02, WebTV	&	Ampersand
		&#39;	N: 1, 2, 3, 4, 4.5, 4.7, 6 IE: 3, 4, 5, 5.5, Opera 4.02, WebTV	"	Single quote
		&#40;	N: 1, 2, 3, 4, 4.5, 4.7, 6 IE: 3, 4, 5, 5.5, Opera 4.02, WebTV	(	Opening parenthesis
		&#41;	N: 1, 2, 3, 4, 4.5, 4.7, 6 IE: 3, 4, 5, 5.5, Opera 4.02, WebTV	)	Closing parenthesis
		&#42;	N: 1, 2, 3, 4, 4.5, 4.7, 6 IE: 3, 4, 5, 5.5, Opera 4.02, WebTV	*	Asterisk
		&#43;	N: 1, 2, 3, 4, 4.5, 4.7, 6 IE: 3, 4, 5, 5.5, Opera 4.02, WebTV	+	Plus sign
		&#44;	N: 1, 2, 3, 4, 4.5, 4.7, 6 IE: 3, 4, 5, 5.5, Opera 4.02, WebTV	,	Comma

3

Named Entity	Browser Support	Numbered Entity	Browser Support	Intended Rendering	Description
		&#45;	N: 1, 2, 3, 4, 4.5, 4.7, 6 IE: 3, 4, 5, 5.5, Opera 4.02, WebTV	-	Minus sign (hyphen)
		&#46;	N: 1, 2, 3, 4, 4.5, 4.7, 6 IE: 3, 4, 5, 5.5, Opera 4.02, WebTV	.	Period
		&#47;	N: 1, 2, 3, 4, 4.5, 4.7, 6 IE: 3, 4, 5, 5.5, Opera 4.02, WebTV	/	Slash/virgul e/bar
		&#48;	N: 1, 2, 3, 4, 4.5, 4.7, 6 IE: 3, 4, 5, 5.5, Opera 4.02, WebTV	0	Zero
		&#49;	N: 1, 2, 3, 4, 4.5, 4.7, 6 IE: 3, 4, 5, 5.5, Opera 4.02, WebTV	1	One
		&#50;	N: 1, 2, 3, 4, 4.5, 4.7, 6 IE: 3, 4, 5, 5.5, Opera 4.02, WebTV	2	Two
		&#51;	N: 1, 2, 3, 4, 4.5, 4.7, 6 IE: 3, 4, 5, 5.5, Opera 4.02, WebTV	3	Three
		&#52;	N: 1, 2, 3, 4, 4.5, 4.7, 6 IE: 3, 4, 5, 5.5, Opera 4.02, WebTV	4	Four

Named Entity	Browser Support	Numbered Entity	Browser Support	Intended Rendering	Description
		&#53;	N: 1, 2, 3, 4, 4.5, 4.7, 6 IE: 3, 4, 5, 5.5, Opera 4.02, WebTV	5	Five
		&#54;	N: 1, 2, 3, 4, 4.5, 4.7, 6 IE: 3, 4, 5, 5.5, Opera 4.02, WebTV	6	Six
		&#55;	N: 1, 2, 3, 4, 4.5, 4.7, 6 IE: 3, 4, 5, 5.5, Opera 4.02, WebTV	7	Seven
		&#56;	N: 1, 2, 3, 4, 4.5, 4.7, 6 IE: 3, 4, 5, 5.5, Opera 4.02, WebTV	8	Eight
		&#57;	N: 1, 2, 3, 4, 4.5, 4.7, 6 IE: 3, 4, 5, 5.5, Opera 4.02, WebTV	9	Nine
		&#58;	N: 1, 2, 3, 4, 4.5, 4.7, 6 IE: 3, 4, 5, 5.5, Opera 4.02, WebTV	:	Colon
		&#59;	N: 1, 2, 3, 4, 4.5, 4.7, 6 IE: 3, 4, 5, 5.5, Opera 4.02, WebTV	;	Semicolon
&lt;	N: 1, 2, 3, 4, 4.5, 4.7, 6 IE: 3, 4, 5, 5.5, Opera 4.02, WebTV	&#60;	N: 1, 2, 3, 4, 4.5, 4.7, 6 IE: 3, 4, 5, 5.5, Opera 4.02, WebTV	<	Less than symbol

3

Named Entity	Browser Support	Numbered Entity	Browser Support	Intended Rendering	Description
		&#61;	N: 1, 2, 3, 4, 4.5, 4.7, 6 IE: 3, 4, 5, 5.5, Opera 4.02, WebTV	=	Equal sign
&gt;	N: 1, 2, 3, 4, 4.5, 4.7, 6 IE: 3, 4, 5, 5.5, Opera 4.02, WebTV	&#62;	N: 1, 2, 3, 4, 4.5, 4.7, 6 IE: 3, 4, 5, 5.5, Opera 4.02, WebTV	>	Greater than symbol
		&#63;	N: 1, 2, 3, 4, 4.5, 4.7, 6 IE: 3, 4, 5, 5.5, Opera 4.02, WebTV	?	Question mark
		&#64;	N: 1, 2, 3, 4, 4.5, 4.7, 6 IE: 3, 4, 5, 5.5, Opera 4.02, WebTV	@@	At symbol
		&#65;	N: 1, 2, 3, 4, 4.5, 4.7, 6 IE: 3, 4, 5, 5.5, Opera 4.02, WebTV	A	
		&#66;	N: 1, 2, 3, 4, 4.5, 4.7, 6 IE: 3, 4, 5, 5.5, Opera 4.02, WebTV	B	
		&#67;	N: 1, 2, 3, 4, 4.5, 4.7, 6 IE: 3, 4, 5, 5.5, Opera 4.02, WebTV	C	
		&#68;	N: 1, 2, 3, 4, 4.5, 4.7, 6 IE: 3, 4, 5, 5.5, Opera 4.02, WebTV	D	

Named Entity	Browser Support	Numbered Entity	Browser Support	Intended Rendering	Description
		&#69;	N: 1, 2, 3, 4, 4.5, 4.7, 6 IE: 3, 4, 5, 5.5, Opera 4.02, WebTV	E	
		&#70;	N: 1, 2, 3, 4, 4.5, 4.7, 6 IE: 3, 4, 5, 5.5, Opera 4.02, WebTV	F	
		&#71;	N: 1, 2, 3, 4, 4.5, 4.7, 6 IE: 3, 4, 5, 5.5, Opera 4.02, WebTV	G	
		&#72;	N: 1, 2, 3, 4, 4.5, 4.7, 6 IE: 3, 4, 5, 5.5, Opera 4.02, WebTV	H	
		&#73;	N: 1, 2, 3, 4, 4.5, 4.7, 6 IE: 3, 4, 5, 5.5, Opera 4.02, WebTV	I	
		&#74;	N: 1, 2, 3, 4, 4.5, 4.7, 6 IE: 3, 4, 5, 5.5, Opera 4.02, WebTV	J	
		&#75;	N: 1, 2, 3, 4, 4.5, 4.7, 6 IE: 3, 4, 5, 5.5, Opera 4.02, WebTV	K	
		&#76;	N: 1, 2, 3, 4, 4.5, 4.7, 6 IE: 3, 4, 5, 5.5, Opera 4.02, WebTV	L	

3

Named Entity	Browser Support	Numbered Entity	Browser Support	Intended Rendering	Description
		&#77;	N: 1, 2, 3, 4, 4.5, 4.7, 6 IE: 3, 4, 5, 5.5, Opera 4.02, WebTV	M	
		&#78;	N: 1, 2, 3, 4, 4.5, 4.7, 6 IE: 3, 4, 5, 5.5, Opera 4.02, WebTV	N	
		&#79;	N: 1, 2, 3, 4, 4.5, 4.7, 6 IE: 3, 4, 5, 5.5, Opera 4.02, WebTV	O	
		&#80;	N: 1, 2, 3, 4, 4.5, 4.7, 6 IE: 3, 4, 5, 5.5, Opera 4.02, WebTV	P	
		&#81;	N: 1, 2, 3, 4, 4.5, 4.7, 6 IE: 3, 4, 5, 5.5, Opera 4.02, WebTV	Q	
		&#82;	N: 1, 2, 3, 4, 4.5, 4.7, 6 IE: 3, 4, 5, 5.5, Opera 4.02, WebTV	R	
		&#83;	N: 1, 2, 3, 4, 4.5, 4.7, 6 IE: 3, 4, 5, 5.5, Opera 4.02, WebTV	S	
		&#84;	N: 1, 2, 3, 4, 4.5, 4.7, 6 IE: 3, 4, 5, 5.5, Opera 4.02, WebTV	T	

Named Entity	Browser Support	Numbered Entity	Browser Support	Intended Rendering	Description
		&#85;	N: 1, 2, 3, 4, 4.5, 4.7, 6 IE: 3, 4, 5, 5.5, Opera 4.02, WebTV	U	
		&#86;	N: 1, 2, 3, 4, 4.5, 4.7, 6 IE: 3, 4, 5, 5.5, Opera 4.02, WebTV	V	
		&#87;	N: 1, 2, 3, 4, 4.5, 4.7, 6 IE: 3, 4, 5, 5.5, Opera 4.02, WebTV	W	
		&#88;	N: 1, 2, 3, 4, 4.5, 4.7, 6 IE: 3, 4, 5, 5.5, Opera 4.02, WebTV	X	
		&#89;	N: 1, 2, 3, 4, 4.5, 4.7, 6 IE: 3, 4, 5, 5.5, Opera 4.02, WebTV	Y	
		&#90;	N: 1, 2, 3, 4, 4.5, 4.7, 6 IE: 3, 4, 5, 5.5, Opera 4.02, WebTV	Z	
		&#91;	N: 1, 2, 3, 4, 4.5, 4.7, 6 IE: 3, 4, 5, 5.5, Opera 4.02, WebTV	[	Opening bracket
		&#92;	N: 1, 2, 3, 4, 4.5, 4.7, 6 IE: 3, 4, 5, 5.5, Opera 4.02, WebTV	\	Backslash

3

Named Entity	Browser Support	Numbered Entity	Browser Support	Intended Rendering	Description
		&#93;	N: 1, 2, 3, 4, 4.5, 4.7, 6 IE: 3, 4, 5, 5.5, Opera 4.02, WebTV	]	Closing bracket
		&#94;	N: 1, 3, 4, 4.5, 4.7, 6 IE: 3, 4, 5, 5.5, Opera 4.02, WebTV	^	Caret
		&#95;	N: 1, 2, 3, 4, 4.5, 4.7, 6 IE: 3, 4, 5, 5.5, Opera 4.02, WebTV	_	Underscore
		&#96;	N: 1, 2, 3, 4, 4.5, 4.7, 6 IE: 3, 4, 5, 5.5, Opera 4.02, WebTV	`	Grave accent, no letter
		&#97;	N: 1, 2, 3, 4, 4.5, 4.7, 6 IE: 3, 4, 5, 5.5, Opera 4.02, WebTV	a	
		&#98;	N: 1, 2, 3, 4, 4.5, 4.7, 6 IE: 3, 4, 5, 5.5, Opera 4.02, WebTV	b	
		&#99;	N: 1, 2, 3, 4, 4.5, 4.7, 6 IE: 3, 4, 5, 5.5, Opera 4.02, WebTV	c	
		&#100;	N: 1, 2, 3, 4, 4.5, 4.7, 6 IE: 3, 4, 5, 5.5, Opera 4.02, WebTV	d	

Named Entity	Browser Support	Numbered Entity	Browser Support	Intended Rendering	Description
		&#101;	N: 1, 2, 3, 4, 4.5, 4.7, 6 IE: 3, 4, 5, 5.5, Opera 4.02, WebTV	e	
		&#102;	N: 1, 2, 3, 4, 4.5, 4.7, 6 IE: 3, 4, 5, 5.5, Opera 4.02, WebTV	f	
		&#103;	N: 1, 2, 3, 4, 4.5, 4.7, 6 IE: 3, 4, 5, 5.5, Opera 4.02, WebTV	g	
		&#104;	N: 1, 2, 3, 4, 4.5, 4.7, 6 IE: 3, 4, 5, 5.5, Opera 4.02, WebTV	h	
		&#105;	N: 1, 2, 3, 4, 4.5, 4.7, 6 IE: 3, 4, 5, 5.5, Opera 4.02, WebTV	i	
		&#106;	N: 1, 2, 3, 4, 4.5, 4.7, 6 IE: 3, 4, 5, 5.5, Opera 4.02, WebTV	j	
		&#107;	N: 1, 2, 3, 4, 4.5, 4.7, 6 IE: 3, 4, 5, 5.5, Opera 4.02, WebTV	k	
		&#108;	N: 1, 2, 3, 4, 4.5, 4.7, 6 IE: 3, 4, 5, 5.5, Opera 4.02, WebTV	l	

3

Named Entity	Browser Support	Numbered Entity	Browser Support	Intended Rendering	Description
		&#109;	N: 1, 2, 3, 4, 4.5, 4.7, 6 IE: 3, 4, 5, 5.5, Opera 4.02, WebTV	m	
		&#110;	N: 1, 2, 3, 4, 4.5, 4.7, 6 IE: 3, 4, 5, 5.5, Opera 4.02, WebTV	n	
		&#111;	N: 1, 2, 3, 4, 4.5, 4.7, 6 IE: 3, 4, 5, 5.5, Opera 4.02, WebTV	o	
		&#112;	N: 1, 2, 3, 4, 4.5, 4.7, 6 IE: 3, 4, 5, 5.5, Opera 4.02, WebTV	p	
		&#113;	N: 1, 2, 3, 4, 4.5, 4.7, 6 IE: 3, 4, 5, 5.5, Opera 4.02, WebTV	q	
		&#114;	N: 1, 2, 3, 4, 4.5, 4.7, 6 IE: 3, 4, 5, 5.5, Opera 4.02, WebTV	r	
		&#115;	N: 1, 2, 3, 4, 4.5, 4.7, 6 IE: 3, 4, 5, 5.5, Opera 4.02, WebTV	s	
		&#116;	N: 1, 2, 3, 4, 4.5, 4.7, 6 IE: 3, 4, 5, 5.5, Opera 4.02, WebTV	t	

Named Entity	Browser Support	Numbered Entity	Browser Support	Intended Rendering	Description
		&#117;	N: 1, 2, 3, 4, 4.5, 4.7, 6 IE: 3, 4, 5, 5.5, Opera 4.02, WebTV	u	
		&#118;	N: 1, 2, 3, 4, 4.5, 4.7, 6 IE: 3, 4, 5, 5.5, Opera 4.02, WebTV	v	
		&#119;	N: 1, 2, 3, 4, 4.5, 4.7, 6 IE: 3, 4, 5, 5.5, Opera 4.02, WebTV	w	
		&#120;	N: 1, 2, 3, 4, 4.5, 4.7, 6 IE: 3, 4, 5, 5.5, Opera 4.02, WebTV	x	
		&#121;	N: 1, 2, 3, 4, 4.5, 4.7, 6 IE: 3, 4, 5, 5.5, Opera 4.02, WebTV	y	
		&#122;	N: 1, 2, 3, 4, 4.5, 4.7, 6 IE: 3, 4, 5, 5.5, Opera 4.02, WebTV	z	
		&#123;	N: 1, 2, 3, 4, 4.5, 4.7, 6 IE: 3, 4, 5, 5.5, Opera 4.02, WebTV	{	Opening brace
		|	N: 1, 2, 3, 4, 4.5, 4.7, 6 IE: 3, 4, 5, 5.5, Opera 4.02, WebTV	|	Vertical bar

3

Named Entity	Browser Support	Numbered Entity	Browser Support	Intended Rendering	Description
		&#125;	N: 1, 2, 3, 4, 4.5, 4.7, 6 IE: 3, 4, 5, 5.5, Opera 4.02, WebTV	}	Closing brace
		&#126;	N: 1, 2, 3, 4, 4.5, 4.7, 6 IE: 3, 4, 5, 5.5, Opera 4.02, WebTV	~	Equivalency symbol (tilde)
		&#127;	n/a		No character (Note: In the standard, the values from 127 to 159 are not assigned. Authors are advised not to use them. Many of them only work under Windows or produce different characters on other operating systems or with different default font sets.)
		&#128;	WebTV (non-standard)*		No character defined
&trade;	IE: 3, 4, 5, 5.5	&#129;	WebTV (non-standard) †	™	Trademark symbol (Non-standard numeric value; use ™ or ™ instead.)

Named Entity	Browser Support	Numbered Entity	Browser Support	Intended Rendering	Description
		&#130;	N: 2, 3, 4, 4.5 IE: 3, 4, 5, 5.5, Opera 4.02, WebTV	,	Low-9 quote (non-standard)
		&#131;	N3, N4, N4.5, 4.7, 6 IE: 3, 4, 5, 5.5, Opera 4.02, WebTV	ƒ	Small "f" with hook (non-standard)
		&#132;	N: 2, 3, 4, 4.5, 4.7, 6 IE: 3, 4, 5, 5.5, Opera 4.02, WebTV	„	Low-9 double quotes (non-standard)
		&#133;	N: 2, 3, 4, 4.5, 4.7, 6 IE: 3, 4, 5, 5.5, Opera 4.02, WebTV	...	Ellipsis (non-standard)
		&#134;	N: 2, 3, 4, 4.5, 4.7, 6 IE: 3, 4, 5, 5.5, Opera 4.02, WebTV	†	Dagger (non-standard)
		&#135;	N: 2, 3, 4, 4.5, 4.7, 6 IE: 3, 4, 5, 5.5, Opera 4.02, WebTV	‡	Double dagger (non-standard)
		&#136;	N3, N4, N4.5, 4.7, 6 IE: 3, 4, 5, 5.5, Opera 4.02, WebTV	^	Circumflex accent, no letter (non-standard)
		&#137;	N: 2, 3, 4, 4.5, 4.7, 6 IE: 3, 4, 5, 5.5, Opera 4.02, WebTV	‰	Per thousand (non-standard)

3

Named Entity	Browser Support	Numbered Entity	Browser Support	Intended Rendering	Description
		&#138;	N3, N4, N4.5, 4.7, 6 IE: 3, 4, 5, 5.5, Opera 4.02, WebTV	Š	Uppercase S with caron (non-standard)
		&#139;	N: 2, 3, 4, 4.5, 4.7, 6 IE: 3, 4, 5, 5.5, Opera 4.02, WebTV	‹	Opening single-angle quote (non-standard)
		&#140;	N: 3, 4, 4.5, 4.7, 6 IE: 3, 4, 5, 5.5, Opera 4.02, WebTV	Œ	Uppercase "OE" ligature (non-standard)
		&#141;	None	Ÿ	Uppercase "Y" with umlaut (non-standard)
		&#142;	n/a		No character
		&#143;	n/a		No character
		&#144;	n/a		No character
		&#145;	N: 1, 2, 3, 4, 4.5, 4.7, 6 IE: 3, 4, 5, 5.5, Opera 4.02, WebTV	`	Opening "smart" single quote (non-standard)
		&#146;	N: 1, 2, 3, 4, 4.5, 4.7, 6 IE: 3, 4, 5, 5.5, Opera 4.02, WebTV	'	Closing "smart" single quote (non-standard)
		&#147;	N: 2, 3, 4, 4.5, 4.7, 6 IE: 3, 4, 5, 5.5, Opera 4.02, WebTV	"	Opening "smart" double quote (non-standard)

3

Named Entity	Browser Support	Numbered Entity	Browser Support	Intended Rendering	Description
		&#148;	N: 2, 3, 4, 4.5, 4.7, 6 IE: 3, 4, 5, 5.5, Opera 4.02, WebTV	"	Closing "smart" double quote (non-standard)
		&#149;	N: 2, 3, 4, 4.5, 4.7, 6 IE: 3, 4, 5, 5.5, Opera 4.02, WebTV	•	Bullet (non-standard)
		&#150;	N: 2, 3, 4, 4.5, 4.7, 6 IE: 3, 4, 5, 5.5, Opera 4.02, WebTV	–	En dash (non-standard)
		&#151;	N: 2, 3, 4, 4.5, 4.7, 6 IE: 3, 4, 5, 5.5, Opera 4.02, WebTV	—	Em dash (non-standard)
		&#152;	N3, N4, N4.5, 4.7, 6 IE: 3, 4, 5, 5.5, Opera 4.02, WebTV	~	Tilde (non-standard)
&trade;	IE: 3, 4, 5, 5.5 N: 2, 3, 4, 4.5, 4.7, 6 O: 4, WebTV	™‡	N: 2, 3, 4, 4.5, 4.7, 6 IE: 3, 4, 5, 5.5, O:4, WebTV	™	Trademark symbol
		&#154;	N3, N4, N4.5, 4.7, 6 IE: 3, 4, 5, 5.5, Opera 4.02, WebTV	š	Lowercase S with caron (non-standard)

Named Entity	Browser Support	Numbered Entity	Browser Support	Intended Rendering	Description
		`&#155;`	N: 2, 3, 4, 4.5, 4.7, 6 IE: 3, 4, 5, 5.5, Opera 4.02, WebTV	>	Closing single-angle quote (non-standard)
		`&#156;`	N3, N4, N4.5, 4.7, 6 IE: 3, 4, 5, 5.5, Opera 4.02, WebTV	œ	Lowercase "oe" ligature (non-standard)
		`&#157;`	n/a		No character
		`&#158;`	n/a		No character
		`&#159;`	N: 4, 4.5, 4.7, 6 IE: 3, 5, 5.5	Ÿ	Uppercase "Y" with umlaut (non-standard)
` `	N: 1, 3, 4, 4.5, 4.7, 6 IE: 3, 4, 5, 5.5, O: 4	` `	N: 1, 2, 3, 4, 4.5, 4.7, 6 IE: 3, 4, 5, 5.5		Nonbreaking space
`&iexcl;`	N3, N4, N4.5, 4.7, 6 IE: 3, 4, 5, 5.5, Opera 4.02, WebTV	`&#161;`	N: 1, 3, 4, 4.5, 4.7, 6 IE: 3, 4, 5, 5.5, Opera 4.02, WebTV	¡	Inverted exclamation point
`&cent;`	N3, N4, N4.5, 4.7, 6 IE: 3, 4, 5, 5.5, Opera 4.02, WebTV	`&#162;`	N: 1, 3, 4, 4.5, 4.7, 6 IE: 3, 4, 5, 5.5, Opera 4.02, WebTV	¢	Cent symbol
`&pound;`	N3, N4, N4.5, 4.7, 6 IE: 3, 4, 5, 5.5, Opera 4.02, WebTV	`&#163;`	N: 1, 3, 4, 4.5, 4.7, 6 IE: 3, 4, 5, 5.5, Opera 4.02, WebTV	£	Pound sterling symbol
`&curren;`	N3, N4, N4.5, 4.7, 6 IE: 3, 4, 5, 5.5, Opera 4.02, WebTV	`&#164;`	N: 1, 2, 3, 4, 4.5, 4.7, 6 IE: 3, 4, 5, 5.5, Opera 4.02, WebTV	¤	Currency symbol

Named Entity	Browser Support	Numbered Entity	Browser Support	Intended Rendering	Description
&yen;	N3, N4, N4.5, 4.7, 6 IE: 3, 4, 5, 5.5, Opera 4.02, WebTV	&#165;	N: 1, 3, 4, 4.5, 4.7, 6 IE: 3, 4, 5, 5.5, Opera 4.02, WebTV	¥	Japanese Yen
&brvbar;	N3, N4, N4.5, 4.7, 6 IE: 3, 4, 5, 5.5, Opera 4.02, WebTV	&#166;	N: 2, 3, 4, 4.5, 4.7, 6 IE: 3, 4, 5, 5.5, Opera 4.02, WebTV	¦	Broken vertical bar
&sect;	N3, N4, N4.5, 4.7, 6 IE: 3, 4, 5, 5.5, Opera 4.02, WebTV	&#167;	N: 1, 2, 3, 4, 4.5, 4.7, 6 IE: 3, 4, 5, 5.5, Opera 4.02, WebTV	§	Section symbol
&uml;	N3, N4, N4.5, 4.7, 6 IE: 3, 4, 5, 5.5, Opera 4.02, WebTV	&#168;	N: 1, 3, 4, 4.5, 4.7, 6 IE: 3, 4, 5, 5.5, Opera 4.02, WebTV	¨	Umlaut, no letter
&copy;	N: 1, 2, 3, 4, 4.5, 4.7, 6 IE: 3, 4, 5, 5.5, Opera 4.02, WebTV	&#169;	N: 1, 2, 3, 4, 4.5, 4.7, 6 IE: 3, 4, 5, 5.5, Opera 4.02, WebTV	©	Copyright symbol
&ordf;	N3, N4, N4.5, 4.7, 6 IE: 3, 4, 5, 5.5, Opera 4.02, WebTV	&#170;	N: 1, 3, 4, 4.5, 4.7, 6 IE: 3, 4, 5, 5.5, Opera 4.02, WebTV	ª	Feminine ordinal indicator
&laquo;	N3, N4, N4.5, 4.7, 6 IE: 3, 4, 5, 5.5, Opera 4.02, WebTV	&#171;	N: 1, 2, 3, 4, 4.5, 4.7, 6 IE: 3, 4, 5, 5.5, Opera 4.02, WebTV	<<	Opening double-angle quote
&not;	N3, N4, N4.5, 4.7, 6 IE: 3, 4, 5, 5.5, Opera 4.02, WebTV	&#172;	N: 1, 2, 3, 4, 4.5, 4.7, 6 IE: 3, 4, 5, 5.5, Opera 4.02, WebTV	¬	Logical "not" symbol

Named Entity	Browser Support	Numbered Entity	Browser Support	Intended Rendering	Description
&shy;	N3, N4, N4.5, 4.7, 6 IE: 3, 4, 5, 5.5, Opera 4.02, WebTV	&#173;	N: 1, 2, 3, 4, 4.5, 4.7, 6 IE: 3, 4, 5, WebTV	-	Soft hyphen [no display in IE 5.5]
&reg;	N: 1, 2, 3, 4, 4.5, 4.7, 6 IE: 3, 4, 5, 5.5, Opera 4.02, WebTV	&#174;	N: 1, 2, 3, 4, 4.5, 4.7, 6 IE: 3, 4, 5, 5.5, Opera 4.02, WebTV	®	Registration mark
&macr;	N3, N4, N4.5, 4.7, 6 IE: 3, 4, 5, 5.5, Opera 4.02, WebTV	&#175;	N: 1, 3, 4, 4.5, 4.7, 6 IE: 3, 4, 5, 5.5, Opera 4.02, WebTV	–	Macron
&deg;	N3, N4, N4.5, 4.7, 6 IE: 3, 4, 5, 5.5, Opera 4.02, WebTV	&#176;	N: 1, 2, 3, 4, 4.5, 4.7, 6 IE: 3, 4, 5, 5.5, Opera 4.02, WebTV	°	Degree symbol
&plusmn;	N3, N4, N4.5, 4.7, 6 IE: 3, 4, 5, 5.5, Opera 4.02, WebTV	&#177;	N: 1, 2, 3, 4, 4.5, 4.7, 6 IE: 3, 4, 5, 5.5, Opera 4.02, WebTV	±	Plus/minus symbol
&sup2;	N3, N4, N4.5, 4.7, 6 IE: 3, 4, 5, 5.5, Opera 4.02, WebTV	&#178;	N: 1, 3, 4, 4.5, 4.7, 6 IE: 3, 4, 5, 5.5, Opera 4.02, WebTV	^{2}	Superscript 2
&sup3;	N3, N4, N4.5, 4.7, 6 IE: 3, 4, 5, 5.5, Opera 4.02, WebTV	&#179;	N: 1, 3, 4, 4.5, 4.7, 6 IE: 3, 4, 5, 5.5, Opera 4.02, WebTV	^{3}	Superscript 3
&acute;	N3, N4, N4.5, 4.7, 6 IE: 3, 4, 5, 5.5, Opera 4.02, WebTV	&#180;	N: 1, 3, 4, 4.5, 4.7, 6 IE: 3, 4, 5, 5.5, Opera 4.02, WebTV	´	Acute accent, no letter

Named Entity	Browser Support	Numbered Entity	Browser Support	Intended Rendering	Description
&micro;	N3, N4, N4.5, 4.7, 6 IE: 3, 4, 5, 5.5, Opera 4.02, WebTV	&#181;	N: 1, 2, 3, 4, 4.5, 4.7, 6 IE: 3, 4, 5, 5.5, Opera 4.02, WebTV	µ	Micron
&para;	N3, N4, N4.5, 4.7, 6 IE: 3, 4, 5, 5.5, Opera 4.02, WebTV	&#182;	N: 1, 2, 3, 4, 4.5, 4.7, 6 IE: 3, 4, 5, 5.5, Opera 4.02, WebTV	¶	Paragraph symbol
&middot;	N3, N4, N4.5, 4.7, 6 IE: 3, 4, 5, 5.5, Opera 4.02, WebTV	&#183;	N: 1, 3, 4, 4.5, 4.7, 6 IE: 3, 4, 5, 5.5, Opera 4.02, WebTV	·	Middle dot
&cedil;	N3, N4, N4.5, 4.7, 6 IE: 3, 4, 5, 5.5, Opera 4.02, WebTV	&#184;	N: 1, 3, 4, 4.5, 4.7, 6 IE: 3, 4, 5, 5.5, Opera 4.02, WebTV	¸	Cedilla
&sup1;	N3, N4, N4.5, 4.7, 6 IE: 3, 4, 5, 5.5, Opera 4.02, WebTV	&#185;	N: 1, 3, 4, 4.5, 4.7, 6 IE: 3, 4, 5, 5.5, Opera 4.02, WebTV	^{1}	Superscript 1
&ordm;	N3, N4, N4.5, 4.7, 6 IE: 3, 4, 5, 5.5, Opera 4.02, WebTV	&#186;	N: 1, 3, 4, 4.5, 4.7, 6 IE: 3, 4, 5, 5.5, Opera 4.02, WebTV	º	Masculine ordinal indicator
&raquo;	N3, N4, N4.5, 4.7, 6 IE: 3, 4, 5, 5.5, Opera 4.02, WebTV	&#187;	N: 1, 2, 3, 4, 4.5, 4.7, 6 IE: 3, 4, 5, 5.5, Opera 4.02, WebTV	»	Closing double-angle quotes
&frac14;	N3, N4, N4.5, 4.7, 6 IE: 3, 4, 5, 5.5, Opera 4.02, WebTV	&#188;	N: 1, 3, 4, 4.5, 4.7, 6 IE: 3, 4, 5, 5.5, Opera 4.02, WebTV	¼	One-quarter fraction

3

Named Entity	Browser Support	Numbered Entity	Browser Support	Intended Rendering	Description
&frac12;	N3, N4, N4.5, 4.7, 6 IE: 3, 4, 5, 5.5, Opera 4.02, WebTV	&#189;	N: 1, 3, 4, 4.5, 4.7, 6 IE: 3, 4, 5, 5.5, Opera 4.02, WebTV	½	One-half fraction
&frac34;	N3, N4, N4.5, 4.7, 6 IE: 3, 4, 5, 5.5, Opera 4.02, WebTV	&#190;	N: 1, 3, 4, 4.5, 4.7, 6 IE: 3, 4, 5, 5.5, Opera 4.02, WebTV	¾	Three-fourths fraction
&iquest;	N3, N4, N4.5, 4.7, 6 IE: 3, 4, 5, 5.5, Opera 4.02, WebTV	&#191;	N: 1, 3, 4, 4.5, 4.7, 6 IE: 3, 4, 5, 5.5, Opera 4.02, WebTV	¿	Inverted question mark
&Agrave;	N: 1, 3, 4, 4.5, 4.7, 6 IE: 3, 4, 5, 5.5, Opera 4.02, WebTV	&#192;	N: 1, 3, 4, 4.5, 4.7, 6 IE: 3, 4, 5, 5.5, Opera 4.02, WebTV	À	Uppercase "A" with grave accent
&Aacute;	N: 1, 3, 4, 4.5, 4.7, 6 IE: 3, 4, 5, 5.5, Opera 4.02, WebTV	&#193;	N: 1, 3, 4, 4.5, 4.7, 6 IE: 3, 4, 5, 5.5, Opera 4.02, WebTV	Á	Uppercase "A" with acute accent
&Acirc;	N: 1, 3, 4, 4.5, 4.7, 6 IE: 3, 4, 5, 5.5, Opera 4.02, WebTV	&#194;	N: 1, 3, 4, 4.5, 4.7, 6 IE: 3, 4, 5, 5.5, Opera 4.02, WebTV	Â	Uppercase "A" with circumflex
&Atilde;	N: 1, 3, 4, 4.5, 4.7, 6 IE: 3, 4, 5, 5.5, Opera 4.02, WebTV	&#195;	N: 1, 3, 4, 4.5, 4.7, 6 IE: 3, 4, 5, 5.5, Opera 4.02, WebTV	Ã	Uppercase "A" with tilde
&Auml;	N: 1, 3, 4, 4.5, 4.7, 6 IE: 3, 4, 5, 5.5, Opera 4.02, WebTV	&#196;	N: 1, 3, 4, 4.5, 4.7, 6 IE: 3, 4, 5, 5.5, Opera 4.02, WebTV	Ä	Uppercase "A" with umlaut

Named Entity	Browser Support	Numbered Entity	Browser Support	Intended Rendering	Description
&Aring;	N: 1, 3, 4, 4.5, 4.7, 6 IE: 3, 4, 5, 5.5, Opera 4.02, WebTV	&#197;	N: 1, 3, 4, 4.5, 4.7, 6 IE: 3, 4, 5, 5.5, Opera 4.02, WebTV	Å	Uppercase "A" with ring
&AElig;	N: 1, 3, 4, 4.5, 4.7, 6 IE: 3, 4, 5, 5.5, Opera 4.02, WebTV	&#198;	N: 1, 3, 4, 4.5, 4.7, 6 IE: 3, 4, 5, 5.5, Opera 4.02, WebTV	Æ	Uppercase "AE" ligature
&Ccedil;	N: 1, 3, 4, 4.5, 4.7, 6 IE: 3, 4, 5, 5.5, Opera 4.02, WebTV	&#199;	N: 1, 3, 4, 4.5, 4.7, 6 IE: 3, 4, 5, 5.5, Opera 4.02, WebTV	Ç	Uppercase "C" with cedilla
&Egrave;	N: 1, 3, 4, 4.5, 4.7, 6 IE: 3, 4, 5, 5.5, Opera 4.02, WebTV	&#200;	N: 1, 3, 4, 4.5, 4.7, 6 IE: 3, 4, 5, 5.5, Opera 4.02, WebTV	È	Uppercase "E" with grave accent
&Eacute;	N: 1, 3, 4, 4.5, 4.7, 6 IE: 3, 4, 5, 5.5, Opera 4.02, WebTV	&#201;	N: 1, 3, 4, 4.5, 4.7, 6 IE: 3, 4, 5, 5.5, Opera 4.02, WebTV	É	Uppercase "E" with acute accent
&Ecirc;	N: 1, 3, 4, 4.5, 4.7, 6 IE: 3, 4, 5, 5.5, Opera 4.02, WebTV	&#202;	N: 1, 3, 4, 4.5, 4.7, 6 IE: 3, 4, 5, 5.5, Opera 4.02, WebTV	Ê	Uppercase "E" with circumflex
&Euml;	N: 1, 3, 4, 4.5, 4.7, 6 IE: 3, 4, 5, 5.5, Opera 4.02, WebTV	&#203;	N: 1, 3, 4, 4.5, 4.7, 6 IE: 3, 4, 5, 5.5, Opera 4.02, WebTV	Ë	Uppercase "E" with umlaut
&Igrave;	N: 1, 3, 4, 4.5, 4.7, 6 IE: 3, 4, 5, 5.5, Opera 4.02, WebTV	&#204;	N: 1, 3, 4, 4.5, 4.7, 6 IE: 3, 4, 5, 5.5, Opera 4.02, WebTV	Ì	Uppercase "I" with grave accent

3

Named Entity	Browser Support	Numbered Entity	Browser Support	Intended Rendering	Description
&Iacute;	N: 1, 3, 4, 4.5, 4.7, 6 IE: 3, 4, 5, 5.5, Opera 4.02, WebTV	&#205;	N: 1, 3, 4, 4.5, 4.7, 6 IE: 3, 4, 5, 5.5, Opera 4.02, WebTV	Í	Uppercase "I" with acute accent
&Icirc;	N: 1, 3, 4, 4.5, 4.7, 6 IE: 3, 4, 5, 5.5, Opera 4.02, WebTV	&#206;	N: 1, 3, 4, 4.5, 4.7, 6 IE: 3, 4, 5, 5.5, Opera 4.02, WebTV	Î	Uppercase "I" with circumflex
&Iuml;	N: 1, 3, 4, 4.5, 4.7, 6 IE: 3, 4, 5, 5.5, Opera 4.02, WebTV	&#207;	N: 1, 3, 4, 4.5, 4.7, 6 IE: 3, 4, 5, 5.5, Opera 4.02, WebTV	Ï	Uppercase "I" with umlaut
&ETH;	N: 1, 3, 4, 4.5, 4.7, 6 IE: 3, 4, 5, 5.5, Opera 4.02, WebTV	&#208;	N: 1, 3, 4, 4.5, 4.7, 6 IE: 3, 4, 5, 5.5, Opera 4.02, WebTV	Ð	Capital "ETH"
&Ntilde;	N: 1, 3, 4, 4.5, 4.7, 6 IE: 3, 4, 5, 5.5, Opera 4.02, WebTV	&#209;	N: 1, 3, 4, 4.5, 4.7, 6 IE: 3, 4, 5, 5.5, Opera 4.02, WebTV	Ñ	Uppercase "N" with tilde
&Ograve;	N: 1, 3, 4, 4.5, 4.7, 6 IE: 3, 4, 5, 5.5, Opera 4.02, WebTV	&#210;	N: 1, 3, 4, 4.5, 4.7, 6 IE: 3, 4, 5, 5.5, Opera 4.02, WebTV	Ò	Uppercase "O" with grave accent
&Oacute;	N: 1, 3, 4, 4.5, 4.7, 6 IE: 3, 4, 5, 5.5, Opera 4.02, WebTV	&#211;	N: 1, 3, 4, 4.5, 4.7, 6 IE: 3, 4, 5, 5.5, Opera 4.02, WebTV	Ó	Uppercase "O" with acute accent
&Ocirc;	N: 1, 3, 4, 4.5, 4.7, 6 IE: 3, 4, 5, 5.5, Opera 4.02, WebTV	&#212;	N: 1, 3, 4, 4.5, 4.7, 6 IE: 3, 4, 5, 5.5, Opera 4.02, WebTV	Ô	Uppercase "O" with circumflex

Named Entity	Browser Support	Numbered Entity	Browser Support	Intended Rendering	Description
&Otilde;	N: 1, 3, 4, 4.5, 4.7, 6 IE: 3, 4, 5, 5.5, Opera 4.02, WebTV	&#213;	N: 1, 3, 4, 4.5, 4.7, 6 IE: 3, 4, 5, 5.5, Opera 4.02, WebTV	Õ	Uppercase "O" with tilde
&Ouml;	N: 1, 3, 4, 4.5, 4.7, 6 IE: 3, 4, 5, 5.5, Opera 4.02, WebTV	&#214;	N: 1, 3, 4, 4.5, 4.7, 6 IE: 3, 4, 5, 5.5, Opera 4.02, WebTV	Ö	Uppercase "O" with umlaut
&times;	N3, N4, N4.5, 4.7, 6 IE: 3, 4, 5, 5.5, Opera 4.02, WebTV	&#215;	N: 1, 3, 4, 4.5, 4.7, 6 IE: 3, 4, 5, 5.5, Opera 4.02, WebTV	×	Multiplication symbol
&Oslash;	N: 1, 3, 4, 4.5, 4.7, 6 IE: 3, 4, 5, 5.5, Opera 4.02, WebTV	&#216;	N: 1, 3, 4, 4.5, 4.7, 6 IE: 3, 4, 5, 5.5, Opera 4.02, WebTV	Ø	Uppercase "O" with slash
&Ugrave;	N: 1, 3, 4, 4.5, 4.7, 6 IE: 3, 4, 5, 5.5, Opera 4.02, WebTV	&#217;	N: 1, 3, 4, 4.5, 4.7, 6 IE: 3, 4, 5, 5.5, Opera 4.02, WebTV	Ù	Uppercase "U" with grave accent
&Uacute;	N: 1, 3, 4, 4.5, 4.7, 6 IE: 3, 4, 5, 5.5, Opera 4.02, WebTV	&#218;	N: 1, 3, 4, 4.5, 4.7, 6 IE: 3, 4, 5, 5.5, Opera 4.02, WebTV	Ú	Uppercase "U" with acute accent
&Ucirc;	N: 1, 3, 4, 4.5, 4.7, 6 IE: 3, 4, 5, 5.5, Opera 4.02, WebTV	&#219;	N: 1, 3, 4, 4.5, 4.7, 6 IE: 3, 4, 5, 5.5, Opera 4.02, WebTV	Û	Uppercase "U" with circumflex accent
&Uuml;	N: 1, 3, 4, 4.5, 4.7, 6 IE: 3, 4, 5, 5.5, Opera 4.02, WebTV	&#220;	N: 1, 3, 4, 4.5, 4.7, 6 IE: 3, 4, 5, 5.5, Opera 4.02, WebTV	Ü	Uppercase "U" with umlaut

3

Named Entity	Browser Support	Numbered Entity	Browser Support	Intended Rendering	Description
&Yacute;	N: 1, 3, 4, 4.5, 4.7, 6 IE: 3, 4, 5, 5.5, Opera 4.02, WebTV	&#221;	N: 1, 3, 4, 4.5, 4.7, 6 IE: 3, 4, 5, 5.5, Opera 4.02, WebTV	Ý	Uppercase "Y" with acute accent
&THORN;	N: 1, 3, 4, 4.5, 4.7, 6 IE: 3, 4, 5, 5.5, Opera 4.02, WebTV	&#222;	N: 1, 3, 4, 4.5, 4.7, 6 IE: 3, 4, 5, 5.5, Opera 4.02, WebTV	Þ	Capital "thorn"
&szlig;	N: 1, 3, 4, 4.5, 4.7, 6 IE: 3, 4, 5, 5.5, Opera 4.02, WebTV	&#223;	N: 1, 3, 4, 4.5, 4.7, 6 IE: 3, 4, 5, 5.5, Opera 4.02, WebTV	ß	"SZ" ligature
&agrave;	N: 1, 3, 4, 4.5, 4.7, 6 IE: 3, 4, 5, 5.5, Opera 4.02, WebTV	&#224;	N: 1, 3, 4, 4.5, 4.7, 6 IE: 3, 4, 5, 5.5, Opera 4.02, WebTV	à	Lowercase "a" with grave accent
&aacute;	N: 1, 3, 4, 4.5, 4.7, 6 IE: 3, 4, 5, 5.5, Opera 4.02, WebTV	&#225;	N: 1, 3, 4, 4.5, 4.7, 6 IE: 3, 4, 5, 5.5, Opera 4.02, WebTV	á	Lowercase "a" with acute accent
&acirc;	N: 1, 3, 4, 4.5, 4.7, 6 IE: 3, 4, 5, 5.5, Opera 4.02, WebTV	&#226;	N: 1, 3, 4, 4.5, 4.7, 6 IE: 3, 4, 5, 5.5, Opera 4.02, WebTV	â	Lowercase "a" with circumflex
&atilde;	N: 1, 3, 4, 4.5, 4.7, 6 IE: 3, 4, 5, 5.5, Opera 4.02, WebTV	&#227;	N: 1, 3, 4, 4.5, 4.7, 6 IE: 3, 4, 5, 5.5, Opera 4.02, WebTV	ã	Lowercase "a" with tilde
&auml;	N: 1, 3, 4, 4.5, 4.7, 6 IE: 3, 4, 5, 5.5, Opera 4.02, WebTV	&#228;	N: 1, 3, 4, 4.5, 4.7, 6 IE: 3, 4, 5, 5.5, Opera 4.02, WebTV	ä	Lowercase "a" with umlaut

Named Entity	Browser Support	Numbered Entity	Browser Support	Intended Rendering	Description
&aring;	N: 1, 3, 4, 4.5, 4.7, 6 IE: 3, 4, 5, 5.5, Opera 4.02, WebTV	&#229;	N: 1, 3, 4, 4.5, 4.7, 6 IE: 3, 4, 5, 5.5, Opera 4.02, WebTV	å	Lowercase "a" with ring
&aelig;	N: 1, 3, 4, 4.5, 4.7, 6 IE: 3, 4, 5, 5.5, Opera 4.02, WebTV	&#230;	N: 1, 3, 4, 4.5, 4.7, 6 IE: 3, 4, 5, 5.5, Opera 4.02, WebTV	æ	Lowercase "ae" ligature
&ccedil;	N: 1, 3, 4, 4.5, 4.7, 6 IE: 3, 4, 5, 5.5, Opera 4.02, WebTV	&#231;	N: 1, 3, 4, 4.5, 4.7, 6 IE: 3, 4, 5, 5.5, Opera 4.02, WebTV	ç	Lowercase "c" with cedilla
&egrave;	N: 1, 3, 4, 4.5, 4.7, 6 IE: 3, 4, 5, 5.5, Opera 4.02, WebTV	&#232;	N: 1, 3, 4, 4.5, 4.7, 6 IE: 3, 4, 5, 5.5, Opera 4.02, WebTV	è	Lowercase "e" with grave accent
&eacute;	N: 1, 3, 4, 4.5, 4.7, 6 IE: 3, 4, 5, 5.5, Opera 4.02, WebTV	&#233;	N: 1, 3, 4, 4.5, 4.7, 6 IE: 3, 4, 5, 5.5, Opera 4.02, WebTV	é	Lowercase "e" with acute accent
&ecirc;	N: 1, 3, 4, 4.5, 4.7, 6 IE: 3, 4, 5, 5.5, Opera 4.02, WebTV	&#234;	N: 1, 3, 4, 4.5, 4.7, 6 IE: 3, 4, 5, 5.5, Opera 4.02, WebTV	ê	Lowercase "e" with circumflex
&euml;	N: 1, 3, 4, 4.5, 4.7, 6 IE: 3, 4, 5, 5.5, Opera 4.02, WebTV	&#235;	N: 1, 3, 4, 4.5, 4.7, 6 IE: 3, 4, 5, 5.5, Opera 4.02, WebTV	ë	Lowercase "e" with umlaut
&igrave;	N: 1, 3, 4, 4.5, 4.7, 6 IE: 3, 4, 5, 5.5, Opera 4.02, WebTV	&#236;	N: 1, 3, 4, 4.5, 4.7, 6 IE: 3, 4, 5, 5.5, Opera 4.02, WebTV	ì	Lowercase "i" with grave accent

3

Named Entity	Browser Support	Numbered Entity	Browser Support	Intended Rendering	Description
&iacute;	N: 1, 3, 4, 4.5, 4.7, 6 IE: 3, 4, 5, 5.5, Opera 4.02, WebTV	&#237;	N: 1, 3, 4, 4.5, 4.7, 6 IE: 3, 4, 5, 5.5, Opera 4.02, WebTV	í	Lowercase "i" with acute accent
&icirc;	N: 1, 3, 4, 4.5, 4.7, 6 IE: 3, 4, 5, 5.5, Opera 4.02, WebTV	&#238;	N: 1, 3, 4, 4.5, 4.7, 6 IE: 3, 4, 5, 5.5, Opera 4.02, WebTV	î	Lowercase "i" with circumflex
&iuml;	N: 1, 3, 4, 4.5, 4.7, 6 IE: 3, 4, 5, 5.5, Opera 4.02, WebTV	&#239;	N: 1, 3, 4, 4.5, 4.7, 6 IE: 3, 4, 5, 5.5, Opera 4.02, WebTV	ï	Lowercase "i" with umlaut
&eth;	N: 1, 3, 4, 4.5, 4.7, 6 IE: 3, 4, 5, 5.5, Opera 4.02, WebTV	&#240;	N: 1, 3, 4, 4.5, 4.7, 6 IE: 3, 4, 5, 5.5, Opera 4.02, WebTV	ð	Lowercase "eth"
&ntilde;	N: 1, 3, 4, 4.5, 4.7, 6 IE: 3, 4, 5, 5.5, Opera 4.02, WebTV	&#241;	N: 1, 3, 4, 4.5, 4.7, 6 IE: 3, 4, 5, 5.5, Opera 4.02, WebTV	ñ	Lowercase "n" with tilde
&ograve;	N: 1, 3, 4, 4.5, 4.7, 6 IE: 3, 4, 5, 5.5, Opera 4.02, WebTV	&#242;	N: 1, 3, 4, 4.5, 4.7, 6 IE: 3, 4, 5, 5.5, Opera 4.02, WebTV	ò	Lowercase "o" with grave accent
&oacute;	N: 1, 3, 4, 4.5, 4.7, 6 IE: 3, 4, 5, 5.5, Opera 4.02, WebTV	&#243;	N: 1, 3, 4, 4.5, 4.7, 6 IE: 3, 4, 5, 5.5, Opera 4.02, WebTV	ó	Lowercase "o" with acute accent
&ocirc;	N: 1, 3, 4, 4.5, 4.7, 6 IE: 3, 4, 5, 5.5, Opera 4.02, WebTV	&#244;	N: 1, 3, 4, 4.5, 4.7, 6 IE: 3, 4, 5, 5.5, Opera 4.02, WebTV	ô	Lowercase "o" with circumflex accent

Named Entity	Browser Support	Numbered Entity	Browser Support	Intended Rendering	Description
&otilde;	N: 1, 3, 4, 4.5, 4.7, 6 IE: 3, 4, 5, 5.5, Opera 4.02, WebTV	&#245;	N: 1, 3, 4, 4.5, 4.7, 6 IE: 3, 4, 5, 5.5, Opera 4.02, WebTV	õ	Lowercase "o" with tilde
&ouml;	N: 1, 3, 4, 4.5, 4.7, 6 IE: 3, 4, 5, 5.5, Opera 4.02, WebTV	&#246;	N: 1, 3, 4, 4.5, 4.7, 6 IE: 3, 4, 5, 5.5, Opera 4.02, WebTV	ö	Lowercase "o" with umlaut
&divide;	N3, N4, N4.5, 4.7, 6 IE: 3, 4, 5, 5.5, Opera 4.02, WebTV	&#247;	N: 1, 3, 4, 4.5, 4.7, 6 IE: 3, 4, 5, 5.5, Opera 4.02, WebTV	÷	Division symbol
&oslash;	N: 1, 3, 4, 4.5, 4.7, 6 IE: 3, 4, 5, 5.5, Opera 4.02, WebTV	&#248;	N: 1, 3, 4, 4.5, 4.7, 6 IE: 3, 4, 5, 5.5, Opera 4.02, WebTV	ø	Lowercase "o" with slash
&ugrave;	N: 1, 3, 4, 4.5, 4.7, 6 IE: 3, 4, 5, 5.5, Opera 4.02, WebTV	&#249;	N: 1, 3, 4, 4.5, 4.7, 6 IE: 3, 4, 5, 5.5, Opera 4.02, WebTV	ù	Lowercase "u" with grave accent
&uacute;	N: 1, 3, 4, 4.5, 4.7, 6 IE: 3, 4, 5, 5.5, Opera 4.02, WebTV	&#250;	N: 1, 3, 4, 4.5, 4.7, 6 IE: 3, 4, 5, 5.5, Opera 4.02, WebTV	ú	Lowercase "u" with acute accent
&ucirc;	N: 1, 3, 4, 4.5, 4.7, 6 IE: 3, 4, 5, 5.5, Opera 4.02, WebTV	&#251;	N: 1, 3, 4, 4.5, 4.7, 6 IE: 3, 4, 5, 5.5, Opera 4.02, WebTV	û	Lowercase "u" with circumflex
&uuml;	N: 1, 3, 4, 4.5, 4.7, 6 IE: 3, 4, 5, 5.5, Opera 4.02, WebTV	&#252;	N: 1, 3, 4, 4.5, 4.7, 6 IE: 3, 4, 5, 5.5, Opera 4.02, WebTV	ü	Lowercase "u" with umlaut

3

Named Entity	Browser Support	Numbered Entity	Browser Support	Intended Rendering	Description
&yacute;	N: 1, 3, 4, 4.5, 4.7, 6 IE: 3, 4, 5, 5.5, Opera 4.02, WebTV	&#253;	N: 1, 3, 4, 4.5, 4.7, 6 IE: 3, 4, 5, 5.5, Opera 4.02, WebTV	ý	Lowercase "y" with acute accent
&thorn;	N: 1, 3, 4, 4.5, 4.7, 6 IE: 3, 4, 5, 5.5, Opera 4.02, WebTV	&#254;	N: 1, 3, 4, 4.5, 4.7, 6 IE: 3, 4, 5, 5.5, Opera 4.02, WebTV	þ	Lowercase "thorn"
&yuml;	N: 1, 3, 4, 4.5, 4.7, 6 IE: 3, 4, 5, 5.5, Opera 4.02, WebTV	&#255;	N: 1, 3, 4, 4.5, 4.7, 6 IE: 3, 4, 5, 5.5, Opera 4.02, WebTV	ÿ	Lowercase "y" with umlaut

* *WebTV renders € as a right-pointing arrowhead.*

† *WebTV renders  as a left-pointing arrowhead.*

‡ Support for ™ (™) is inconsistent across platforms, although this has improved much in more recent browsers. Designers concerned with backward compatibility might want to consider using a workaround such as **<sup><small>**TM**</small></sup>**.

HTML 4.0 Character Entities

The HTML 4.0 specification introduced a wide array of new character entities that expand the presentation possibilities of HTML, particularly in the presentation of foreign languages. These include additional Latin characters, the Greek alphabet, special spacing characters, arrows, technical symbols, and various shapes. Some of these entities have yet to be supported by browser vendors. Netscape versions 4.0 through 4.73 support only a few of the extended Latin characters, and some entities that duplicate characters already are available in the "standard" list (32 through 255). Internet Explorer versions 4.0 and higher support many of these entities, including the Greek alphabet and mathematical symbols. Testing in early releases of Netscape 6 shows that Netscape has finally addressed the shortcomings of their earlier browsers.

Latin Extended-A

Named Entity	Browser Support	Numbered Entity	Browser Support	Intended Rendering	Description
&Oelig;	IE: 4, 5, 5.5 N: 6	&#338;	IE: 4, 5, 5.5, N: 4, 4.5, 4.7, 6	Œ	Uppercase ligature "OE"
&oelig;	IE: 4, 5, 5.5 N: 6	&#339;	IE: 4, 5, 5.5, N: 4, 4.5, 4.7, 6	œ	Lowercase ligature "oe"
&Scaron;	IE: 4, 5, 5.5 N: 6	&#352;	IE: 4, 5, 5.5, N: 4, 4.5, 4.7, 6	Š	Uppercase "S" with caron
&scaron;	IE: 4, 5, 5.5 N: 6	&#353;	IE: 4, 5, 5.5, N: 4, 4.5, 4.7, 6	š	Lowercase "s" with caron
&Yuml;	IE: 4, 5, 5.5 N: 6	&#376;	IE: 4, 5, 5.5, N: 4, 4.5, 4.7, 6	Ÿ	Uppercase "Y" with umlaut

NOTE: Internet Explorer 5 for Macintosh displays Š, Š, š, and š with the caron shifted one space to the left of the "s" or "S" character it should be over.

Latin Extended-B

Named Entity	Browser Support	Numbered Entity	Browser Support	Intended Rendering	Description
&fnof;	IE: 4, 5, 5.5 N: 6	&#402;	IE: 4, 5, 5.5, N: 4, 4.5, 4.7, 6	ƒ	Latin small "f" with hook

Spacing Modifier Letters

Named Entity	Browser Support	Numbered Entity	Browser Support	Intended Rendering	Description
&circ;	IE: 4, 5, 5.5 N: 6, O: 4	&#710;	IE: 4, 5, 5.5, N: 4, 4.5, 4.7, 6, O: 4	^	Circumflex accent

3

Named Entity	Browser Support	Numbered Entity	Browser Support	Intended Rendering	Description
&tilde;	IE: 4, 5, 5.5 N: 6, O: 4	&#732;	IE: 4, 5, 5.5, N: 4, 4.5, 4.7, 6, O: 4	~	Small tilde

General Punctuation

Named Entity	Browser Support	Numbered Entity	Browser Support	Intended Rendering	Description
	N: 6		N: 6		En space
	N: 6		N: 6		Em space
	N: 6		N: 6		Thin space
&zwnj;	IE: 4, 5, 5.5	&#8204;	IE: 4, 5, 5.5	|	Zero width nonjoiner
&zwj;	IE: 4, 5, 5.5	&#8205;	IE: 4, 5, 5.5	Ɏ	Zero width joiner
&lrm;	None	&#8206;	None	Unknown	Left-to-right mark
&rlm;	None	&#8207;	None	Unknown	Right-to-left mark
&ndash;	IE: 4, 5, 5.5 N: 6	&#8211;	IE: 4, 5, 5.5, N: 4, 4.5, 4.7, 6	–	En dash
&mdash;	IE: 4, 5, 5.5 N: 6	&#8212;	IE: 4, 5, 5.5, N: 4, 4.5, 4.7, 6	—	Em dash
&lsquo;	IE: 4, 5, 5.5 N: 6	&#8216;	IE: 4, 5, 5.5, N: 4, 4.5, 4.7, 6	'	Left single quotation mark
&rsquo;	IE: 4, 5, 5.5 N: 6	&#8217;	IE: 4, 5, 5.5, N: 4, 4.5, 4.7, 6	'	Right single quotation mark
&sbquo;	IE: 4, 5, 5.5 N: 6	&#8218;	IE: 4, 5, 5.5, N: 4, 4.5, 4.7, 6	,	Single low-9 quotation mark
&ldquo;	IE: 4, 5, 5.5 N: 6	&#8220;	IE: 4, 5, 5.5, N: 4, 4.5, 4.7, 6	"	Left double quotation mark
&rdquo;	IE: 4, 5, 5.5 N: 6	&#8221;	IE: 4, 5, 5.5, N: 4, 4.5, 4.7, 6	"	Right double quotation mark
&bdquo;	IE: 4, 5, 5.5 N: 6	&#8222;	IE: 4, 5, 5.5, N: 4, 4.5, 4.7, 6	„	Double low-9 quotation mark

Named Entity	Browser Support	Numbered Entity	Browser Support	Intended Rendering	Description
&dagger;	IE: 4, 5, 5.5 N: 6	&#8224;	IE: 4, 5, 5.5, N: 4, 4.5, 4.7, 6	†	Dagger
&Dagger;	IE: 4, 5, 5.5 N: 6	&#8225;	IE: 4, 5, 5.5, N: 4, 4.5, 4.7, 6	‡	Double dagger
&bull;	IE: 4, 5, 5.5 N: 6	&#8226;	IE: 4, 5, 5.5, N: 4, 4.5, 4.7, 6	•	Bullet
&hellip;	IE: 4, 5, 5.5 N: 6	&#8230;	IE: 4, 5, 5.5, N: 4, 4.5, 4.7, 6	…	Horizontal ellipsis
&permil;	IE: 4, 5, 5.5 N: 6	&#8240;	IE: 4, 5, 5.5, N: 4, 4.5, 4.7, 6	‰	Per thousand sign
&prime;	IE: 4, 5, 5.5 N: 6	&#8242;	IE: 4, 5, 5.5 N: 6	′	Prime, minutes, or feet
&Prime;	IE: 4, 5, 5.5 N: 6	&#8243;	IE: 4, 5, 5.5 N: 6	″	Double prime, seconds, or inches
&lsaquo;	IE: 4, 5, 5.5 N: 6, O: 4	&#8249;	IE: 4, 5, 5.5, N: 4, 4.5, 4.7, 6, O: 4	‹	Single left-pointing angle quotation mark
&rsaquo;	IE: 4, 5, 5.5 N: 6, O: 4	&#8250;	IE: 4, 5, 5.5, N: 4, 4.5, 4.7, 6, O: 4	›	Single right-pointing angle quotation mark
&oline;	IE: 4, 5, 5.5 N: 6	&#8254;	IE: 4, 5, 5.5 N: 6	‾	Overline
&frasl;	IE: 4, 5, 5.5 N: 6, O: 4	&#8260;	IE: 4, 5, 5.5 N: 6, O: 4	⁄	Fraction slash

Greek

Named Entity	Browser Support	Numbered Entity	Browser Support	Intended Rendering	Description
&Alpha;	IE: 4, 5, 5.5 N: 6	&#913;	IE: 4, 5, 5.5 N: 6	A	Greek capital letter alpha

Named Entity	Browser Support	Numbered Entity	Browser Support	Intended Rendering	Description
&Beta;	IE: 4, 5, 5.5 N: 6	&#914;	IE: 4, 5, 5.5 N: 6	Β	Greek capital letter beta
&Gamma;	IE: 4, 5, 5.5 N: 6	&#915;	IE: 4, 5, 5.5 N: 6	Γ	Greek capital letter gamma
&Delta;	IE: 4, 5, 5.5 N: 6	&#916;	IE: 4, 5, 5.5 N: 6	Δ	Greek capital letter delta
&Epsilon;	IE: 4, 5, 5.5 N: 6	&#917;	IE: 4, 5, 5.5 N: 6	Ε	Greek capital letter epsilon
&Zeta;	IE: 4, 5, 5.5 N: 6	&#918;	IE: 4, 5, 5.5 N: 6	Ζ	Greek capital letter zeta
&Eta;	IE: 4, 5, 5.5 N: 6	&#919;	IE: 4, 5, 5.5 N: 6	Η	Greek capital letter eta
&Theta;	IE: 4, 5, 5.5 N: 6	&#920;	IE: 4, 5, 5.5 N: 6	Θ	Greek capital letter theta
&Iota;	IE: 4, 5, 5.5 N: 6	&#921;	IE: 4, 5, 5.5 N: 6	Ι	Greek capital letter iota
&Kappa;	IE: 4, 5, 5.5 N: 6	&#922;	IE: 4, 5, 5.5 N: 6	Κ	Greek capital letter kappa
&Lambda;	IE: 4, 5, 5.5 N: 6	&#923;	IE: 4, 5, 5.5 N: 6	Λ	Greek capital letter lambda
&Mu;	IE: 4, 5, 5.5 N: 6	&#924;	IE: 4, 5, 5.5 N: 6	Μ	Greek capital letter mu
&Nu;	IE: 4, 5, 5.5 N: 6	&#925;	IE: 4, 5, 5.5 N: 6	Ν	Greek capital letter nu
&Xi;	IE: 4, 5, 5.5 N: 6	&#926;	IE: 4, 5, 5.5 N: 6	Ξ	Greek capital letter xi
&Omicron;	IE: 4, 5, 5.5 N: 6	&#927;	IE: 4, 5, 5.5 N: 6	Ο	Greek capital letter omicron
&Pi;	IE: 4, 5, 5.5 N: 6	&#928;	IE: 4, 5, 5.5 N: 6	Π	Greek capital letter pi

Named Entity	Browser Support	Numbered Entity	Browser Support	Intended Rendering	Description
&Rho;	IE: 4, 5, 5.5 N: 6	&#929;	IE: 4, 5, 5.5 N: 6	P	Greek capital letter rho
&Sigma;	IE: 4, 5, 5.5 N: 6	&#931;	IE: 4, 5, 5.5 N: 6	Σ	Greek capital letter sigma
&Tau;	IE: 4, 5, 5.5 N: 6	&#932;	IE: 4, 5, 5.5 N: 6	T	Greek capital letter tau
&Upsilon;	IE: 4, 5, 5.5 N: 6	&#933;	IE: 4, 5, 5.5 N: 6	Y	Greek capital letter upsilon
&Phi;	IE: 4, 5, 5.5 N: 6	&#934;	IE: 4, 5, 5.5 N: 6	Φ	Greek capital letter phi
&Chi;	IE: 4, 5, 5.5 N: 6	&#935;	IE: 4, 5, 5.5 N: 6	X	Greek capital letter chi
&Psi;	IE: 4, 5, 5.5 N: 6	&#936;	IE: 4, 5, 5.5 N: 6	Ψ	Greek capital letter psi
&Omega;	IE: 4, 5, 5.5 N: 6	&#937;	IE: 4, 5, 5.5 N: 6	Ω	Greek capital letter omega
&alpha;	IE: 4, 5, 5.5 N: 6	&#945;	IE: 4, 5, 5.5 N: 6	α	Greek small letter alpha
&beta;	IE: 4, 5, 5.5 N: 6	&#946;	IE: 4, 5, 5.5 N: 6	β	Greek small letter beta
&gamma;	IE: 4, 5, 5.5 N: 6	&#947;	IE: 4, 5, 5.5 N: 6	γ	Greek small letter gamma
&delta;	IE: 4, 5, 5.5 N: 6	&#948;	IE: 4, 5, 5.5 N: 6	δ	Greek small letter delta
&epsilon;	IE: 4, 5, 5.5 N: 6	&#949;	IE: 4, 5, 5.5 N: 6	ε	Greek small letter epsilon
&zeta;	IE: 4, 5, 5.5 N: 6	&#950;	IE: 4, 5, 5.5 N: 6	ζ	Greek small letter zeta
&eta;	IE: 4, 5, 5.5 N: 6	&#951;	IE: 4, 5, 5.5 N: 6	η	Greek small letter eta
&theta;	IE: 4, 5, 5.5 N: 6	&#952;	IE: 4, 5, 5.5 N: 6	θ	Greek small letter theta
&iota;	IE: 4, 5, 5.5 N: 6	&#953;	IE: 4, 5, 5.5 N: 6	ι	Greek small letter iota

3

Named Entity	Browser Support	Numbered Entity	Browser Support	Intended Rendering	Description
&kappa;	IE: 4, 5, 5.5 N: 6	&#954;	IE: 4, 5, 5.5 N: 6	κ	Greek small letter kappa
&lambda;	IE: 4, 5, 5.5 N: 6	&#955;	IE: 4, 5, 5.5 N: 6	λ	Greek small letter lambda
&mu;	IE: 4, 5, 5.5 N: 6	&#956;	IE: 4, 5, 5.5 N: 6	μ	Greek small letter mu
&nu;	IE: 4, 5, 5.5 N: 6	&#957;	IE: 4, 5, 5.5 N: 6	ν	Greek small letter nu
&xi;	IE: 4, 5, 5.5 N: 6	&#958;	IE: 4, 5, 5.5 N: 6	ξ	Greek small letter xi
&omicron;	IE: 4, 5, 5.5 N: 6	&#959;	IE: 4, 5, 5.5 N: 6	o	Greek small letter omicron
&pi;	IE: 4, 5, 5.5 N: 6	&#960;	IE: 4, 5, 5.5 N: 6	π	Greek small letter pi
&rho;	IE: 4, 5, 5.5 N: 6	&#961;	IE: 4, 5, 5.5 N: 6	ρ	Greek small letter rho
&sigmaf;	IE: 4, 5, 5.5 N: 6	&#962;	IE: 4, 5, 5.5 N: 6	ς	Greek small letter final sigma
&sigma;	IE: 4, 5, 5.5 N: 6	&#963;	IE: 4, 5, 5.5 N: 6	σ	Greek small letter sigma
&tau;	IE: 4, 5, 5.5 N: 6	&#964;	IE: 4, 5, 5.5 N: 6	τ	Greek small letter tau
&upsilon;	IE: 4, 5, 5.5 N: 6	&#965;	IE: 4, 5, 5.5 N: 6	υ	Greek small letter upsilon
&phi;	IE: 4, 5, 5.5 N: 6	&#966;	IE: 4, 5, 5.5 N: 6	φ	Greek small letter phi
&chi;	IE: 4, 5, 5.5 N: 6	&#967;	IE: 4, 5, 5.5 N: 6	χ	Greek small letter chi
&psi;	IE: 4, 5, 5.5 N: 6	&#968;	IE: 4, 5, 5.5 N: 6	ψ	Greek small letter psi
&omega;	IE: 4, 5, 5.5 N: 6	&#969;	IE: 4, 5, 5.5 N: 6	ω	Greek small letter omega
&thetasym;	IE: 5 (Mac only), N: 6	&#977;	IE: 5 (Mac only), N: 6	θ	Greek small letter theta symbol
&upsih;	IE: 5 (Mac only), N: 6	&#978;	IE: 5 (Mac only), N: 6	γ	Greek upsilon with hook symbol
&piv	IE: 5 (Mac only), N: 6	&#982;	IE: 5 (Mac only), N: 6	ϖ	Greek pi symbol

Letter-like Symbols

Named Entity	Browser Support	Numbered Entity	Browser Support	Intended Rendering	Description
&weierp;	N: 6	&#8472;	N: 6	℘	Script capital P, power set
&image;	N: 6	&#8465;	N: 6	ℑ	Blackletter capital I, or imaginary part symbol
&real;	N: 6	&#8476;	N: 6	ℜ	Blackletter capital R, or real part symbol
&trade;	IE: 3, 4, 5, 5.5 N: 6, O: 4	&#8482;	IE: 4, 5, 5.5, N: 4, 4.5, 4.7, 6, O: 4	™	Trademark symbol
&alefsym;	N: 6	&#8501;	N: 6	ℵ	Alef symbol, or first transfinite cardinal

Arrows

Named Entity	Browser Support	Numbered Entity	Browser Support	Intended Rendering	Description
&larr;	IE: 4, 5, 5.5 N: 6	&#8592;	IE: 4, 5, 5.5 N: 6	←	Leftward arrow
&uarr;	IE: 4, 5, 5.5 N: 6	&#8593;	IE: 4, 5, 5.5 N: 6	↑	Upward arrow
&rarr;	IE: 4, 5, 5.5 N: 6	&#8594;	IE: 4, 5, 5.5 N: 6	→	Rightward arrow
&darr;	IE: 4, 5, 5.5 N: 6	&#8595;	IE: 4, 5, 5.5 N: 6	↓	Downward arrow
&harr;	IE: 4, 5, 5.5 N: 6	&#8596;	IE: 4, 5, 5.5 N: 6	↔	Left-right arrow
&crarr;	N: 6	&#8629;	N: 6	↵	Downward arrow with corner leftward
&lArr;	N: 6	&#8656;	N: 6	⇐	Leftward double arrow

Named Entity	Browser Support	Numbered Entity	Browser Support	Intended Rendering	Description
&uArr;	N: 6	&#8657;	N: 6	⇑	Upward double arrow
&rArr;	N: 6	&#8658;	N: 6	⇒	Rightward double arrow
&dArr;	N: 6	&#8659;	N: 6	⇓	Downward double arrow
&hArr;	N: 6	&#8660;	N: 6	⇔	Left-right double arrow

Mathematical Operators

Named Entity	Browser Support	Numbered Entity	Browser Support	Intended Rendering	Description
&forall;	N: 6	&#8704;	N: 6	∀	For all
&part;	IE: 4, 5, 5.5 N: 6	&#8706;	IE: 4, 5, 5.5 N: 6	∂	Partial differential
&exist;	N: 6	&#8707;	N: 6	∃	There exists
&empty;	N: 6	&#8709;	N: 6	∅	Empty set, null set, diameter
&nabla;	N: 6	&#8711;	N: 6	∇	Nabla, or backward difference
&isin;	N: 6	&#8712;	N: 6	∈	Element of
&notin;	N: 6	&#8713;	N: 6	∉	Not an element of
&ni;	N: 6	&#8715;	N: 6	∋	Contains as member
&prod;	IE: 4, 5, 5.5 N: 6	&#8719;	IE: 4, 5, 5.5 N: 6	∏	N-ary product, or product sign
&sum;	IE: 4, 5, 5.5 N: 6	&#8721;	IE: 4, 5, 5.5 N: 6	∑	N-ary summation
&minus;	IE: 4, 5, 5.5 N: 6 O: 4	&#8722;	IE: 4, 5, 5.5 N: 6 O: 4	−	Minus sign
&lowast;	N: 6	&#8727;	N: 6	∗	Asterisk operator
&radic;	IE: 4, 5, 5.5 N: 6	&#8730;	IE: 4, 5, 5.5 N: 6	√	Square root, radical sign

Named Entity	Browser Support	Numbered Entity	Browser Support	Intended Rendering	Description
&prop;	N: 6	&#8733;	N: 6	∝	Proportional to
&infin;	IE: 4, 5, 5.5 N: 6	&#8734;	IE: 4, 5, 5.5 N: 6	∞	Infinity
&ang;	N: 6	&#8736;	N: 6	∠	Angle
&and;	N: 6	&#8869;	N: 6	⊥	Logical and
&or;	N: 6	&#8870;	N: 6	⊢	Logical or
&cap;	IE: 4, 5, 5.5 N: 6	&#8745;	IE: 4, 5, 5.5 N: 6	∩	Intersection, cap
&cup;	N: 6	&#8746;	N: 6	∪	Union, cup
&int;	IE: 4, 5, 5.5 N: 6	&#8747;	IE: 4, 5, 5.5 N: 6	∫	Integral
&there4;	N: 6	&#8756;	N: 6	∴	Therefore
&sim;	N: 6	&#8764;	N: 6	~	Tilde operator
&cong;	N: 6	&#8773;	N: 6	≅	Approximately equal to
&asymp;	IE: 4, 5, 5.5 N: 6	&#8776;	IE: 4, 5, 5.5 N: 6	≈	Almost equal to, asymptotic to
&ne;	IE: 4, 5, 5.5 N: 6	&#8800;	IE: 4, 5, 5.5 N: 6	≠	Not equal to
&equiv;	IE: 4, 5, 5.5 N: 6	&#8801;	IE: 4, 5, 5.5 N: 6	≡	Identical to
&le;	IE: 4, 5, 5.5 N: 6	&#8804;	IE: 4, 5, 5.5 N: 6	≤	Less than or equal to
&ge;	IE: 4, 5, 5.5 N: 6	&#8805;	IE: 4, 5, 5.5 N: 6	≥	Greater than or equal to
&sub;	N: 6	&#8834;	N: 6	⊂	Subset of
&sup;	N: 6	&#8835;	N: 6	⊃	Superset of
&nsub;	N: 6	&#8836;	N: 6	⊄	Not a subset of
&sube;	N: 6	&#8838;	N: 6	⊆	Subset of or equal to
&supe;	N: 6	&#8839;	N: 6	⊇	Superset of or equal to
&oplus;	N: 6	&#8853;	N: 6	⊕	Circled plus, direct sum
&otimes;	N: 6	&#8855;	N: 6	⊗	Circled times, vector product

3

Named Entity	Browser Support	Numbered Entity	Browser Support	Intended Rendering	Description
&perp;	N: 6	&#8869;	N: 6	⊥	Perpendicular
&sdot;	N: 6	&#8901;	N: 6	·	Dot operator

Technical Symbols

Named Entity	Browser Support	Numbered Entity	Browser Support	Intended Rendering	Description
&lceil;	N: 6	&#8968;	N: 6	⌈	Left ceiling
&rceil;	N: 6	&#8969;	N: 6	⌉	Right ceiling
&lfloor;	N: 6	&#8970;	N: 6	⌊	Left floor
&rfloor;	N: 6	&#8971;	N: 6	⌋	Right floor
&lang;	None	&#9001;	None	<	Left-pointing angle bracket
&rang;	None	&#9002;	None	>	Right-pointing angle bracket

Geometric Shapes

Named Entity	Browser Support	Numbered Entity	Browser Support	Intended Rendering	Description
&loz;	IE: 4, 5, 5.5 N: 6	&#9674;	IE: 4, 5, 5.5 N: 6	◊	Lozenge

Miscellaneous Symbols

Named Entity	Browser Support	Numbered Entity	Browser Support	Intended Rendering	Description
&spades;	IE: 4, 5, 5.5 N: 6	&#9824;	IE: 4, 5, 5.5 N: 6	♠	Spade suit
&clubs;	IE: 4, 5, 5.5 N: 6	&#9827;	IE: 4, 5, 5.5 N: 6	♣	Club suit
&hearts;	IE: 4, 5, 5.5 N: 6	&#9829;	IE: 4, 5, 5.5 N: 6	♥	Heart suit
&diams;	IE: 4, 5, 5.5 N: 6	&#9830;	IE: 4, 5, 5.5 N: 6	♦	Diamond suit

Chapter 4
Color Reference

This chapter provides basic information about the use of colors on the Web, from how to calculate browser-safe colors, adjust unsafe colors, and form hybrid colors, to the use of color names and their numerical equivalents as used in HTML and CSS, and browser support of color names.

Browser-Safe Colors

While 8-bit GIF images support 256 colors, cross-platform issues leave a palette of only 216 colors that are completely safe to use on the Web. This group of Web-safe colors is often called the *browser-safe palette*. Because it is difficult to present this information visually in a black-and-white book, the palette can be viewed online at http://www.htmlref.com/reference//safepalette.htm. Use of other colors beyond this safe set can lead to poor-looking images when viewed under limited color conditions such as 8-bit (256 color) VGA. Selecting a set of colors from the safe color palette and mixing them together in a process called *dithering* will approximate colors outside the safe range. In short, dithering attempts to imitate colors by placing similar colors near them, but generally creates irregularities that render the image unappealing.

The selection of the 216 safe colors is fairly obvious if you consider the additive nature of RGB color. Consider a color to be made up of varying amounts of red, green, or blue that could be set by adjusting an imaginary color dial from the extremes of no color to maximum color saturation. The safe colors suggest six possible intensity settings for each value of red, green, or blue. The settings are 0%, 20%, 40%, 60%, 80%, and 100%. A value of 0%, 0%, 0% on the imaginary color dial would be equivalent to black. A value of 100%, 100%, 100% would indicate pure white, while a value of 100%, 0%, 0% is pure red, and so on. The safe colors are those that have an RGB value set only at one of the safe intensity settings. The hex conversions for saturation are shown in Table 4-1.

Color Intensity	Hex Value	Decimal Value
100%	FF	255
80%	CC	204
60%	99	153
40%	66	102
20%	33	51
0%	00	0

Table 4-1. Color Intensity Conversion Table

Setting a safe color is simply a matter of selecting a combination of safe hex values. In this case, #9966FF is a safe hex color; #9370DB is not. Most Web design tools like Macromedia Dreamweaver or Allaire HomeSite contain safe color pickers; so do imaging tools like Macromedia Fireworks or recent versions of Adobe PhotoShop. Designers looking for color palettes, including improved color pickers and swatches, should visit http://www.visibone.com/colorlab/.

Setting an unsafe color to its nearest safe color is fairly easy—just round each particular red, green, or blue value up or down to the nearest safe value. A complete conversion of hex to decimal values is shown in Table 4-2. Safe values are indicated in bold.

00=00	01=01	02=02	03=03	04=04	05=05
06=06	07=07	08=08	09=09	10=0A	11=0B
12=0C	13=0D	14=0E	15=0F	16=10	17=11
18=12	19=13	20=14	21=15	22=16	23=17
24=18	25=19	26=1A	27=1B	28=1C	29=1D
30=1E	31=1F	32=20	33=21	34=22	35=23
36=24	37=25	38=26	39=27	40=28	41=29
42=2A	43=2B	44=2C	45=2D	46=2E	47=2F
48=30	49=31	50=32	**51=33**	52=34	53=35
54=36	55=37	56=38	57=39	58=3A	59=3B

Table 4-2. RGB to Hexadecimal Color Conversion Chart

60=3C	61=3D	62=3E	63=3F	64=40	65=41
66=42	67=43	68=44	69=45	70=46	71=47
72=48	73=49	74=4A	75=4B	76=4C	77=4D
78=4E	79=4F	80=50	81=51	82=52	83=53
84=54	85=55	86=56	87=57	88=58	89=59
90=5A	91=5B	92=5C	93=5D	94=5E	95=5F
96=60	97=61	98=62	99=63	100=64	101=65
102=66	103=67	104=68	105=69	106=6A	107=6B
108=6C	109=6D	110=6E	111=6F	112=70	113=71
114=72	115=73	116=74	117=75	118=76	119=77
120=78	121=79	122=7A	123=7B	124=7C	125=7D
126=7E	127=7F	128=80	129=81	130=82	131=83
132=84	133=85	134=86	135=87	136=88	137=89
138=8A	139=8B	140=8C	141=8D	142=8E	143=8F
144=90	145=91	146=92	147=93	148=94	149=95
150=96	151=97	152=98	**153=99**	154=9A	155=9B
156=9C	157=9D	158=9E	159=9F	160=A0	161=A1
162=A2	163=A3	164=A4	165=A5	166=A6	167=A7
168=A8	169=A9	170=AA	171=AB	172=AC	173=AD
174=AE	175=AF	176=B0	177=B1	178=B2	179=B3
180=B4	181=B5	182=B6	183=B7	184=B8	185=B9
186=BA	187=BB	188=BC	189=BD	190=BE	191=BF
192=C0	193=C1	194=C2	195=C3	196=C4	197=C5
198=C6	199=C7	200=C8	201=C9	202=CA	203=CB
204=CC	205=CD	206=CE	207=CF	208=D0	209=D1
210=D2	211=D3	212=D4	213=D5	214=D6	215=D7
216=D8	217=D9	218=DA	219=DB	220=DC	221=DD
222=DE	223=DF	224=E0	225=E1	226=E2	227=E3
228=E4	229=E5	230=E6	231=E7	232=E8	233=E9
234=EA	235=EB	236=EC	237=ED	238=EE	239=EF
240=F0	241=F1	242=F2	243=F3	244=F4	245=F5
246=F6	247=F7	248=F8	249=F9	250=FA	251=FB
252=FC	253=FD	254=FE	**255=FF**		

4

Table 4-2.   RGB to Hexadecimal Color Conversion Chart
(*continued*)

Although mathematically translating to the closest browser-safe color seems appropriate, it might not look correct to many people. Consider creating a hybrid color by combining multiple safe colors together. This is done simply by creating a checkerboard effect with a GIF image, in which two or more non-dithering colors are placed side by side to give the appearance of a third color. A variety of PhotoShop plug-ins such as Colorsafe (www.boxtopsoft.com) exist for mixing colors.

Color Names and Numerical Equivalents

Table 4-3 lists all the color names commonly supported by the major browsers (Netscape 3.0 and better, Internet Explorer 3.0 and better, Opera 4.02, and WebTV). The HTML specification defines sixteen named colors (aqua, black, blue, fuchsia, gray, green, lime, maroon, navy, olive, purple, red, silver, teal, white, and yellow). (Out of these colors, only seven are considered safe in the reproduction sense discussed previously.) Many other color names have been introduced by the browser vendors—particularly Netscape—and are fairly commonly used. Color names are easier to remember than numerical codes, but might cause trouble when viewed under old or uncommon browsers. It is advisable to stick with the hexadecimal approach to colors, as it is generally safer. The corresponding hexadecimal code is shown next to each color name shown in Table 4-3, and generally is interchangeable with the corresponding name. Thus, the code <**BODY BGCOLOR= "lightsteelblue"**> would produce the same result as <**BODY BGCOLOR="#B0C4DE"**> under any browser that supported these color names. Identical colors might be reproducible with different names. For example, "magenta" and "fuchsia" are both equivalent to #FF00FF. Regardless of named color support, keep in mind that not all numeric values are completely browser safe either. Although these names and numbers probably won't be an issue for users with high-resolution monitors and higher degrees of color support, don't forget that these users are not the only people on the Web. Browser-safe colors in Table 4-3 appear in bold; RGB equivalents are also included.

NOTE: If designing with the Opera browser in mind, beware that the current version of Opera tested (4.02) supports numerical values well but has highly inconsistent support of color names. Only 18 color names match their numeric equivalents when viewed in Opera. These are marked with a dagger (†) in the chart. Opera approximates the correct display of most of the remaining color names, but shows such significant variations that, again, the best—and perhaps only—option is to use numeric values exclusively. Finally, there are some color names that Opera does not support at all, or supports in ways radically different from their intended values; these are marked with a double dagger (‡). Hopefully this will be improved with a future release of this browser.

Hexadecimal Code	Name	RGB Equivalent	Notes
#F0F8FF	aliceblue ‡	240,248,255	The name "aliceblue" is not supported by versions of Netscape prior to version 4.0.
#FAEBD7	antiquewhite	250,235,215	
#00FFFF	aqua †	0,255,255	
#7FFFD4	aquamarine	127,255,212	
#F0FFFF	azure	240,255,255	
#F5F5DC	beige	245,245,220	
#FFE4C4	bisque	255,228,196	
#000000	black †	0,0,0	
#FFEBCD	blanchedalmond	255,235,205	
#0000FF	blue †	0, 0,255	
#8A2BE2	blueviolet	138, 43,226	WebTV displays "blueviolet" the same as "blue" (0000EE).
#A52A2A	brown	165, 42, 42	
#DEB887	burlywood ‡	222,184,135	
#5F9EA0	cadetblue	95,158,160	

Table 4-3. Color Names and Their Numerical Equivalents

Hexadecimal Code	Name	RGB Equivalent	Notes
#7FFF00	chartreuse	127,255, 0	
#D2691E	chocolate	210,105, 30	
#FF7F50	coral	255,127, 80	
#6495ED	cornflowerblue	100,149,237	
#FFF8DC	cornsilk	255,248,220	
#DC143C	crimson ‡	220,20,60	
#00FFFF	cyan †	0,255,255	
#00008B	darkblue ‡	0,0,139	
#008B8B	darkcyan ‡	0,139,139	
#B8860B	darkgoldenrod	184,134, 11	
#A9A9A9	darkgray ‡	169,169,169	
#006400	darkgreen ‡	0,100, 0	
#BDB76B	darkkhaki	189,183,107	
#8B008B	darkmagenta ‡	139, 0,139	
#556B2F	darkolivegreen ‡	85,107, 47	
#FF8C00	darkorange	255,140, 0	
#9932CC	darkorchid ‡	153, 50,204	
#8B0000	darkred	139, 0, 0	
#E9967A	darksalmon	233,150,122	
#8FBC8F	darkseagreen	143,188,143	
#483D8B	darkslateblue ‡	72, 61,139	
#2F4F4F	darkslategray ‡	47, 79, 79	
#00CED1	darkturquoise ‡	0,206,209	
#9400D3	darkviolet	148, 0,211	
#FF1493	deeppink	255, 20,147	
#00BFFF	deepskyblue	0,191,255	
#696969	dimgray ‡	105,105,105	
#1E90FF	dodgerblue	30,144,255	
#B22222	firebrick ‡	178, 34, 34	
#FFFAF0	floralwhite	255,250,240	
#228B22	forestgreen ‡	34,139, 34	
#FF00FF	fuchsia †	255,0,255	
#DCDCDC	gainsboro	220,220,220	
#F8F8FF	ghostwhite	248,248,255	
#FFD700	gold ‡	255,215, 0	

Table 4-3. Color Names and Their Numerical Equivalents
(*continued*)

Hexadecimal Code	Name	RGB Equivalent	Notes
#DAA520	goldenrod ‡	218,165, 32	WebTV displays "goldenrod" the same as "gold" (#FFD700).
#808080	gray	127,127,127	
#008000	green †	0,128,0	
#ADFF2F	greenyellow	173,255, 47	WebTV displays "greenyellow" the same as "green" (#008000).
#F0FFF0	honeydew	240,255,240	
#FF69B4	hotpink	255,105,180	
#CD5C5C	indianred ‡	205, 92, 92	
#4B0082	indigo ‡	75,0,130	
#FFFFF0	ivory	255,255,240	
#F0E68C	khaki ‡	240,230,140	
#E6E6FA	lavender	230,230,250	
#FFF0F5	lavenderblush	255,240,245	
#7CFC00	lawngreen	124,252, 0	
#FFFACD	lemonchiffon	255,250,205	
#ADD8E6	lightblue	173,216,230	
#F08080	lightcoral	240,128,128	
#E0FFFF	lightcyan †	224,255,255	
#FAFAD2	lightgolden-rodyellow	250,250,210	
#90EE90	lightgreen ‡	144,238,144	
#D3D3D3	lightgrey ‡	211,211,211	
#FFB6C1	lightpink	255,182,193	
#FFA07A	lightsalmon	255,160,122	
#20B2AA	lightseagreen	32,178,170	
#87CEFA	lightskyblue	135,206,250	
#778899	lightslategray	119,136,153	
#B0C4DE	lightsteelblue ‡	176,196,222	
#FFFFE0	lightyellow	255,255,224	
#00FF00	lime †	0,255,0	

Table 4-3.   Color Names and Their Numerical Equivalents *(continued)*

Hexadecimal Code	Name	RGB Equivalent	Notes
#32CD32	limegreen ‡	50,205, 50	WebTV displays "limegreen" the same as "lime" (#00FF00).
#FAF0E6	linen	250,240,230	
#FF00FF	magenta †	255, 0,255	
#800000	maroon †	128,0,0	
#66CDAA	medium-aquamarine ‡	102,205,170	
#0000CD	mediumblue ‡	0,0,205	
#BA55D3	mediumorchid ‡	186, 85,211	
#9370DB	mediumpurple	147,112,219	
#3CB371	medium-seagreen ‡	60,179,113	
#7B68EE	medium-slateblue ‡	123,104,238	
#00FA9A	medium-springgreen ‡	0,250,154	According to the WebTV specification, WebTV supports "mediumspring-green," but the name display does not match the numerical code display.
#48D1CC	mediumturquoise	72,209,204	
#C71585	mediumvioletred	199, 21,133	
#191970	midnightblue	25, 25,112	
#F5FFFA	mintcream	245,255,250	
#FFE4E1	mistyrose	255,228,225	
#FFE4B5	moccasin	255,228,181	
#FFDEAD	navajowhite	255,222,173	
#000080	navy †	0, 0,128	
#9FAFDF	navyblue ‡	159,175,223	WebTV displays "navyblue" the same as "navy" (#000080).
#FDF5E6	oldlace	253,245,230	

Table 4-3.   Color Names and Their Numerical Equivalents
(continued)

Hexadecimal Code	Name	RGB Equivalent	Notes
#808000	olive †	128,128,0	
#6B8E23	olivedrab	107,142, 35	WebTV displays "olivedrab" the same as "olive" (#808000).
#FFA500	orange	255,165, 0	
#FF4500	orangered	255, 69, 0	WebTV displays "orangered" the same as "orange" (#FFA500).
#DA70D6	orchid	218,112,214	
#EEE8AA	palegoldenrod	238,232,170	
#98FB98	palegreen	152,251,152	
#AFEEEE	paleturquoise	175,238,238	
#DB7093	palevioletred	219,112,147	
#FFEFD5	papayawhip	255,239,213	
#FFDAB9	peachpuff	255,218,185	
#CD853F	peru	205,133, 63	
#FFC0CB	pink	255,192,203	
#DDA0DD	plum	221,160,221	
#B0E0E6	powderblue	176,224,230	
#800080	purple †	128,0,128	
#FF0000	red †	255, 0, 0	
#BC8F8F	rosybrown	188,143,143	
#4169E1	royalblue	65,105,225	
#8B4513	saddlebrown ‡	139,69,19	
#FA8072	salmon ‡	250,128,114	
#F4A460	sandybrown	244,164, 96	
#2E8B57	seagreen	46,139, 87	
#FFF5EE	seashell	255,245,238	
#A0522D	sienna	160, 82, 45	
#C0C0C0	silver †	192,192,192	
#87CEEB	skyblue	135,206,235	
#6A5ACD	slateblue	106, 90,205	
#708090	slategray	112,128,144	
#FFFAFA	snow	255,250,250	
#00FF7F	springgreen	0,255,127	

Table 4-3.   Color Names and Their Numerical Equivalents
(continued)

Hexadecimal Code	Name	RGB Equivalent	Notes
#4682B4	steelblue	70,130,180	
#D2B48C	tan	210,180,140	
#008080	teal †	0,128,128	
#D8BFD8	thistle	216,191,216	
#FF6347	tomato	255, 99, 71	
#40E0D0	turquoise	64,224,208	
#EE82EE	violet	238,130,238	
#F5DEB3	wheat	245,222,179	
#FFFFFF	white †	255,255,255	
#F5F5F5	whitesmoke	245,245,245	
#FFFF00	yellow †	255,255, 0	
#9ACD32	yellowgreen	139,205,50	WebTV displays "yellowgreen" the same as "yellow" (#FFFF00).

Table 4-3.   Color Names and Their Numerical Equivalents *(continued)*

NOTE: WebTV supports the color names but displays several colors (noted in the table) differently. General WebTV color support might also vary because of essential differences between computer monitors and television screens.

Many online color references claim that further color variations can be introduced by adding the numbers 1 through 4 to color names. If this were correct, cadetblue1, cadetblue2, cadetblue3, and cadetblue4 would display as different shades of the same color, with 1 being the lightest and 4 the darkest. Opera seems to support this concept to some degree, but given the inconsistency of that browser's overall color name support and the complete lack of support by the major browsers, there seems little sense in using this approach.

Some online color references also claim that gray supports up to 100 color variations (gray10, gray50, gray90, and so forth). Testing reveals that this does not work under Netscape, Internet Explorer, or WebTV. Opera supports this concept by displaying lighter grays for higher numerical values.